C000134528

A CLOSER LOOK AT SCIENCE FICTION

Live long and prosper!

Anthony Thorlius

To
Chris, Sandy and Stephen

A Closer Look at
Science Fiction

ANTHONY THACKER

KINGSWAY PUBLICATIONS
EASTBOURNE

Copyright © Anthony Thacker 2001

The right of Anthony Thacker to be identified
as the author of this work has been asserted by him in
accordance with the Copyright, Designs
and Patents Act 1988.

First published 2001

All rights reserved.
No part of this publication may be reproduced or
transmitted in any form or by any means, electronic
or mechanical, including photocopy, recording or any
information storage and retrieval system, without
permission in writing from the publisher.

Unless otherwise indicated, biblical quotations are
from the New International Version © 1973, 1978, 1984
by the International Bible Society.

ISBN 0 85476 888 2

Cartoons by Roy Mitchell

Published by
KINGSWAY PUBLICATIONS
Lottbridge Drove, Eastbourne, BN23 6NT, England.
Email: books@kingsway.co.uk

Book design and production for the publishers by
Bookprint Creative Services, P.O. Box 827, BN21 3YJ, England.
Printed in Great Britain.

Contents

Acknowledgements

I'd like to thank my wife Helen for her patience, as it must have seemed as though I lived and breathed TV science fiction. Also my boys, Chris, Sandy and Stephen, who enjoyed helping me with the research: Sandy, for sorting out the *Doctor Who Magazines* with their telesnap and other archives; Chris, for helping with the *Star Trek Fact Files*; and Stephen, for pretending to be the monsters! And I want to thank my sister, Maggie, for providing me with a wealth of *Star Trek* material; those who have videoed various episodes for me; my mother Doreen Thacker; Alan Cook, Linda Beckingham, Andy Mitchell and Mark Goodrum; and many friends who read and commented on an earlier stage of this book, including Shelly Melia, Alan Cook, Jane Jervis and Bill Wilson.

I also want to thank the staff at the International Baptist Theological Seminary in Prague, where I was able to write the first draft, and the people of Oadby Baptist Church, for their generosity in giving me the space on sabbatical over the summer of 1998 to write up the first draft, and for their tolerance of my spending time on revisions.

I want to thank the *Baptist Times* for their permission to reuse some of the words and ideas that I originally wrote in an April 1998 article under the title 'To boldly go – and make disciples?'. And Richard Herkes of Kingsway, for spotting that article and asking me to write this book, and for his comments and suggestions at different stages.

Like any writer, I am indebted to other books and magazines, and also other people for their comments. Many of these will become obvious in the pages of this book, and are cited in the Notes and Further Reading sections. However, any mistakes are of course my own.

Introduction: The Strange New World of Science Fiction

I was a child of the space age – the time that saw President Kennedy's vision of an American on the Moon by the end of the 1960s survive his assassination and become a reality. I also saw the new BBC time travel programme, *Doctor Who,* from its first episode on 23 November 1963 (the day after that world-shaking assassination). A little later, US viewers first saw the science fiction series *Star Trek*, and by the end of the decade it began to capture British audiences too, with its imaginative exploration of the stars, and use of concepts like 'warp speed', 'matter/anti-matter power', etc.

It has to be said that this seemed to have little to do with my experience of faith, beyond the obvious point that as a Christian I believed God made these stars and planets that the *Enterprise* and TARDIS were exploring in our imaginations. One of the joys of having children is that it has given me a good excuse to revisit childhood as videos of *Doctor Who* have become available. What's more, with frequent repeats of *Star Trek* and the appearance of other series like *Babylon 5*, this voyage of discovery has never been easier. The imaginary worlds of science fiction also provide a context to discuss certain issues. My son Christopher, for example, once rather neatly described the character of Mike Baldwin from *Coronation Street* as a kind of 'human Ferengi'!

But the striking thing about science fiction at the turn of the millennium is that the old gap between SF and religion has changed radically. There's been a discovery – maybe a rediscovery – that real faith sparks issues and tensions that can play out well in a sci-fi context. What's more, the best SF raises questions about 'life, the universe and everything', often in a striking way. Sometimes, as in *The Hitch-hiker's Guide to the Galaxy*, classic questions about God and the meaning of life are posed for their comic potential. Meanwhile, other issues thrown up, like the paranormal and the occult, the stock-in-trade of *The X-Files*, press for a proper answer.

Science fiction has of course had a precarious existence in TV, as the increased sophistication of viewers requires a corresponding improvement in special effects, which has often meant greater expenditure. Quiz shows, chat shows and soaps are cheaper, so sci-fi often has to justify itself, and indeed *Doctor Who*, *Star Trek* and *Babylon 5* have all faced threats of being cut. The launch of *Doctor Who* in 1963 was significant for a generation of British children. Unusually, it had been promised a year of programmes, but after just a few weeks, Verity Lambert, its initial producer, was told it would end after 13 episodes.[1] The phenomenal success of its second story, *The Daleks*, took everyone by surprise and changed all that, with its UK viewing figures reaching over 10 million! These exterminating aliens captured the imagination of an entire generation of children and teenagers, combining the traditional children's fantasy world of monsters, 'goodies' and 'baddies' with the ultra-modern world of space travel, computers and in this first sci-fi story a stretching morality tale of survivors of a nuclear holocaust.

After that, *Doctor Who* went on to be the longest ever running TV science fiction series, transmitted every season but one from 1963 to 1989. TV chiefs tried to close it – and succeeded for 17 months in 1985–86, and again in 1989 – but its many fans ensured it was briefly revived on TV in 1986–89 and with a film in 1996. Its success lay in its simplicity of format. The Doctor and his companions could end up anywhere in space and time, or even out of it. The strength of each story would depend on the imagination of the writer, the coherence of the plot, the credibility of the monsters and the charisma of the actors, especially the Doctor. This formula proved remarkably successful, sustaining the series all that time. Even now, rumours of reviving the series or producing a new film periodically resurface.

Later in the 1960s the classic *Star Trek* series faced similar problems: funding was restricted after the first year, and after just three years the plug was pulled. But after that it took off! The shortsightedness of those who pulled the plug has been proved by the way in which those original programmes are still being repeated in many countries, and the way it has spawned to date three new spin-off series and nine films. TV science fiction in many countries consists of little other than the many *Star Trek* series, *Babylon 5*, *The X-Files*, occasionally *Doctor Who*, and other British and American programmes, either with subtitles or dubbed into the local language. *Babylon 5* also suffered, with its fourth season unduly hurried by the threat of closure before the story was completed after all, and its short-lived but brilliant successor series *Crusade* was sadly cut short!

Science fiction history

The term 'science fiction' was first coined in the 1920s, but had existed for a long time before that. There are many books we would now think of as science fiction, or quite similar to it. In the twentieth century we have George Orwell's *Nineteen Eighty-Four*, and Aldous Huxley's *Brave New World*. Famous in the nineteenth century were Mary Shelley's *Frankenstein*, and the many works of Jules Verne, like *Journey to the Centre of the Earth* and *20,000 Leagues Under the Sea*, and of H. G. Wells with *The Time Machine* and *War of the Worlds*, etc.

The best known eighteenth-century example is of course Jonathan Swift's *Gulliver's Travels*, with its sea travel to strange new worlds and encounters with new civilisations. Meanwhile, other writers featured trips to the Moon – for example, *A Trip to the Moon* by Murtagh McDermot in 1728, and the idea of a visit from an extraterrestrial visitor in *The Adventures of Eovaai* (or *The Unfortunate Princess*) by Eliza Haywood in 1736. Earlier fiction included some written by the great scientists of the day, like *The New Atlantis* (1627) by Francis Bacon, and *Utopia* (1516) by Thomas More. Further back still, David Pringle's *The Ultimate Encyclopedia of Science Fiction* sees Lucian of Samosata's *Satires* from the second century as similar to the fantasy end of the science fiction spectrum.

Science fiction today

The space age saw SF successes on TV like *Doctor Who, Star Trek* and *Blake's 7*. Since the late 1980s we've had *Star Trek*'s three new spin-off series (so far!): the SF comedy *Red Dwarf, The X-Files* and *Babylon 5*. More recently there's been *Farscape, Earth: Final Conflict, Stargate SG-1* and, best of the lot, the abortive *Babylon: Crusade* series, not to mention pure fantasy series like *Buffy the Vampire Slayer* and *Xena:*

Warrior Princess. Radio in the 1970s saw the brilliant spoof *The Hitch-hiker's Guide to the Galaxy*, which was far better in its original radio form than it was on TV. And radio/audio is the current context for the new *Doctor Who.* Meanwhile, films running science fiction themes have caught the imagination, like *2001: A Space Odyssey, Blade Runner,* the *Star Wars* trilogies, *E.T.* and *Jurassic Park.*

These stories bring a new world (such as *Doctor Who*'s 'Whoniverse') to the imagination. Many have devoted fans, with clubs and conventions for 'Trekkers', 'Whovians', 'X-Philes' and others. While some people hate science fiction, its influence so permeates the culture that everyone recognises catchphrases like 'Beam me up, Scotty!' and knows what it means to say a politician 'speaks like a Dalek'!

During the 1995 Conservative leadership election, candidate John Redwood was portrayed as rather coldly rational, so he was shown to be like Mr Spock. Tabloid headlines called Redwood a Vulcan, and said that John Major tried to 'Klingon' to power. And after William Hague became Conservative leader, comic impersonator Rory Bremner parodied Hague in the Commons, quoting a 'letter' to him supposedly by Redwood, ending with 'John Redwood, aged 46 of your Earth years'. Back in 1980, *Private Eye* satirised the succession of Michael Foot as new leader of the Labour Party with a picture of him with a Tom Baker hat and scarf.

Meanwhile a news report in *The Times* (18 August 2000) tells how 'Star Trek engines fly from fiction to fact' as ion engines, used in reserve in the *USS Enterprise*, have successfully been used in NASA's latest craft – rejoicing in the name of *Deep Space 1.*

FOOT IS NEW DR WHO

The 67-year-old Michael Foot is to be the new Dr Who, it was revealed today. The part of the eccentric doctor who spends his life in another world was left vacant when James Callaghan decided last month that he had 'had enough'.

Tardis & emotional

Said Foot, 67, 'I am over the moon. It is a part I have always coveted and it is a great honour to be chosen.' In his first series Foot, 67, will do battle with the ruler of the dreaded Tory Party, the extraordinary so-called Leaderene, a statuesque blonde with staring blue eyes and high-pitched mechanical voice.

'I haven't seen the script yet,' said the Doctor-elect, 'but I know the character is in for a hard time.'

Hello, Dalek!

Meanwhile a searing question mark hangs over the dog-like robot K-Benn, which has proved an especially unpopular feature of the story. 'We shall just have to see,' said Mr Foot, putting on his long scarf and disappearing into the Tardis. Michael Foot is 81.

Original source: *Private Eye* (November, 1980)

Science fiction is pervasive and influential. What's more, it has a unique capacity to open up pictures of who we are, what our possibilities are in the universe and where we're going. And I think it can help us explore some of the issues that have traditionally been worked through in theology and personal faith. So that's what I'm trying to do in this book.

The opening chapters set the scene in the space age, and we will then go on to look at many of the big issues of faith and life raised by the main TV series, *Doctor Who*, *Star Trek*, *Babylon 5* and *The X-Files*, and major films like the *Star Wars* series:

▶ Is the truth 'out there'?
▶ Are we 'all alone in the night' – or do we have company?
▶ Do aliens exist? Indeed, does God, or is he an alien invention?
▶ What is the Force?
▶ Will technology lead people to outgrow God?
▶ What about these heroes who save the universe each week? What does that say about who we are?
▶ What would meeting a real Vulcan mean for discovering our own humanity?
▶ In face of hostiles chanting, 'Resistance is futile!' what about the struggle with evil?
▶ And finally, where are we going ultimately?

Whether, like me, you wonder how Christian faith and science fiction go together, or whether you're interested in sci-fi and are attracted by the religious questions it raises, I hope this journey together will be fun and helpful.

Part One:
To Boldly Go

 IN THIS SECTION . . .

▶ **Science fiction comes of age**

After *Sputnik*, science fiction took off – especially with new TV shows like *Doctor Who* and *Star Trek*.

▶ **What will the future be?**

Science fiction imagines the future, but often mirrors the present. In the 1960s writers often assumed religion would die out in the near future.

▶ *Doctor Who* and *Star Trek*

Religion is usually set in the past in *Doctor Who*, and seen as invented or primitive in *Star Trek*.

▶ **The future is a-changing**

With *Star Trek*'s films and even more its new series, together with *Babylon 5*, *The X-Files* and *Farscape*, religion is far from absent, and often more positively seen.

▶ **The truth is out there**

The X-Files shows a more postmodern attitude to science and religion, with a mixture of doubt and faith about both.

The Dawn of a New Age

A space odyssey

It was the dawn of a new age of mankind, twelve years after the Second World War, at the height of the cold war and the arms race. The United Nations was a dream that resolved nothing. Its goal: to prevent another war by creating a place of diplomacy for communists and democrats to work out their differences peacefully. It failed. Instead, it proved a vehicle for mutual denunciation and competition.

It was the start of a new age of adventure, the exploration of space. The Astronomer Royal had said on 2 January 1956 that the idea of space travel was 'bilge'. But 20 months later, 'bilge' became fact. This is also the era when science fiction came of age; the time when the dreams and the fantasy came true. The year was 1957.

Babylon 5

It was the dawn of the third age of mankind, ten years after the Earth/Minbari War. The Babylon Project was a dream given form – its goal, to prevent another war by creating a place where humans and aliens could work out their differences peacefully . . . Humans and aliens, wrapped in two million, five hundred thousand tons of spinning metal, all alone in the night. It can be a dangerous place, but it's our last, best hope for peace . . . The year is 2258. The name of the place is *Babylon 5*.

The introduction to *Babylon 5* episodes in Season 1

Sputnik was not the only thing launched in 1957: science fiction arrived in a new way, as its fantastic ideas, long laughed off as impossible, were suddenly actually happening. The space age gave a credibility to science fiction. Suddenly, SF authors were being treated as maligned prophets.

 Life on Mars or Venus?

1898 – H. G. Wells's famous *The War of the Worlds* is based on invasion by Martians.

1938 – C. S. Lewis's *Out of the Silent Planet* and *Perelandra* tell of an inhabited Mars and Venus.

1960s – *Star Trek*'s Mr Spock was first conceived as half-Martian. *Doctor Who* sees Mars as a dying planet, which its 'Ice Warriors' want to escape. The Doctor also learned Venusian lullabies.

1975 – The Russian probe *Venera 9* lands on Venus and shows a planet extremely hostile to life: it is 500°C, with an oppressive atmosphere of carbon dioxide and sulphuric acid gas.

1976 – The American *Viking* lands on Mars, and shows a lifeless desert.

1992 – Kim Stanley Robinson's *Red Mars* tells of humans terraforming the dead planet.

1993 – Mars on *Babylon 5* is also seen as a human colony.

Johannes Kepler, the astronomer famous for showing how the Earth went round the Sun, is less well known for his science fiction work *Somnium* (1634). This includes an imaginary flight to the Moon, in which Kepler used the best scientific detail of the day to add realism to the story. But suddenly, in the space age, this old dream of fantasy became real. Back in 1870, Jules Verne wrote a book called *Round the Moon*. In it astronauts successfully blast off in a rocket from Florida, travel around the Moon and splash down in the Pacific. Ninety-eight years later, the crew of *Apollo 8* did just that. Arthur C. Clarke's 1951 story *The Sentinel*, with its trip to the Moon, was expanded into the classic film *2001: A Space Odyssey* in 1968. A year later, television used its theme tune, Richard Strauss's *Also Sprach Zarathustra*, for the actual *Apollo 11* landing on the Moon. The trips to the Moon and other planets had long been the setting for stories about Utopia. And now this age seemed upon us: science and technology were opening up the whole universe. The Utopian vision of Gene Roddenberry, which is part of the attraction of *Star Trek*, reflects this. It is faith in the future.

Things changed rapidly. Facts required that old fantasies be changed to reflect new realities. Even in the more fantasy-based world of *Doctor Who*, the story *The Space Pirates* (1969) was written to include a lot of realistic space travel. The production team worked hard to make the view in space reflect what people were used to seeing in *Apollo* missions. Furthermore, the idea that space flights took time was reflected, having the unintended effect of slowing down the story.

Meanwhile, by the 1990s, earlier stories of life on Venus and Mars became increasingly anachronistic. That reports of the supposed discovery of extinct Martian bacteria should have excited people shows how hopes for advanced life have shifted beyond the solar system. Newer tales of Mars take 'human terraforming' of the planet as their context – like *Babylon 5*, or Kim Stanley Robinson's brilliant character-driven trilogy, *Red Mars, Green Mars* and *Blue Mars*.

The 1950s and 60s saw the height of the arms race

between NATO and the communists of the Soviet Union, but who would get the decisive lead? It was the time of the doctrine of MAD: Mutually Assured Destruction. And the cold war flared up in places like Korea and Vietnam and, in a more indirect way, all over the Third World. With *Sputnik* in October 1957, the arms race now went up into space. The power commanding space could rain missiles over its foe. Which power would defeat the other: communism with its workers' revolution or Western-style democracy? The answer seemed to be in gaining the upper hand through new technologies. When the race moved into space, for the first time it seemed the Soviets were way ahead. Nowhere (outside Russia!) was this felt more acutely than in America.

For years the Russians were first in space with everything: first rocket, first animal, first man, first woman, first spacewalk and first crew. With the Moon, they had the first fly-by, first crash-landing, first orbit and first photographs of the Moon's hidden side. Beyond the Moon, despite failure at Mars, they had the only soft landings on Venus. Even today they have been far ahead with their working space station, MIR, despite its problems, and with long-duration space flights. It seemed that Soviet dominance of space spelled the future; that Soviet leader Khrushchev's boast against the West – 'We will bury you!' – was being proved true in space.

In the mid-1960s, Russian was the language of the future. Our school's Latin teacher saw the decline of Latin was following that of Greek. He trained in Russian, along with many others, and in 1967 I was one of the many who opted to learn this language. But the Americans were stung by the seeming effortlessness of the Russian dominance of space, and determined to fight back.

Kennedy boldly declared his vision to see a man on the Moon by the end of the 1960s:
' For the eyes of the world now look into space, to the moon and to the planets beyond. And we have vowed that we shall not see it governed by a hostile flag of conquest, but by a banner of freedom. And therefore we intend to be first.

'To be sure, we are behind, and will be behind for some time in manned flight. But we do not intend to stay behind, and in this decade we shall make up and move ahead.

'We choose to go to the moon in this decade and do the other things, not because they are easy, but because they are hard, because that goal will serve to organise and measure the best of our energies and skills, because that challenge is one that we're willing to accept, one we are unwilling to postpone, and one we intend to win – and the others too.'

But the space race first saw disasters on the launch pad: many rockets exploded and a fatal fire killed the crew of *Apollo 1*. Years followed before the first US unmanned crash landing on the Moon – and the Russians were still ahead.

With this goal seemingly out of reach, and NASA still far away from sorting out the technologies for landing on the Moon, Christmas 1968 was unforgettable in my memory. NASA took the risky step of advancing its programme by sending people to orbit the Moon without landing. Suddenly people were out there, all alone in the night, 250,000 miles away, hidden by the Moon and totally out of contact with the rest of the human race. Then they emerged, awed by the sight of Earthrise over the Moon, and in turn awing those

who heard them, as Frank Borman gave a message. It was
Christmas Eve 1968.

 'For all the people back on Earth, the crew of
Apollo 8 has a message that we would like to
send to you: "In the beginning, God created
the heaven and the earth. And the earth was without form,
and void: and darkness was upon the face of the deep. And
the Spirit of God moved upon the face of the waters. And
God said, 'Let there be light: and there was light.' And God
saw the light, that it was good: and God divided the light
from the darkness." And from the crew of *Apollo 8*, good
night, good luck, a merry Christmas, and God bless all of
you on the good Earth.'

Frank Borman

It was still very moving to hear when the story was repeated
on TV in 1994 and 1999 for the twenty-fifth and thirtieth
anniversaries of the first Moon landing. Though spontaneous, it provided a response to the famous atheistic comment of an early Soviet cosmonaut who said that he had been
up into the heavens and God was not there, therefore God
didn't exist! In the words of Psalm 139:8: 'If I go up to the
heavens, you are there.'

The following July, the American success in the race to the
Moon was confirmed with the historic Moon-landing by
Apollo 11, Neil Armstrong and Buzz Aldrin actually stepping
onto the surface of the Moon, and Michael Collins the third
crew member remaining above the surface in the main
rocket. This was the space age, and increasingly the science
fiction of space affected the real world. The language of *Star*

Wars coloured the US 'strategic defence initiative' of the 1980s, and though it was not clear at the time, this was the prelude to the end of the cold war. Just 20 years after the Moon-landing, in 1989, the Soviet empire crumbled in eastern Europe, and the communism of Lenin fell in its country of origin in 1991. It was the dawn of a new era, an age of new forms of co-operation, on Earth and in space.

In the 1990s, *Babylon 5* was pictured as just such a base of co-operation and set 'deep in neutral territory' but not too deep: around the third planet of the star Epsilon Eridani, less than eleven light years away. By one of those pleasing coincidences by which science follows science fiction, August 2000 saw the reported discovery of a Jupiter-like planet and a suspected whole solar system around this very star!

The 1960s proved to be the decade in which science fiction came of age. Soon, rockets sent off to the planets would be followed by human conquest, and the universe itself was a short step away. In time we would 'boldly go where no man has gone before' – way out among the stars. The British Labour Party leader, Harold Wilson, caught the mood of the times with his sound-bite about 'the white-heat of this scientific revolution'.

Mirror, mirror

TV made its response to this new 'final frontier' with *Doctor Who* and *Star Trek*. It was an age in which the future belonged to science and youth, in art, architecture, fashion and pop music. Science fiction pictures the future, but often reflects exaggerations of the present, as these fashions show. The 1960s were the age of the miniskirt, so in *Star Trek* it reached almost vanishing point with the skant. It was an age of gleaming new towers and the white heat of the technological revolution, so in *2001: A Space Odyssey* and the TARDIS interior all the technology was clean and white. The 1970s were an age of bright colours, so in *Buck Rogers* bright lycra was everywhere. The turn of the millennium, meantime, is a darker period and black is more fashionable, so the sets are darker on *Babylon 5*, *The X-Files*, *DS9*, *Batman*, *Millennium* and the Doctor's TARDIS in the 1996 film.

As science fiction shifted from far-fetched fantasy towards the imagined future of hard science, how much sheer fantasy would remain and how true would it be to the possibilities of science and technology, not to mention those of fashion, let alone society and religion? Would it be a true mirror to the future? This is our next theme.

• 2 •
Space: The Final Frontier

Science fiction and fantasy

A useful distinction, if not overdone, is between science fiction and fantasy, where science fiction stories maximise the scientific accuracy. In addition, some people talk of 'science fantasy' as a halfway house, but perhaps 'space fantasy' is better. In practice, we see a spectrum from space fantasies to science fiction, which has a lot of 'hard science', with pure fantasy and pure scientific predictions at the infra-red and ultra-violet ends of the spectrum.

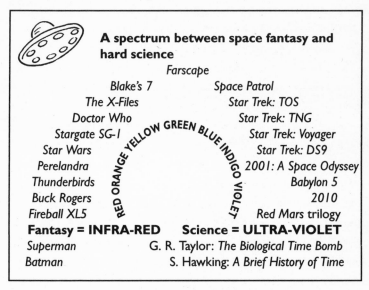

A spectrum between space fantasy and hard science

Farscape

Blake's 7   *Space Patrol*

The X-Files   *Star Trek: TOS*

Doctor Who   *Star Trek: TNG*

Stargate SG-1   *Star Trek: Voyager*

Star Wars   *Star Trek: DS9*

Perelandra   *2001: A Space Odyssey*

Thunderbirds   *Babylon 5*

Buck Rogers   *2010*

Fireball XL5   *Red Mars trilogy*

RED ORANGE YELLOW GREEN BLUE INDIGO VIOLET

Fantasy = INFRA-RED   **Science = ULTRA-VIOLET**

Superman   G. R. Taylor: *The Biological Time Bomb*

Batman   S. Hawking: *A Brief History of Time*

The film *2010*, the sequel to *2001: A Space Odyssey*, tries to maximise the accuracy of its science. But picturing the future requires more imaginative and even fantastic elements. *Star Trek* tries to include a fair element of things that might be scientifically imaginable in the far future, though its picture of society is fantasy, while *Babylon 5* is more realistic. Meanwhile, *Doctor Who* has a far greater proportion of pure fantasy.

So you can analyse the 'technobabble' of *Star Trek*, spotting the scientifically prescient, the technically imaginable as well as the downright impossible. Lawrence Krauss set the trend in his book *The Physics of Star Trek* (Flamingo, 1997), telling us that *Star Trek*'s talk of 'black stars' (before anyone coined the term 'black hole') and even of 'dilithium crystals' has more scientific accuracy than might have been expected. Robert and Susan Jenkins have followed, with *The Biology of Star Trek* (Boxtree, 1999), which discusses the plausibility of Ferengi ears, Quark's synthehol and many other features. You could discuss the science of *Babylon 5* too. But any attempt to analyse the scientific credibility of the details of *Doctor Who* would be fruitless, as its fluid links, sonic screwdrivers, Taranium and Dalekenium are pure make-believe.

Most science fiction is set in the future, but the future societies pictured are a revealing mix of expectations of the future and the present. It is said that when George Orwell began writing *Nineteen Eighty-Four* in 1948, he originally planned to call it *Nineteen Forty-Eight*, as it was a parody of the emerging cold war. Swift's strange new worlds in *Gulliver's Travels* also presented a satire on the Europe of his day. But *Star Trek* is more than this: it is a myth for our time, picturing a Utopian goal. And it is a summons to create this ideal society. It is no accident that at the crankier end of fandom there are those starting a *Star Trek*-based religion.

In the real world, there were difficulties. Gene Roddenberry wanted his original *Star Trek* to include a female first officer and an alien – the Vulcan Mr Spock. His backers rejected the actress, and famously wanted to airbrush Spock's pointed ears off! In the end he managed to retain Spock. Just as well, because without him the show would never have succeeded. And his casting of a black female communications officer – ostensibly a black African, as 'Uhuru' is Swahili for 'freedom' – was genuinely ahead of its time, and an inspiration to blacks at the time.

In 1995, a female captain, pictured in the twenty-fourth century in *Star Trek: Voyager*, is no longer so remarkable in an age used to female government leaders and captains of industry. What is more striking is that in the current series *all* the alien races are portrayed with increasing sexual equality, whether Vulcan, Romulan, Bajoran or Klingon. Even Ferengi women were suddenly given equal rights, at least temporarily, in *DS9: Profit and Lace* (May 1998). This reflects today's gender politics, which has overtaken *Star Trek*'s dream.

Doctor Who has had far more difficulty in responding to such feminist desires, partly because its lead is as much a man as the Bionic Woman has to be a woman, and the lead has to dominate the show because that's what the storyline is: 'stranger saves the world'. In a way the Doctor is a kind of space age Lone Ranger. Even so, summer 1998 speculation about a possible new *Doctor Who* film included talk not only of yet another change of lead actor, but also that it might be a woman, a hope finally realised in the 1999 Comic Relief affectionate parody 'Doctor Who and the Curse of Fatal Death'.

Incidentally, there's nothing new in that speculation. In a

Doctor Who Magazine interview, Peter Davison records that around the time he was appointed as the new Doctor, 'John [Nathan-Turner] had been putting out these rumours that a woman was going to take over . . . He used to do that all the time.' But as Davison said, 'It happens to be that the Doctor is male. I don't think it would work with a female Doctor. I think it would be hogwash, really. If you start off with a female character, if you start off with Miss Marple, then great. If you start with Helen Mirren in *Prime Suspect*, great, absolutely great. I'm all for more programmes with women in them, but I don't think that means programmes with male stars can't be made.'

In practice its real troubles stem from the laziness of writers who allowed a constant flow of strong female personalities to degenerate into ignorant screamers and pin-ups, from astrophysicist Zoe to scientist Nyssa. The strongest exceptions were arguably streetwise Ace, knife-wielding Leela, journalist Sarah and schoolteacher Barbara (despite her famous scream on meeting the first Dalek).

Religion in the future

The futuristic side to science fiction leads writers to imagine future societies, and as religion is a part of life, these pictures reflect various attitudes to the future role (or lack of it) of religion in society. This aspect has too often been overlooked. But this is our theme. Science fiction can deal with issues not open to other forms of writing, because of its setting at the edge of current human existence. What's more, many of the issues traditionally given religious answers crop up: 'Are we alone in the universe?', 'What is the meaning of life?', 'Is there any form of existence after death?' and so on.

But is science fiction therefore a substitute for faith? And what about all the talk of alien abductions and people contacting UFOs telepathically? Indeed, some SF has been promoted as fact, particularly the idea that aliens have already visited Earth.

▶ George Adamski had failed in writing fiction, so presented his themes as fact, claiming to have been taken by aliens – blonde female Venusians – to the Moon. Eventually he was discredited.

▶ Similarly, most famously, Erich von Däniken's journalistic *Chariots of the Gods* asked 'Was God an astronaut?'

▶ R. L. Dione proposed that *God Drives a Flying Saucer* from some alien world, and that this powerful alien caused all religious history!

Further conflict with Christian faith can be seen in the overlap with horror and the occult in some science fiction (an issue we must return to). The fantasy of C. S. Lewis, *The Lion, the Witch and the Wardrobe*, was more of a religious allegory, and some forms of SF can be interpreted that way, like *Star Wars* with its talk of 'the Force'. The suggestion that *Star Trek* was also an allegory of Christianity in a way is harder to justify. This could be only in a very loose sort of way – perhaps in its future vision of individuals and races increasingly working together, as a realisation of Jesus' command to love one another.

Language and realism

One interesting test of whether a TV programme is more sci-ence fiction than fantasy is how it deals with the problem of language. On this little planet we are aware of over 7,000 dif-ferent languages, with very different structures. Difficulties in communication between different linguistic groups are a fea-ture of life. It is clear that if life on other planets existed, then communication would be a significant hazard, and a major feature in relations.

Doctor Who of course was first written for children as a fan-tasy, so the question of how English is spoken and under-stood by people living 100,000 years ago, not to mention by Thals and Daleks from a remote planet where they have never heard of Earth, was ignored. Once the cast was placed in revolutionary France, or apparently in the First World War with French and German soldiers, in *The War Games* (1969), the problem was greater: children learn French and know it's different, and so a nod or two in that direction was required.

To the growing teenage and adult audiences, this became more anachronistic. So by the time Tom Baker was the Doctor in *The Masque of Mandragora* (1976), a rationalisa-tion of this ability to speak in and understand all languages was felt necessary, and in a throw-away remark he says, 'It's a Time Lord's gift I allow you to share.' *The Hitch-hiker's Guide to the Galaxy* solved the problem with the Babel fish, which, as we will see, raised questions about faith in God.

Perhaps it was the great fantasy writer J. R. R. Tolkien who inspired the drive towards linguistic realism, with his development of an imaginary language in Middle Earth. First *Star Wars* used alien language with subtitles in 1978, then

Star Trek followed. In the original series, there was the same lack of explanation as in *Doctor Who*, with the cast able to speak to and understand everyone, wherever they landed. Obviously the dramatic requirements of the stories precluded communication snarl-ups at every new 'first contact', and the desire to avoid odd head-gear ruled out headphones. The first solution was the 'universal translator' in the computer, though this still does not explain one-to-one communication with strange *new* worlds.

Once *Star Trek* matured with the films, a new realism developed. So with *Star Trek: The Motion Picture* (1979) we have real alien language, Vulcan, with Spock's attempts to attain *kolinahr* (pure, dispassionate Vulcan logic), and later in *The Wrath of Khan* (1982) as Spock and Saavik speak Vulcan together (with English subtitles).

But the future was Klingon. In the following film, *The Search for Spock*, it became a plot theme, with Kirk speaking Klingon to capture their spaceship. As for the sixth film, *The Undiscovered Country* (1991), the Klingon villain – almost an attractive anti-hero, Chang – exclaims that Shakespeare is better in the Klingon language! At the Klingon trial of Kirk and 'Bones', matters are conducted in Klingon (with English subtitles), the humans using visible simultaneous translators. And then, after a few such subtitled scenes, the film of the trial continues in English, the viewers having being per-suaded the 'real thing' is all happening in Klingon.

Most amusing of all is where Uhura and the *Enterprise* crew need to speak in Klingon, rather than use the 'giveaway' of a Federation 'universal translator', and so we are treated to their faulty Klingon duly translated literally, to the mirth of the Klingon defence team.

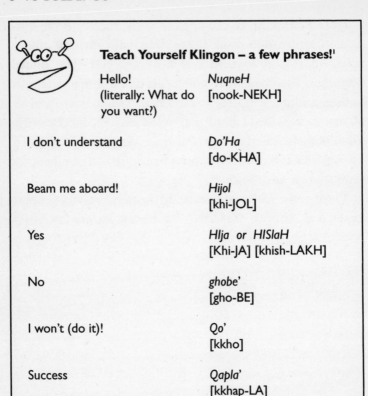

Teach Yourself Klingon – a few phrases![1]

Hello! (literally: What do you want?)	*NuqneH*	[nook-NEKH]
I don't understand	*Do'Ha*	[do-KHA]
Beam me aboard!	*Hijol*	[khi-JOL]
Yes	*HIja* or *HISlaH*	[Khi-JA] [khish-LAKH]
No	*ghobe'*	[gho-BE]
I won't (do it)!	*Qo'*	[kkho]
Success	*Qapla'*	[kkhap-LA]
Religion	*lalDan*	[lal-DAN]

Klingon is now a growth industry, and the interested linguist or Trekker can buy tapes on conversational Klingon (full of guttural expletives) and books of a 'Teach Yourself Klingon' kind. A wonderful syntax, grammar, pronunciation guide and vocabulary has been designed, to which I can only say, *'Qapla!'* And indeed, the parties where people dress as Klingons and speak Klingon are among the more popular with Trekkers.

With *Babylon 5*, the action has usually been set in human territory – sometimes Earth or Mars – but most often *B5* itself, which, set up by the Earth Alliance, uses the human language English by convention. However, if Minbari speak to one another, or a Ranger familiar with their language, like Marcus, speaks it, then we have the language spoken with subtitles added. Furthermore, in *And Now for a Word* (2:15) we are told that there are three basic Minbari languages – Lenann, Feek and Adronato – plus 97 dialects.

As for realism about religion in society, that is our next theme.

• 3 •
Dalek Gods? Vulcan Mystics? Vorlons?

The 1960s was an age in which science ruled. Architecture reflected the future dream. The pop music revolution showed that the future belonged to the young, the next generation. But what was to be the place of religion in this bold new world? Next to nothing! The 1960s and early 70s saw a serious decline in church attendance and particularly in sending children to Sunday school. The future for our children did not include religion, and the world of science fiction reflected that: the decline of religion was assumed to be permanent in science fiction's future. Where do you see a believer in the heroes of *Star Trek* or *Doctor Who*? You don't. There's no trace of Buddhism in Mr Sulu, and no Christianity in any of the crew of the *Enterprise*, whether under Kirk or Picard. The same is true of *Doctor Who*. The Doctor and his companions never express a personal religious faith, with the exception of Katarina from legendary ancient Troy, and she was quickly killed off by the editors as she was felt to be too primitive. Religion does occasionally play a role, however. But before the 1990s, religion was nearly always seen as ancient, primitive, invented, superstitious or at best an obsolete stage in evolution.

Religions in British TV science fiction before the 1990s

Doctor Who and *Blake's 7*

Quatermass and the Pit (1959) and *Doctor Who: The*

Daemons (1971)
▶ Problem: alien menace unearthed, where alien proves to be basis of all experiences of the devil.
▶ Faith: fear of the devil.
▶ Religion: superstition.
▶ Outlook: science ends fears/evil.

Doctor Who: The Daleks (1963–4)
▶ Problem: after the Daleks are defeated, how can the Thals rebuild their future?
▶ Religion/faith: 'Always search for truth . . . My truth is . . . in the stars. And yours . . . is here' (the Doctor).
▶ Outlook: scientific rationalism.

Doctor Who: The Aztecs (1964)
▶ Problem: as Barbara is mistaken for the goddess Yetaxa, could she end human sacrifice and so change history?
▶ Faith/religion: historical Aztec.
▶ Outlook: historical fatalism – the Doctor can't stop past evil, but often stops future evil.

Doctor Who: The Romans (1964)
▶ Problem: Tavius, a Roman, admires Barbara's help of a slave as an unusual 'Christian' attitude.
▶ Faith: violence v. compassion.
▶ Religion: Tavius is a secret Christian.
▶ Outlook: historical faith fleetingly portrayed positively.

Doctor Who: Doctor Who and the Crusaders (1965/novelisation 1973)
▶ Problem: Saladin says that 'the Will of Allah' means

nothing to Ian.
- ▶ Faith: Ian believes all religions have much in common.
- ▶ Religion: Saladin's – Islam.
- ▶ Outlook: religions are relative.

Doctor Who: Mythmakers (1965)
- ▶ Problem: Doctor seen as Zeus, his TARDIS as a temple.
- ▶ Religion/faith: ancient Trojan.
- ▶ Outlook: light-hearted history: 'whether it's sorcery, or palmistry, or tea leaves, or just time travelling . . .'

Doctor Who: Peladon (1972 and 74)
- ▶ Problem: will Peladon remain medieval or modernise?
- ▶ Religion/faith: conflicts with science.
- ▶ Outlook: religion looks backward.

Doctor Who: Death to the Daleks (1974)
- ▶ Problem: a super-advanced city absorbing all energy reduces Exxilons to stone age existence.
- ▶ Faith: most Exxilons 'have made the city their god. They worship and fear it. They even sacrifice to it.' Others, like rebel Bellal, risk 'sacrilege' and aim to destroy it.
- ▶ Religion: invented.
- ▶ Outlook: science ends ignorance.

Doctor Who: Planet of the Spiders (1974)
- ▶ Problem: a mind-enhancing crystal has enabled spiders to oppress a human colony.
- ▶ Faith: Buddhism plus.
- ▶ Religion: heroes the Doctor and Captain Yates have practised Buddhist meditation (but the alien crystal causes

odd events).
▶ Outlook: Buddhism affirmed.

Doctor Who: Genesis of the Daleks (1975)
▶ Problem: Davros creates the Daleks, unleashing untold evil.
▶ Faith: megalomania.
▶ Religion: Kaleds who became Daleks once had gods. Davros wants to *be* God. He says that this 'power would set me among the gods. And through the Daleks I shall have that power!'
▶ Outlook: against megalomania.

Blake's 7: Cygnus Alpha (1979)
▶ Problem: dark age penal colony, subjugated by religious obedience and maintained by dependence on a drug, set up by power-mad couple.
▶ Faith: local religious authorities and devotees seem sincere, but it's a power game, shown as hero Roj Blake frees them.
▶ Religion: a con trick.
▶ Outlook: (some) religions enslave.

While the Daleks themselves are clearly godless (genetically programmed hatred of all non-Dalek life leaves no room for any God to challenge them!), presumably it was not always so. In *Genesis of the Daleks*, Davros thinks his Daleks will set him 'among the gods'. The Daleks' ancestors, the Kaleds, and presumably also the Thals, may have worshipped gods once. But Davros's determination to *be* God has left them with the evil of the Daleks. Maybe that is a parable for all religions in *Doctor Who*.

First, the devil is seen as an alien in *The Daemons* (1971), Satan is Sutekh in *The Pyramids of Mars* (1975) and occult themes drive *K-9 and Company* (1981). Meanwhile, pagan star-worshippers gain power from an alien power in *The Masque of Mandragora* (1976), and vampires are the subject of *State of Decay* (1981) and *The Curse of Fenric* (1989). Second, there are gods and spirits feared superstitiously in *The Tribe of Gum* (1963) and *Marco Polo* (1964). Indeed such people see the TARDIS as work of the gods or of witch-craft in *The Crusade* (1964), *The Mythmakers* and *The Daleks' Masterplan* (1965–6) and *The Massacre* (1966). Meanwhile, alien faiths are usually primitive and artificial, as in Terry Nation's *Death to the Daleks* and *Cygnus Alpha* and the vol-cano god of *Planet of Fire* (1984). Even where religion is seen more sympathetically, as in Robert Holmes's Peladon stories, it still emerges as a primitive and backward-looking phenomenon. Most positive is the Menoptera's light-god in *The Web Planet* (1964).

In most of the historical stories, the historical religions are duly recorded. There is even a momentary implied affirma-tion of Tavius as a Christian in *The Romans*, and rather more positive views of Buddhism, with the third Doctor suppos-edly a student of Buddhist meditation (a bit odd considering all his activism). *Kinda* (1982) is unusually rich in a positive use of both Christian and Buddhist imagery. But these are the most positive exceptions: such religions are more in the past than the future.

Generally, *Doctor Who* pictures religion as set in the past. But it would be an exaggeration to say that it presents an atheistic view of religion. It does assert that the future is with science and rational investigation, but from time to time a bit more emerges, perhaps nowhere more than in *The Massacre of St Bartholomew's Eve* (1966). Here the Doctor takes advantage of being the double of the fanatical Abbot of Amboise, and goes beyond impersonating the true Abbot (who has now been killed by a fanatic) to pressing matters (within a historic Christendom context) towards his own view. In the novelisation, the Doctor says that Catholic and Huguenot should not fight.

 'We are all God's children, each and every one of us, and it is not by acts of war nor bloody deeds that His Kingdom shall be attained, rather should we look to our own hearts and find therein those three blessed precepts of Love, Humility and Charity.'

The Doctor

In context, that sounds like a vague Christian humanism. Of course, the Doctor could just be dressing up an atheistic humanism in Christian terms for his hearers, but as spoken, the words, like Ian's to Saladin, imply that historic religions are equally valid paths to God in their common view of us all as God's children, who should be inspired by their common call to virtue. In practice, in *Doctor Who* faith is not in religion but in science. The scientific faith of the future of those days is shown in the comment of Leela, the fourth Doctor's 'savage' companion in *The Horror of Fang Rock* (1977), combating faith in astrology: 'A waste of time. I, too, used to believe in magic, but the Doctor has taught me about science. It is better to believe in science.' The other 'faith', selectively applied, is in fate; selectively, because in historical stories past evils cannot be changed, but in the SF stories the Doctor changes them all the time.

Incidentally, religion in *Doctor Who* could have developed in a rather different way. Famously, Sydney Newman had been keen to avoid 'bug-eyed monsters', but after Anthony Coburn's *The Masters of Luxor* had been rejected, Terry Nation's *The Daleks* was allowed to be screened despite the Daleks, because there was no time left to find a further replacement. But if Nation's script had been the one rejected first, Coburn's excellent script would have left us not only with equally engaging robots and androids, but also with a different attitude to God. In Coburn's script, Susan exclaims, 'Why are you Earth people afraid of the word "God"?' The Doctor himself kneels at least in sympathy with Tabon's act of prayer, and argues that Karl Marx was wrong to reject religion: 'It would have been truer to say, "Religion sneering at scientific progress . . . or scientific progress sneering at religion . . . either of them can lull people to sleep." Each needs the other.'

Star Trek: The Original Series and The Next Generation

Star Trek: Who Mourns for Adonais? (1967)

▶ Problem: the ancient Greek god Apollo is really an alien abusing his power.
▶ Faith: ancient Greeks unknowingly worshipped aliens as gods.
▶ Religion/outlook: historical faith an alien con trick.

Star Trek: The Apple (1967)

▶ Problem: the gentle people of Gamma Trianguli VI are in

danger of destruction from their god Vaal (a computer).
▶ Faith: dependent childish worship.
▶ Religion: invented.
▶ Outlook: religion can end growth, creating dependent attitudes.

Star Trek: Bread and Circuses (1968)
▶ Problem: 'What if Rome never fell?' – a world with death in the arena on TV, versus rebels.
▶ Faith: rebels worship the Son of God, first misread as the Sun-god.
▶ Religion: *ersatz* Christianity.
▶ Outlook: such worship is an obsolete evolutionary stage from superstition towards 'many beliefs' held in harmony.

The Next Generation: Lonely Among Us (1987)
▶ Problem: two alien races 'feel such passionate hatred over matters of customs, God-concepts [and economics]'.
▶ Faith: Riker says, 'I never understood this sort of hostility [in] history.'
▶ Religion: warring.
▶ Outlook: such religion is long past.

The Next Generation: Justice (1987)
▶ Problem: the Edo worship an entity, which creates simple but deadly rules for dependent Edo.
▶ Faith: in a transdimensional thing.
▶ Religion: invented by aliens.
▶ Outlook: according to Picard, this is appropriate for the Edo's stage of religious evolutionary growth.

As the examples above show, the picture in *Star Trek* is slightly different. While it too presents religion as a past phenomenon, it is more explicitly humanistic and atheistic, and more clear in seeing all religion including Christianity as an obsolete evolutionary phase. This is clearest in *Bread and Circuses*, which adopts a regular theme of SF: an alternative history. We might ask, for example, 'What if Hitler had won the Second World War?' (as in the brilliant *City on the Edge of Forever*). Here it is 'What if Rome never fell?' However, *Star Trek* only commends this *ersatz* Christian 'faith in the Son', with its 'love and brotherhood', by making it an evolutionary stage between 'primitive superstition religion' and Dr McCoy's post-Christian, secular, humanistic future in which 'we represent many beliefs', all working together in harmony. This evolutionary picture strengthened with *Star Trek: The Next Generation*. Its future heroes would be democratic, humanistic and completely secular.

Closure of the final frontier?

Though President Kennedy's vision was realised in 1969, it was not succeeded by trips to Mars and beyond. In 1972 manned space trips to 'strange new worlds' came to an abrupt halt because of the *realpolitik* of changing economic priorities. President Bush's 1988 public commitment to send a manned mission to Mars failed to ignite sufficient public interest, so didn't happen. Barnstorming of interplanetary space was over. If in the real world mankind had given up on space, would SF fade? Initially it seemed possible, and even *Doctor Who* was wound up in 1989. But the end of the space race has not meant the end of science fiction. In the 1990s

SF was resurgent and with a far greater maturity, including in its picture of religion.

The strange new world of religion: Vulcans and Vorlons

The success of the film *Star Wars* in 1977 led to a renewal of *Star Trek*, not as first envisaged, as a new TV series, but with a string of successful films. However, this development has helped promote a new realism. We have seen this in the use of alien languages, but it has also gradually extended to culture and religion. So we see the original *Star Trek* crew beginning to interact with some religious themes. By *Star Trek III*, Mr Spock and his fellow Vulcans are not only rational and scientific, their culture is said to be 'full of mysticism'. As Spock is reintegrated, body and soul, we find the Vulcans engaged in rather spiritual-looking practices (while the humans look on, seemingly unsure of what to do!).

Roddenberry on *Star Trek V*:

'I didn't object to it being an alien claiming to be God, but there was too much in it that an audience could have thought was really God or really the devil, and I very strongly resist believing in either.'[1]

And in *Star Trek V*, the crew, in reaching 'the final frontier', are given to believe they are encountering God, before it turns out to be one of his many impersonators! Even so, the idea that there might be a Reality who deserves the title 'God' is far from being rubbished as before. This film is famous for the line of Captain Kirk to the impostor: 'Excuse me – excuse me, but what does *God* need with a starship?'

Since the 1990s, the strange absence of religion from the future has been changing. There is a real shift in the profile of spirituality and religion, and even Christians, in SF on TV. It is a straw in the wind, reflecting a potential greater openness among people in society towards spirituality in particular. There are, I believe, positive and negative implications for Christians in this.

One feature of the 1990s was the proliferation of new novels based on *Doctor Who, Star Trek, Star Wars* and *Babylon 5.* These have allowed a greater depth to character and situation, including personal and social religion. So in *Star Wars,* while the first two films never mentioned beliefs in God or gods, *Return of the Jedi* (1983) and even more so *The Phantom Menace* (1999) do so. And even in the world of *Doctor Who,* there has been a shift. Take *Love and War* (1992), for example. We are told that Brewer, an early character in the book, 'believed in Allah' and that new companion Bernice Summerfield has a Catholic mother. Meanwhile, the *Doctor Who* spin-off *Auton 2: The Sentinel* (1999) assumes there is 'psychic power' in prayer. There is no real hint in any *Doctor Who* on TV that there would be any Catholics or Muslims in the twenty-fifth century, but the idea that there will be faith in the future started to become widespread in science fiction in the 1990s.

One side of this is the growth of occult fascination in our spiritually starved culture, clearest in the cult series *The X-Files,* which is centred on the paranormal and the possibility of UFOs, etc. It is modern-day Hammer Horror, but it also presses the boundaries, presenting as credibly real what

1960s science would have laughed off as superstition; its openness to the inexplicable reflects the current less rigid scientific dogmatism. It presents occult and spiritual themes that make it both more religious than anything in the 1960s and potentially more spiritually disturbing. People following it will be more inclined to accept occultism. This reflects a continuing rise in exposure to the occult, a theme we must cover carefully as we consider the struggle with evil that is all too real today in pastoral and spiritual experience in helping people get disentangled from openness to occult powers.

The religious dimension is clear in the way the two main characters are drawn. Back in the 1960s and 70s, on one side we would have had scientific heroes and on the other religion and superstition. But in *The X-Files*, the rational and more sceptical scientist (Dana Scully) is the religious believer, the Catholic, while the credulous one (Fox Mulder) is the pagan. Mulder is a paranormal pagan, wide open to the wild and conflicting elements in the world of *The X-Files*, where alien abductions, genetic mutations and demonic manifestations abound.

Then there's telepathy. In SF on TV it began as Mr Spock famously 'mind-melded' with a sentient rock, and Deanna Troi benignly used empathy in her counselling in *The Next Generation*. Cally, one of *Blake's 7*, is an alien telepath. Similarly, the author of *Thunderbirds*, Gerry Anderson, in his latest *Space Precinct* presents alien telepathy as a fact. And *Babylon 5* gives us the 'psi-corps': telepathy among humans enhanced by the mysterious Vorlons, and taken for granted and developed with the 'psi cops' as a worse version of the 'thought police' of George Orwell's *Nineteen Eighty-Four*.

But it's with the newer series in the *Star Trek* franchise, and in *Babylon 5*, that the positive openness to spirituality, faith and religion is clearest. *Deep Space Nine* has a distinctly New Age feel, and in several episodes the story hinges on spiritual awareness, especially with the religious Bajorans. In the pilot story *The Emissary* the captain needs to discover his *pagh* – which sounds like an equivalent of the Chinese *ch'i* or Hindu *prana*. Bajorans are the key alien race in *Star Trek: DS9* and their prophets and prophecies, mystics and spiritual experiences regularly shape the stories. Technobabble mixes with New Age mysticism, and the supernatural and miraculous are taken for granted. The star, Captain Sisko, becomes the Bajorans' religious 'emissary'. And his first officer, Major Kira Nerys, is a Bajoran, whose religious convictions are increasingly visibly portrayed. Recent tales, *Rapture* (1996) and *Far Beyond the Stars* (1998), centre on Captain Sisko having accurate visions and 'words of knowledge' – the miracles are presented as real, not explained away. The latter episode even includes talk of God and the Bible.

The changes are also visible in *Star Trek: Voyager*. The ancestral spirit world of First Officer Chakotay features in several stories. What's more, although *Voyager*, like *The Original Series* and *The Next Generation*, gives us stand-alone stories about a spaceship meeting new situations each week, it has pursued the religious themes more strongly and positively than the original series and *The Next Generation*. One early example was *Emanations* (1995), which explores different religious practices and beliefs about the afterlife.

Religion is central to *Babylon 5*. The appearance of a Baptist minister (a sort of Jesse Jackson) in a Season 3 episode – the '2260' of *Babylon 5* – gave Baptists, especially the *Baptist Times,* a thrill. But more prominent was Brother Theo and his Catholic monks, who are on *B5* because they want to study alien experiences of God, and who save the day in *Convictions* (1996).

But the religious element goes beyond such features. Season 3 centred on an escalating Armageddon between 'Vorlons' shown as angels in disguise, and the demonic 'Shadows' (though in Season 4 that simple picture was modified). Delenn, the religious Minbari ambassador, castigates the corrupt Centauri ambassador Londo for his evil: 'You have lost much more than a friend. But that is between you and whatever gods you worship!' Mira Furlan, the actress who plays Delenn, is a Croat married to a Serb. She said, 'A friend of mine in New York said to me, "When are they going to do an episode that doesn't deal with Yugoslavia?"'[2]

Religions in *Babylon 5*

Minbari

Nearest human equivalent: a mixture of Hindu and Buddhist, with reincarnation and castes. Delenn feels at home in the Zen garden.

Narn

Nearest human equivalent: a mixture of Islam, Judaism and Christianity, centred on Holy Books, which tells of historical experiences of the divine, for example of G'Lan and G'Quan.

Centauri

Nearest human equivalent: ancient Roman (and Greek) religion and culture, with its decadence, many gods, real prophecy and delight in the achievements of empire.

Human

Historic religions continue: Jews, Buddhists, Baptists, Catholics and 150 others mentioned or implied.

Foundationist

A human/alien religion started after 2100, as humans try to integrate the foundational experiences of human and alien religions. Dr Stephen Franklin is a Foundationist.

Vorlons

These don't so much show they have a religion, as try to foster spirituality. They appear as creatures of light, angels, in the indigenous form to each race. They are paternalistic.

Shadows

Like the Vorlons they foster a response, but they encourage violent conflict, to precipitate rapid growth through the desperate struggle to survive. They appear as creatures in the shadow, and of darkness. They seem demonic.

We not only see alien religions, but human religions are sympathetically treated, with lively Baptists, Catholic monks interested in alien spirituality, and the Jewish, semi-agnostic commander, Susan Ivanova, who is surprisingly indebted to these monks for their computer skills. There is an openness to the religious, including Christian, experience in the world of *Babylon 5*. Jane Curtis, who was a curate in my home town, was right to spot this in the episode *Comes the Inquisitor* (2:21). Captain Sheridan and Ambassador Delenn are subjected to a painful test. At length they show the incredulous Inquisitor that each would die to save the other. He then concedes: 'No greater love hath a man, than he lay down his life for his brother. The darkness might only be overcome by an honest man willing to die . . . not for fame, but in the dark, where no-one will ever know or see.' It is not too hard to see the religious parallel affirmed here, and Jane was quick to draw it in the local parish magazine: 'The Inquisitor . . . might as well have been speaking of Jesus Christ . . . who in order to overcome the darkness . . . humbled himself.'

Meanwhile *Farscape* continues this trend, with Zhaan, the Delvian priestess and prophetess. All this is a far cry from the religion-less future pictured in theology and science fiction alike in the 1960s and 70s. In many ways this reflects a broader, deeper series of changes in outlook as we enter the third millennium. We are moving from the modern, scientific era, where all religion has been dismissed, into a more confused, uncertain 'postmodern' culture, where the supernatural is widely, even superstitiously, sought. It is an age where faith and spirituality and even the miraculous are more easily accepted. But it is a time when belief in the 'truth' is more uncertain, and where consistency and commitment are far more precarious.

Today, people in modern societies can more easily believe in miracles, though they have a harder job believing in commitment and permanence.

• 4•
The Truth Is Out There

Millennial Watergate

It has been suggested that in the 1990s we were suffering
from an acute dose of 'Pre-Millennial Tension'. This cultural
angst was well expressed by the most popular new programme of the 1990s, *The X-Files*, which almost as much as
Babylon 5 was the vision of one man, its creator, and author
of many of its stories – Chris Carter. His second TV series
was the even darker *Millennium*. Meanwhile, the ironic slogan of *The X-Files* is 'The truth is out there'.

The X-Files, with its fascination with the occult and paranormal, dominated much of the sci-fi scene internationally in
the 1990s. The most successful *Doctor Who* spin-off, *The
Auton Trilogy*, shows clear influence. The 1990s were a much
darker time than the 1960s and 1970s and yet also more
open to the possibility of religious experience. Chris Carter
puts it this way: 'I'm a non-religious person in search of religious experience.'

A question we must return to is: What sort of religious
experience is being sought after, not just within the stories of
The X-Files, but within the approach behind it? We can ask:
What sort of experiences might heroes Fox Mulder and Dana
Scully (and their families and associates) endure? What sort
of religious experiences might viewers of the programme also
have?

The X-Files: the context

America lost its trust in its leaders during Vietnam and Watergate. The year 1968 was one of radical protest the world over, and in the US the main focus was Vietnam. By the time Uncle Sam flew home, cynicism was widespread. But what killed it off was the way in which over two years it was shown that the President, Richard Nixon, had not only arranged the burglary of his opponents during the election, but sought ever after to cover it up. Ever since, each president has been scrutinised closely and found wanting. The highlights of this are the Iran/Contra arms scandal of the Reagan and Bush administrations, and the fiasco of Clinton's Zippergate and repeated Bimbo scandals.

What's more, history is now looked at differently. Most obviously, the assassination of President John F. Kennedy is not seen as a simple tragedy. Instead, especially as assassin Lee Harvey Oswald was killed before he could spill any beans, in a culture cynical of politicians and Pentagon, a conspiracy and cover-up is assumed. It is only a short step from this to seeing conspiracies, murders and cover-ups everywhere. Was Marilyn Monroe murdered? Or Elvis? Indeed, is Elvis still alive, hidden by some conspirators? Add to this the growing feeling since 1978 that there was a major cover-up regarding the Roswell incident of 1947, with its tales of alien crashes, autopsies and even survival, together with military censorship, and the background to *The X-Files* is clear. Such fascination with Roswell, encouraged by *The X-Files*, also lies behind *Roswell High*.

The assumption is that government, and the FBI, are as aware of claims of UFO sightings as the rest of us. The difference is that they will also know which ones are really secret plans of the government, and which ones are genuinely still *unidentified* flying objects. They also have an ability to check sightings through with a thoroughness unavailable to the rest of us.

There's a range of possibilities that the FBI might have encountered, from the odd vague UFO sighting, through the famous allegation of the alien 'crash' at Roswell, New Mexico, in 1947, on to alleged 'hard evidence of alien abductions'. *The X-Files* is based on the 'what if?' premise: 'What if all these wackier possibilities were true?'

What happened at Roswell?[1]

Date: 8 July 1947
Explanation: 'Flying Disc Captured'. The first comment said a UFO was found. Some later comments suggest five aliens were also found, one of whom may have still been alive. Allegations include an alien autopsy (on photograph) and a massive cover-up.

Date: 9 July 1947
Explanation: '"Flying Disc" a Weather Balloon'. The official military answer for many years: just a damp squib. But rumours of a cover-up grew after 1978.

Date: July 1994
Explanation: Project Mogul: a highly sensitive and classified radiation experiment to test whether the Soviet Union was setting off nuclear weapons in the atmosphere.

Conclusion: Conspiracy theorists have a field day, with two exciting fears: the military may have wanted to hide their mistakes with aliens, or else hide a military scandal. With Roswell near the nuclear test sites, many terrible ideas can be imagined.

And it's not just alien sightings, but the whole range of unexplained, paranormal and occult phenomena that forms the backcloth of *The X-Files*. Attempts to use telepathy in the cold war provide a historical reference point. But again *The X-Files* is written on the 'what if?' basis: 'What if all sorts of paranormal phenomena have a basis in reality?' 'What if the FBI has its secret files on all these things, and wants them to remain a military secret?'

Author Chris Carter says that it was his research for a programme on alien abductions that inspired him. He comments that the consultant 'told me that 3% (sic) of the public believed in this syndrome. I was astounded. I realised there was a topicality to this theme of the unknown, and *The X-Files* grew out of that fascination.'[2]

Enter Mulder and Scully. We add to this toxic brew the idea of a junior FBI agent stumbling across these 'X-Files', and trying to uncover what is really going on. He meets obstruction from more senior figures and apparently from aliens (who for very different reasons want to hide what is really going on), and finds his colleague more sceptical, doubting his bizarre findings as unscientific, but testing the data.

Meanwhile, in keeping with its cloak-and-dagger suspense of conspiracy and cover-up, most of the characters seem shadowy, unnamed, hidden: Deep Throat, Mr X, the Smoking Man, the 'well-manicured man', and a host of unnamed higher-up figures. Even some names, like Alan Krycek, seem to be pseudonyms, or are ambiguous in some other way. The slogans intensify the sense of ambiguity and malaise: Deep Throat's dying words are, 'Trust no one!' After his death and that of Mr X, Marita Covarrubias provided

Mulder's third source of inside information. Her ambiguous and plausibly ironic motto is: 'Not everything dies'.

As for Fox Mulder himself, his approach is a model in relation to theories about Roswell. He is the agent who believes there is something sinister going on between the secret governmental 'syndicate' and the aliens. Gradually, the storyline suggests he is right, but keeps us in long-term uncertainty as to how. He tends to be the intuitive but reckless one of the duo. His faith is paranormal paganism. He began with interest in serial killers and the occult. He went on to accept the theory that all the 'alien' leads were a cover-up for the *real* military secrets, only to return to accepting the alien reality later still.

Meanwhile, Dana Scully, his colleague, is more than the foil of Mulder. A more traditional approach, like *Doctor Who* or its imitation *Invasion Earth*, has a doubter with a myopic prejudice based on the current scientific consensus. This is then neatly contrasted with the true openness of the hero. But Scully's cautiousness is a genuine contrast to Mulder's recklessness. She has a physics degree and medical school training. She has a broadly Catholic faith in God – and also faith in science.

The X-Files: the story

The story centres on the mysteries and cover-ups surrounding suspected alien/human encounters – like the Roswell incident. The first two episodes set up this theme clearly, with eerie or blinding light; strange, alien-looking carcasses with odd implants; weird bumps on the back of a corpse; odd suicides; events at a site supposedly storing Roswell debris;

and threatening and disruptive agents.

Early episodes give us the following:

- ▶ Talk of abductions and sand turned by massive heat into glass at the site.
- ▶ Alien larvae in Alaska from an ammonia-based environment.
- ▶ The ghostly 'Martian face' alien (so called because of the Sphinx-like phenomenon, with pyramids, on Mars) that 'possesses' an astronaut.
- ▶ Aliens capable of shape-shifting into the opposite sex, disguised as a cult, but implicated in sex-attack serial murders.
- ▶ Assumed encounters, past and present, with an Extraterrestrial Biological Entity; and so on.

Other 'conspiracy'-based episodes home in on sinister scientific/military experiments, like gene manipulation, ageing process reversal by reptilian regenerative-cell morphegins, etc.

However, the series is not restricted to this, but wanders widely around the whole range of unexplained mysteries: paranormal and occult phenomena, the weird, gory and scary, and even the wacky and outlandish. But there is little light-heartedness even with the last, as the gory atmosphere of murderous cover-up continues.

The third episode shows this wider type of theme. Mulder and Scully's investigation concerns a serial killer who kills five people in rapid succession for their livers, only to wait another 30 years before repeating the exercise! When caught, the killer seems like a human who's degenerated into a sort of animal life. The sense of mystery stays, as most of the questions about this creature remain unanswered.

Later, such episodes home in on beastly sub-human cannibals, post-mortem psychokinetic manipulation, ghostly shadow-boxing, the artificial intelligence that (as in *2001*) starts killing to save itself, human spontaneous combustion, channelling spirits and demons, an evil spirit jumping from possessing one person to another at death, nasty things in the sewers, vampire-like creatures, and so on. There is a similarity between this element and the Hammer Horror type films of an earlier generation. But there are big, vital differences: the earlier stories, however disturbing, were usually played as fantasies, as phenomena of the 'ghost train', not of everyday life; but in *The X-Files*, these disturbing horrors are played as real events, part of an array of things the government is trying to conceal.

What has sustained it is the sense of 'who-done-it' suspense, all the government cover-up. That changed somewhat with the transition to the big screen in 1998, where a number of the show's questions actually got answered. For example, we are told that the Smoking Man's partners have for the last 50 years been conspiring to develop alien/human 'clones'.

The X-Files: the truth

What is the truth about aliens on Earth, and who's right – the sceptic or the believer? The tension between scepticism and belief is an old trick in science fiction. It was regularly played in a cosy way in *Doctor Who*: the new companion would express disbelief about the TARDIS as a spaceship and time machine, but was proved wrong as the thing landed in 1066 (or whenever). This comfy in-joke was eventually phased out.

The tensions between believing that invaders are aliens versus the scientific/common-sense prejudice that it's just the Russians was also a central theme in the BBC's 1998 series *Invasion Earth*. Flight Lieutenant Drake and Major General David Reece can't convince others of the alien threat. So we have the cosy 'Gotcha!' moments where sceptic Squadron Leader Helen Knox first sees the aliens, and a similar time where Reece's disbelieving boss finally turns up and gets the evidence he needs. Just as well, as half of Scotland has to be nuked!

But what makes *The X-Files* different is not this cosy version, where we the viewers know, and they the doubters are about to get their come-uppance. *The viewers don't know either.* Instead, there's a sinister hide-and-seek not only with the aliens, but also the FBI and the shadowy power-brokers behind the scenes. Who knows what? What is really true? Is the truth out there ever going to be uncovered? Indeed 'The truth is out there' is very much an ironic statement: there may indeed be truth, but it seems we will never get near enough to it, because *they* will fight tooth and nail to stop us finding out.

The colours are unremittingly dark, both as *film noir* for today (it's as filled with dark corridors as *Doctor Who* was with gleaming white ones!) and in the sense of pervasive secrecy, violence and menace, with a sustained Hitchcock-like suspense throughout. As sci-fi entertainment, it has set new standards. But as the truth out there about modern life, it is unjustified paranoia: the conspiracy theory of society is not remotely credible in an age where Bill Clinton can conceal far less than Lloyd George or Edward VII. However, the more things are disclosed, the more is believed to be hidden.

Which truth is 'out there'?

'The truth is out there' is the ironic slogan of *The X-Files*. Ironic for two reasons: it's hidden and it's self-contradictory:

1. The 'truth' is obscured by so much conspiracy and cover-up that it seems unattainable.
2. With the search for the 'truth' about alien sightings, abductions leading in a bewildering variety of directions, the truth seems self-contradictory.

One of the strengths which has helped *The X-Files* acquire its leadership of the TV sci-fi field is its staunch refusal to endorse any single alternative orthodoxy. Not only does the show insist on maintaining the murky visibility of a whole series of alternatives, it also maintains a blithe indifference to the fact that some of these alternatives are flatly contradictory, offering very different and mutually exclusive interpretations of similar phenomena. Aliens and their rogue DNA must compete continually with largely untapped reserves of human psychic power and authentic demonic intrusions.[3]

David Pringle, *Ultimate Encyclopedia of Science Fiction*

There are too many 'truths' that seem plausible – too many possible answers to what's happening in the world. All this shows signs of a new shift in the way people think and feel.

For centuries, people in European-based cultures have felt a tension between the modern, scientific worldview and the traditions of our culture in faith. The new tension, expressed in sci-fi terms by *The X-Files*, is between each of these and a postmodern outlook.

The old outlook, which increasingly dominated our Western culture over the last 350 years and was called the 'modern, scientific' worldview, assumed there was one set of truths. This is often called the 'modern' era. Earlier more traditional approaches also assumed one set of truths, but saw the way to this harmonious truth through spiritual authorities. The 'modern' approach assumed that this one set of truths was discoverable by all who gave up 'primitive, barbaric, superstitious' ideas. It said that it alone was free of all prejudice and presuppositions. Problems were sorted out by a combination of rigorous thinking and rigorous observation. This included religion. So, either Jesus rose from the dead or he didn't – and if the latter, it was either because he never died or he never rose. Either atheistic humanists would be right about there being no God, or they would be wrong and God would be discovered! The truth would also be worked out deductively and analytically. Every scientist was, in a way, a Sherlock Holmes. History and science, conducted with rational, logical consistency, would resolve all issues of faith.

But increasingly in the current era, a new approach is gaining currency. It is often called the 'postmodern' era. The increasing complexity and paradoxical nature of modern mathematics and physics is sometimes taken as inspiration. Examples of how light works, coupled with the theories of relativity and uncertainty, have inspired many to assume a new more 'relativistic' attitude to truth.

Traditional wisdom

▶ Inspiration: includes holy books and/or revered teachers.
▶ Truth: is given
  – for Catholics, by church;
  – for Protestants, in Bible;
  – for Jews: Bible and rabbis;
  – for Muslims: Qur'an and mullahs.
▶ Attitude: trust.
▶ Presuppositions: varied combinations of generally agreed and revealed truths.
▶ Values: integrates facts and values.

Modern enlightenment

▶ Inspiration: includes science and history.
▶ Truth: is discovered – by any person of any faith or none on the basis of direct investigation and enquiry.
▶ Attitude: rugged pursuit of truth.
▶ Presuppositions: claims to be free of them – says it is objective, unbiased, unprejudiced.
▶ Values: promotes facts as true and relegates values to opinions.

Postmodern deconstruction

▶ Inspiration: includes relativity and uncertainty in science.
▶ Truth: is a mirage.
▶ Attitude: irony.
▶ Presuppositions: unavoidable, making all claims relative and subjective.
▶ Values: sees facts and values as both affected by subjectivity.

Einstein showed how, when close to the speed of light, para-doxical things happen to relative speeds and times. Heisenberg showed how there was a fundamental uncer-tainty about subatomic particles (where versus how fast they move). Einstein didn't like that, and said that God doesn't play dice, i.e. he does not leave things to chance. But scien-tists today accept both 'relativity' and 'uncertainty' – 'quan-tum' physics. These ideas, whether understood properly or not, are part of the outlook of our culture.

In Douglas Adams' witty version of space fantasy, *The Hitch-hiker's Guide to the Galaxy*, the heroes are aboard the ship *Heart of Gold*, which is powered by an 'infinite improba-bility drive'. They activate this when they are under attack by a nuclear missile from the legendary planet of Magrathea, escaping 'certain death'. The drive causes extremely unlikely things to happen, so the missile freakishly alters into a whale by virtue of every subatomic particle changing, presumably according to the ultimate randomness implied in Heisenberg's principle!

ZAPHOD: What happened to the missiles?
FORD: Well according to the screen, they've just turned into a bowl of petunias and a very surprised looking whale.
COMPUTER: At an improbability factor of 8,767,128 to one against.

The impact of these ideas on the popular imagination is to strengthen rather different developments of postmodernism and the New Age. If two seemingly contradictory things can be true even in physics, then, the assumption goes, we should expect the rest of life to be full of paradoxes. This has a strong impact on faith. But before we move on to the issues of faith, let's look at spirituality in *The X-Files*.

The X-Files: spirituality and religion

Religious belief and experience among the characters is taken as normal, so there will be believers and unbelievers, as in the world we know. Mulder's faith is not conventional – it is paranormal paganism. But Scully is seen as a Catholic. She also wears a gold cross necklace, given to her by her mother. Navajo Indians are relevant in the trilogy bridging Seasons 2 and 3, and their healing ritual, the days-long Blessing Way Chant, becomes part of the storyline.

However, it is the exploration of off-beat and indeed occult spirituality that *The X-Files* specialises in. So we have the range of ghosts, possessions, vampires, channelling of spirits and demons, odd cults, evil spirits jumping into other people at death, faith healing, supernatural knowledge, resurrections, the curse of legendary evil spirits that turn men into animals, not to mention the whole question of contacts with UFOs and aliens, whether telepathic or physical, etc. Occult spirituality is a question we will tackle later. *The X-Files* is far from unique in occult-based storylines. However, it is stock-in-trade for the programme, and played not as fantastic nonsense (as in *Doctor Who*) but for real. As such it raises the question of the reality of its fantastic ideas.

What do those at the heart of *The X-Files* think? Creator and author Chris Carter once spent nine hours sitting on the ground in a Native American chanting ceremony, hoping to have a paranormal experience. He comments:

I'm equal parts of both characters. I'm a skeptic like Scully, but I'm also ready to be enraptured, like Mulder . . . They are the equal parts of my desire to believe in something and my inability to believe in something. My skepticism and my faith. And the writing of the characters and the voices came very easily to me. I want, like a lot of people do, to have the experience of witnessing a paranormal phenomenon. At the same time I want not to accept it, but to question it. I think those characters and those voices came out of that duality.[4]

David Duchovny, who plays the paranormal believer Mulder, is flippant and uncommitted about the show's themes. Gillian Anderson, who plays the more sceptical Scully, takes up meditation. She comments, 'I am one of the least strait-laced people you will ever meet. I'm a full-fledged believer in the supernatural, alien visitation, and other paranormal paradigms.'[5] She is far from alone. This is what makes *The X-Files* what it is – the fantastic world of horror films as a realistic documentary drama/crime thriller.

The truth is out there. . . . Science fiction has a way of taking on the big issues, the cosmic questions. As we look at the questions ahead – Are we alone in the universe? Is the future going to see our salvation or destruction? What is our true humanity? What about life, the universe and everything? – we tackle religious questions. SF throws some sharp light on them, and helps us see them in a way true to our age.

Does that mean the truth out there is simply things we opt for – just subjective ideas and feelings? Are all thoughts and feelings equally OK, equally 'true'? Like *The X-Files* should we show, to quote David Pringle, 'a blithe indifference to the

. . . flatly contradictory alternatives' around? 'The truth is out . . . of fashion', as the brilliant take on *The X-Files* in the *Babylon 5: Crusade* episode, *Visitors from Down the Street*, had it. Hero Matthew Gideon was not so keen on conspiratorial, made-up truth.

So are beliefs in truth-claims little more than fashion statements, as postmodernists imply? We'll take a shot at that by looking later at the Prime Directive in *Star Trek*, and Foundationism and *The Parliament of Dreams* in *Babylon 5*. But first, the big question: What about that other *X-Files* slogan 'We are not alone'? What really is 'out there'?

Part Two:
All Alone in the Night?

 IN THIS SECTION . . .

▶ **Are we alone?**

Do aliens exist? If it's life, but not as we know it, how different will it be? What religions might aliens have? Could they be godlike?

▶ **Gene Roddenberry and God**

Roddenberry rejected religion, but what replaced it?

▶ **Who made God?**

Was God an astronaut? How about alien telepathy? Do aliens explain religion?

▶ **Proof and faith**

The 'Babel fish' – an amusing example of the tension between proof and faith.

• 5 •
Life – But Not as We Know It

Alone in the universe?

Are we alone in the universe? This is a question at the heart of all SF, and is also the classic religious question. And what follows if we are not alone?

As we have seen, the evocative start to *Babylon 5* in Season 1 talks of 'humans and aliens . . . all alone in the night'. And *B5* is, in Season 2, 'a shining beacon in space, all alone in the night'. In our imaginations, as we live on *B5*, we sustain this fragile existence in the night of space. Like the crew of *Apollo 13*, if things go wrong we are very vulnerable. Space can be lonely.

In another way it points up the heroic nature of the struggle. Imagine *B5* as the United Nations being set up in St Helena, in the mid-Atlantic, with American military forces maintaining it, but then there is a fascist takeover of the US: how isolated those American forces would feel declaring independence. Humans on *B5* feel very much alone.

But actually they are far from alone, of course. Even in military terms, the station has the massive superior military might of the Minbari as a shield. And throughout, this 'lonely' beacon is teeming with life, both human and alien. And this is perhaps the single most asked question of space travel: Are we 'all alone in the night' of space? Are we alone in the universe?

It's rare for space fiction to be written without aliens, as in the 1987 TV series *Star Cops*, which was a sort of futuristic cops and robbers programme set on the Moon, with the odd episode on Mars. Most programmes have a wide range of aliens. Alien plants and animals, and the occasional sub-human, feature usually only as a threat. *Star Wars* is the strongest exception to that trend, with varied animal life, both sentient and non-sentient. But the most common aliens in sci-fi are equal to us – humanoids. Sometimes they are more advanced – post-human monsters, or post-human successes. Sometimes they are amazingly advanced, almost god-like creatures and spirit-type and energy-type entities (good, evil and indifferent), or entities claiming to be God.

Can the existence of alien life be proved? One way is to find it! NASA said it had – with bacteria allegedly from Mars. But the cynics were proved right: it was a false alarm. What it did show is that *The X-Files'* premise – that US agencies want to cover up news of alien life – is suspect. NASA needs mega-bucks. It knows people are interested in discovering alien life, so it tries to persuade them that by spending money on rockets to Mars, Europa and Titan, they could find life. Now if even primitive life were discovered, that would greatly increase the statistical probability of life in other solar systems. But so far, life is still only found for certain on Earth.

Christian faith – and indeed that of many other religions – would have to take account of the discovery of any form of life elsewhere. It would show a wider creative work of God. But the mere existence of life would require no other adjustments to belief. The problem really changes if the form of life discovered is 'human' to the extent of having, like us, the capacity for self-reflection and belief and trust in a God or gods, and the corresponding disbelief and distrust.

Live long and prosper!

The high point of Spielberg's 1977 film, *Close Encounters of the Third Kind*, is of course the moment when the UFO lands and makes contact with our planet. Spielberg is famous for his brilliant special effects and sense of atmosphere, and capturing the 'moment' is more the aim of that film than its plot. The parallel moment on the eighth *Star Trek* film is all the better for the subtlety of its presentation. The title of the film, *First Contact*, is all about this moment. But the drama is about the attempt of the sinister Borg to cut back in time and prevent humanity entering the interstellar warp age, and thus render them unable to resist Borg assimilation in later centuries. For all Trekkers, the final, light moment is one to savour: the *Enterprise* crew has saved the future for humanity, so the 'historic' first contact with aliens can now happen. Then a spaceship descends, and the stunned humans stand and gape as the craft opens and what we see emerging are Vulcans, declaring, 'Live long and prosper!' For any viewer familiar with Vulcans the moment can be imagined: the humans are in for a nice time, though the Vulcans may find us a bit uncivilised and certainly very illogical!

But if there were races out there as advanced as we are, or somewhat more so, what are the chances that they would turn out to be so human in appearance as Vulcans? *Star Trek* is notable for its wide range of aliens that look human apart from the odd difference or two. This is now a fine art, and actors are used to spending several hours in the make-up department! In the beginning there were problems. Mr Spock's ears originally had to be applied by the props department rather than by make-up. This meant glue, and wide variation in ear size in the early pilots. It also meant pain. Actor Leonard Nimoy was frustrated and Roddenberry even promised to write an episode where they needed to be removed surgically if Nimoy could bear it no longer!

The scene in the pilot episode *The Cage,* where Vina has 'become' a green-skinned Orion slave girl, met similar problems. Every time it was shot, the result came through with the green reverting to normal colours, no matter how dark they made the green. Eventually it transpired that the developers were confused by the green. Thinking it their mistake, they kept on chemically correcting the 'mistake'!

A few alien ideas			
	Star Trek	*Doctor Who*	*Babylon 5*
Non-humanoid	Silicon Horta; Reptilian Gorn; many incorporeal creatures of gas or light; Targ; 'Species 8472'; Tribbles; Armus.	Yeti; Zarbi; Ice Warriors; Sea Devils; Silurians; many other animals, insects or reptilians.	Invisible, spidery Shadows; Mafia-like N'Grath, a giant insect; and other methane breathers.
Humanoid	Betazoids; Guinan; Odo, Shapeshifters, Kelvans and the Q don human form.	The Doctor; Time Lords; Thals; Kinda.	Centauri; Techno-mages; Varn.
Cyborgs	The Borg.	Daleks; Cybermen.	Cyberweb telepaths.

Androids and humanoid artificial intelligence	Data; Lore Mudd's women, EMH.	Sharaz Jek's; Taran; Kraal; Drahvins.	
Other artificial intelligence	The computer; Vaal; Nomad.	WOTAN; BOSS; [ORAC, Zen from *Blake's 7*].	
Masked quasi-humanoid		Autons; Sontarans; Voc Robots Voords; etc.	Angelic Vorlons hidden in encounter suits; Pak'ma'ra.
Humanoid with prosthetics	The vast majority of aliens: Romulan/ Vulcan/Mintakan/ Ocampan/Ferengi ears; Bajoran noses; Cardassian/ Klingon/Kazon cranial growths; blue antennaed Andorians; the modest leopard spots of the Trill; and Talosians and other super-advanced aliens with large cranial developments.	Draconians; Sontarans; Ogrons Sensorites; and several others.	Exo-skeletal headed Minbari; lizard-like Narn; and most other aliens, like Drazi, Brokiri and Zathras.

Babylon 5 and *Star Trek* have concentrated on humans with prosthetics, while *Doctor Who* usually hid its monsters behind rubber masks. This may be just a matter of taste. But beyond it are a couple of questions: If aliens exist, what will they look like? Will they look human? And anyway, what does the way we picture aliens say about us? Of course, as Jon Pertwee once commented, where actors' eyes remain visible, aliens can look far more expressive. So we have mainly humanoid aliens for acting. But in reality, life is so varied on *this* planet, it would be incredible that on most other planets it would look human.

Why is the *Star Trek* universe so humanoid? *The Chase* (*TNG*, 1993) gives a surprising and direct answer: a story of how all humanoid races were ultimately one, scattered by a primeval race. That takes and adds to the nineteenth-century Panspermia theory of Svaante Arrhenius, which suggested that very primitive life is scattered through space. Are we alone in the universe – and would the discovery of such humanoid aliens elsewhere end the sense of solitude? Right now we have distant 'cousins' in every race on Earth. *The Chase* would only give us more distant human 'cousins' in the galaxy. That still leaves the real questions unanswered. When Christopher Columbus discovered the New World, and humans living there, their existence did not provide the answer to the meaning of life, or change the sense of human aloneness. Nor would the discovery of humanoids on other planets. It would just make the adventure of discovery more complex.

Do Vulcans exist?

'A planet circling that far left star in Orion's belt – see?' Jim Kirk asked Edith Keeler in *City on the Edge of Forever*. 'That's where in the twenty-first century . . . I believe a famous novelist will write a classic.' If *we* went there, would we find a novelist? Move a little to the right of Orion, to Omicron 2 Eridani: if we went there, would we find the planet Vulcan, with its logical humanoids? Or more generally, as space exploration develops (no doubt for now by Earth-based enquiries), are we likely to find other life-forms similar to ourselves, self-aware creatures, sentient life-forms?

The scientists tell us we can have no firm answer at the moment. It is looking less and less likely that even the most primitive life exists or ever has existed within our own solar system beyond Earth, and the claims of Martian bacterial life have proved hollow. But if it ever is discovered, that will change the guesses about life elsewhere a lot.

Scientists *have* discovered planets around other stars. So far only giant planets have been inferred. But, we are told, sometime within the next 20 years it should be possible to infer Earth-like planets, and whether the organic chemicals associated with life are in that star system. What is needed for life 'as we know it' is an oxygenated planet of sufficient size in the temperate zone. There may be loads of dead planets like the other ones in our solar system, and plenty of other places totally inhospitable to life. But if the list starts with trillions of planets, we could still end up with a large number of 'M Class' and 'L Class' planets (to use the *Star Trek* jargon).

But there is another problem. The chemicals for life may

exist on comets in a star system, but it is a big leap from that to concluding that on a certain planet there could be *intelligent* life. So another track has been the attempt to discover intelligent transmissions, e.g. by artificial radio waves. This has been the heart of the SETI research (the Search for Extra-Terrestrial Intelligence). But this has so far met total silence. Nor can we assume that life is out there but not advanced enough to develop radio waves. If intelligent life were common, then as the scientists usually date the Milky Way as twice as old as the Earth and the rest of our solar system, then life far more advanced than our own would have to be around. There should be many artificial radio waves. That still leaves the possibility of intelligent life existing *rarely* elsewhere. The scientists have not reached a consensus. Indeed biologists tend to argue that life should be common in the universe, while physicists more commonly argue it would seem rare, indeed probably unique here.

But if we did meet other races, intelligent but different, like the Centauri, it would of course be a great adventure – or a great threat. The last time our (Western) culture met a New World, indeed a string of new cultures following the voyages of discovery after Columbus, it proceeded to conquer them. What would have been the European response if it had met with equivalent or at least sufficient power to resist conquering? Japan provides the historical answer: confused messages. The Japanese heard of European conquests and eventually assumed the West intended a similar conquest of Japan. So with extraordinary persecution they obliterated every trace they could of European impact. Imagine if Japan had had far superior technology, particularly military power: maybe a sixteenth-century equivalent of *Babylon 5*'s

Earth/Minbari war could have happened!

Is it true that we are not like that now? What if we discovered a race that some said could wipe us out – unless we got our strike in first, as the gung-ho would put it? Would it be met with a Roddenberry-like 'Let's all be friends', or a reversion to macho panic?

Alien religion

If intelligent aliens with their own culture do exist, this raises a further question: What about the status of these aliens before God? The answer of SF until recently was a bit thin on religion – especially alien religions. They were normally make-believe. Religions, like Terry Nation's on Exxilon and Cygnus Alpha, were humanoid inventions.

As we have seen, *Justice* (*TNG*, 1987) shows an artificial god. The Edo are maintained in what is shown as a paradisal but infantile state. For Troi their planet is an 'Eden'. The locals seem to have nothing to do but run around and play games wearing skimpy clothing, promoting love-making, happiness and sex with gay abandon (no, make that 'straight' abandon!). The one flaw in their society is that every violation of the changing rules – like running on some grass marked out of bounds – has only one unavoidable result: capital punishment. Oops! No one told Wesley Crusher, so he's due for the chop.

The moral dilemma is between conflicting requirements of justice (hence the title). However, it turns out that the Edo worship an entity in the sky, which is normally invisible, and which shifts in and out of reality as we know it. Picard's personal dilemma is whether to overrule the justice of the Prime

Directive, or overrule the locals' lethal justice. Moreover, the Edo's god has the power to thwart his plans.

The plot has a very weak resolution, in that Picard simply appeals to the 'god' that absolute rules are unhelpful, and without further ado Wesley is spared! You wonder how Edo who'd seen their loved ones executed would feel. . . . Here, the god is absurdly flawed; a creature who needs to be taught a lot by humans!

Lonely Among Us

PICARD: But do you understand the basis of all this nonsense between them?

RIKER: No, sir. I never understood that sort of hostility even when I studied Earth history.

PICARD: Really? Oh yes. Well these life-forms feel such passionate hatreds over matters of customs, God-concepts – even, strangely enough, economic systems.

Lonely Among Us is similar, discussing two warring, cannibalistic races, as is *Who Watches the Watchers?* where Picard is mistaken for an 'overseer' – a god – by the Mintakans. Picard exclaims that these rational, proto-Vulcans would be sent back to the 'dark ages of superstition and fear' if they recovered such belief in 'overseers'.

What sort of gods?

These unsympathetic pictures show a debunking of certain types of gods. But what sort of gods are they, and how realistic or credible are they? Gods regularly crop up in science fiction. There are the gods of old, like Apollo (*TOS*), Thor and Osiris (*Stargate SG-1*) or Sutekh (*Doctor Who*). They can be disclosed as alien impostors without any believers getting too shirty about it! Then there are godlike characters like Q, an almost omnipotent prankster. *TNG* began and closed with Q stories, and both *DS9* and *Voyager* have had Q episodes, and the Q episodes are among the most hilarious in the *Star Trek* series.

TNG began with *Encounter at Farpoint*. Its idea was that some day humanity might cross a line at which ultra-powerful beings would think about calling a halt to our desire 'to explore strange new worlds'. If the galaxy really were inhabited by the many superhuman entities encountered by Kirk and Spock, this would be a legitimate possibility. And Q does like to pose as a god – as in the time Picard is seemingly at the point of death, and his next experience is seeing Q say to him, 'Welcome to the after-life, Jean-Luc!'

A few more godlike super-beings

Doctor Who
- ▶ The Celestial Toymaker.
- ▶ Mighty Kronos in *The Time Monster*.
- ▶ The Black Guardian and White Guardian and the 'Eternals' in *Enlightenment*.
- ▶ The Doctor's own race: 'I'm a Time Lord. I walk through eternity.'

Superman II
- ▶ Superman himself, and three evil superhuman entities from his planet of Krypton.

Superman III
▶ A good and an evil Superman (following a snarl-up with Kryptonite).

Babylon 5
▶ The First Ones.
▶ The Vorlons.
▶ The Shadows.

All these entities in *Babylon 5* are first seen as advanced aliens, then as angels and demons, before again being presented as fallible supra-human entities.

These 'gods' are as flawed as the human race. There are differences, of course. Beings that walk in eternity have different problems and interests. So an Eternal seeks Tegan, and Q seeks Vash, to get a cheap thrill by riding on the back of ordinary human experience.

One God or many?

Let's return to our question on the faith that might sustain us in such a space-bound future. We have been reminded that many of the more amusing *Star Trek* stories are almost a throw-back to Greek or Roman gods, with superhuman entities across the galaxy. But will we meet such massively advanced beings, almost godlike entities? What will happen to us if we do?

Maybe the idea of Apollo is not so far-fetched to represent this kind of cosmic entity. For what were the gods of ancient Greece and Rome if not superhuman versions of very human figures, with flaws and sins similar to our own? What was the point of belief in such gods? It was the expression of the feeling that the world does contain hostile powers and forces that need to be appeased. These gods represented the powerful forces within and beyond humanity. Forces like love and war, music and words, ageing, death and the underworld, thunder, storm and sea.

Are we alone in the universe? Those who believed in gods like Apollo certainly didn't think so. They feared the gods' hostility: if these gods were characters like ourselves, with similar desires and a readiness to attack those who angered them, then they were fearsome. To us, this is rightly superstition, but to those caught up in it, it all seemed very natural. You're out on the sea one day and everything's fine, but another day you're in danger of shipwreck. Did you give Neptune (or whoever) that offering? This was very much the attitude of the Mediterraneans who wanted to throw Jonah overboard in the famous Bible story.

But there was one ancient race that 'secularised' the world, and said it was superstition (fear based on false belief) to see the world, or the self, as the plaything of gods, spirits and demonic forces. This was the faith of the Jews. It said that not just the world, but all of space – the stars and planets, the Sun and Moon – were simply creations. They were not gods. Astrology and all other beliefs in mysterious powers of celestial lights are linked with worship or fear of unknown hidden powers in the skies. The account of creation in Genesis 1, in a deliberate belittling of any assumed power of the Sun and Moon, says God made them, and simply calls them matter-of-factly 'the greater light . . . and the lesser light', and adds in a throw-away phrase, 'He also made the stars.'

And not only here, at the start of the Bible, but through-out, the picture of the universe is that it is made by God, and so is orderly. Psalms, like 8, 19, 90, 104 and 136, and prophets, like Amos 5:8, 26 and Isaiah 47:12–15, to name a few, declare that stars are no gods – they are physical cre-ations and part of the coherent universe. It is this belief that formed the basis for the development of early modern sci-ence: the universe is not unpredictable, depending on the moods of gods, but orderly, if complex, and may be observed, discovered and made sense of.

If we boldly travelled among the stars (assuming the well-known question-marks against faster-than-light space travel could be overcome), this biblical attitude says we would not come across mysterious, frightening, unfathomable, godlike powers. Instead, the universe would essentially make sense according to broadly consistent patterns. Orion would not be a hunter thrown by gods into the sky, but a set of stars and planets, nebulae and galaxies. And if we were able to travel to each of its stars or to the famous Orion nebula, the sights would be extraordinary, but they would not include the gods – or indeed Q.

One highly credible aspect of the Centauri culture as por-trayed on *Babylon 5* concerns their religion. They are poly-theistic and polygamous. They have a light-hearted but real faith in many gods and goddesses. And their men have sev-eral wives. Ambassador Londo Mollari has three, and in the story *Soul Mates* we hear that by Imperial decree he is able to divorce two of them. Theologian Helmut Thielicke com-mented on this sort of issue once. He compared the experi-ence of Christian missionaries in polygamous societies. Some operated the hard line that required polygamous men to divorce their wives on accepting the Christian faith. Others took the soft line that tolerated their continuing polygamy after accepting the faith. In both cases, by one generation later, the Christian communities had become monogamous. Thielicke said that they moved to faith in one God, the God of love, from the previous belief in an array of gods, where any overarching God was remote and irrelevant. And this committed relationship with one God led them away from polygamy to the committed, loving relationship of monogamy: '*Agape* [Christian love] as a bond of fidelity tallies with monogamy.'[1]

Centauri religion reminds us that belief in many gods is real. The storylines in many science fiction dramas remind us that belief in godlike powers and forces – things like fate, luck and unseen powers – is not so far from the minds of many people. But belief in many godlike powers is superstitious, and is more easily in tune with polygamous attitudes. Maybe today's confused half-belief in all sorts of things out there that *The X-Files* has tapped into is part of the same cultural shift as today's confused half-belief in monogamy.

The key question is: Should we drop the idea that you can believe in one truth, one God? Is God truly the clue to life, or is he an invention of people in the past – or even of aliens? That is our next question.

• 6 •
Roddenberry's 'The God Thing'

Gene Roddenberry was brought up by his mother as a Baptist, but little of what he heard went in deep and he went on to become a humanist and atheist. In his last few years, he became a high-profile member of the American Humanist Association, and in an interview with *The Humanist*, plus comments to friends, as reported by tell-all biographer Joel Engel, Roddenberry gave various reasons for rejecting religious faith.[1]

It was in 1964 that he developed his first *Star Trek* idea, including a Captain Robert T. April, a logical female 'Number One', a half-Martian called Spock, Navigator José Tylor and a doctor called 'Bones', all in the USS *Yorktown*. In the actual pilot, *The Cage*, with Captain Christopher Pike, Roddenberry's private and public life overlapped, as the logical female Number One was played by Majel Barrett, at that time his mistress. She went on, at his encouragement, to play nurse Chapell in the original series of *Star Trek*, Lwaxana Troi in *The Next Generation*, and the computer's voice throughout. She was born as Majel Lee Hudec, and after Gene divorced his wife Eileen, Majel went on to marry him in a Buddhist-Shinto ceremony conducted in Tokyo in 1969.

After wartime service, he survived a crash as a crewman on a PanAm flight. He recalls that in a situation where other crew and several passengers died, and he was seconds away from possible death himself, he did not for a moment pray: his atheism went all the way down. He became an atheist, suspicious of and hostile towards all faith. He once said of

President Jimmy Carter, 'I worry about a president who claims he has a personal relationship with God.' This shows a fear of God being real. Biographer Joel Engel suggests that Roddenberry allowed himself to become a kind of substitute god for the adoring fans; a god who could never make a mistake, just like his characters.

Roddenberry rejects religion

Problem: In a sermon he heard when he was 14, he believed they said that at communion 'you . . . are supposed to be eating the body of Christ and drinking his blood. My first impression was, "This is a bunch of cannibals they've put me down among."'

Comment: This is an odd mistake. This was not even a Catholic church. American Baptists would say that communion is a ceremony to remember the death of Christ. At most, they say that Christ is present, spiritually, to believers.

Problem: More significant, perhaps, was his decision at this stage to reject Jesus as being like Santa Claus, and treat religion as 'nonsense, magic and superstition'.

Comment: This illustrates the idea that faith is something you grow out of. The fact that 90 per cent of people in the world have some faith is dismissed. Such humanists see themselves as the mature *avant garde*, those who have discovered what everyone will grow into in the future.

Problem: He wanted to be freed from God as 'the guy who knows you masturbate'. Roddenberry resolved to shun religion, 'to extricate himself . . . from any emotion or thought that might undermine the pursuit of pleasure' (as Joel Engel put it).

Comment: This reveals a none-too-hidden motive clear enough in much of Roddenberry's own contributions actual and intended to *Star Trek*. If he had had his way, for example, his Betazoid character (which became Deanna Troi) would have had four breasts and engaged in constant sex.

Problem: He believed that people started with 'negative gods who kept us from all kinds of behaviour' moving on to one, positive god, who was to be feared and who could inculcate shame, guilt and blame.

Comment: This belief is of a piece with a picture of evolution in religion. First primitive then advanced religion, but then on beyond religion to independence from God. What's more, the key is a pleasure principle: first, gods you fear who stop pleasure, then more positive gods who inculcate shame, and then beyond gods into being free to act according to your own desires and motives.

Star Trek II

We have seen that in the original series religion was shown as invented. The series was cancelled, but then in the 1970s interest and indeed cult status grew, with the programme endlessly repeated ever since. An animated version followed. Later, talk began of a new series, first involving the original crew, or an expanded version of it. Scripts were written for this series, starting with Gene L. Coon's *He Walked Among Us*, where a Starfleet officer called Bayne has trashed the Prime Directive, advancing the local culture's technical development by 1,000 years. He is hailed as a god. Kirk has to remove him without plunging the planet into chaos. But it is Roddenberry's own script of 1975, *The God Thing*, that is revealing. Paramount decided they would not run with a script that would amount to Kirk versus God. Richard Colla, who was familiar with the screenplay for this tale, comments:

 That script was much more daring. By the time they got to the spaceship, the alien manifested itself and said, 'Do you know me?' Kirk said, 'No, I don't know who you are.' It said, 'Strange. How could you not know who I am?' So it shapeshifts and became another image and said, 'Do you know me?' Kirk said, 'No, who are you?' It replied, 'The time has passed and you should know me by now.' It changes again and comes up in the form of Christ the carpenter, and says, 'Do you know me?' and Kirk said, 'Oh, now I know who you are.' And he says, 'How strange you didn't know these other forms of me.' Really, what Gene had written was that this 'thing' was sent forth to communicate the law of the universe, and that as time goes on the law needs to be reinterpreted. And at that time, 2,000 years ago, the law was interpreted by this carpenter image. But as time went on, the law was meant to be reinterpreted, and the Christ figure was meant to reappear in different forms. But this machine malfunctioned, and it was like a phonograph record that got caught in a groove and kept grooving back.[2]

Richard Colla

Star Trek II, with such scripts for its new five-year mission with the original crew (with three new characters to replace Spock: Commander Willard Decker, Lieutenant Ilia, and a full Vulcan as science officer: Xon), never happened. And a string of scripts written for this series remained unused. The success of *Star Wars* as a film provided what proved to be the way forward for *Star Trek*, and the increasingly successful films followed, then brand new series.

The trouble with quibbles

It's odd, but when people quibble about God in the name of science, it seems that something unexpected happens. The same month as he wrote *The God Thing*, Roddenberry was approached by a group who wanted him to write a screenplay that focused on their study and experience of paranormal events, including their belief that through psychic channelling they had contacted a group of extraterrestrials called 'The Nine'. The need for the money they offered persuaded him to write what proved to be a highly autobiographical first draft. In *The Nine*, hero Jim NacNorth is in practice Gene Roddenberry. The story is his: a womaniser, sceptical about the paranormal, whose sci-fi movie script has just been rejected. He maintains scepticism despite discovering psychic powers. He achieves reconciliation with his wife, and while the character says that no paranormal phenomena are confirmed, he accepts part of their message: 'I believe I know now that all life is One, that we're part of a wondrous, eternal miracle which we have yet to fully comprehend.'

In real life, Andrija Puharich, who brought Uri Geller and his spoon-bending telekinetic claims to world attention, was part of this group. Roddenberry began to accept at least some of what he was seeing. Indeed, he told his secretary Susan Sackett of his out-of-body experience in childhood. The tape of his conversation through the medium, or 'channeller', Phyllis Schlemmer with 'The Nine' shows him 'unfailingly polite and engaged', as journalist Joel Engel reports. Through Schlemmer's voice, the entities claimed that Roddenberry was the reincarnation of a grandson of Moses and Simon Peter's father Jonah, as well as of the Roman god Jupiter! Regarding reincarnation Roddenberry told Sackett, 'I believe that we continue, but you don't come back with all your thoughts intact. You're not the same being. You become one with the All.' But in practice his beliefs on these matters, particularly the existence of UFOs and of real (i.e. psychic) contact with them, fluctuated, and he became a strong opponent of belief in UFOs and extraterrestrials.

This is perhaps due to the fate of that script. The group had paid for a first draft and a rewrite. Roddenberry accepted the money, but asked Jon Povill to do the rewrite. But that brought the problems for Gene to the fore, as Povill's 'MacNorth', in rejecting 'The Nine' despite evidence, has a breakdown. He showed the script to Harold Livingstone, who went on to produce the planned series *Star Trek II*, and who immediately saw Gene Roddenberry in the script, flaws and all, in particular his massive insecurity about *Star Trek* being his only success. What if it was a success because 'previous lives' had in some way pre-programmed him to write it? Sackett claims Gene was going through a lot of depression in life, especially at that stage. He needed to break free from being Jim MacNorth.

The God Thing was never screened along with the rest of *Star Trek II*. But just as elements of that series ended up in the first film, *Star Trek: The Motion Picture*, so elements of the ideas of *The God Thing* ended up in the fifth film, *The Final Frontier*. This was William Shatner's film, and he was taking up the claims of TV evangelists to hear God, and effectively debunking them. Shatner explained:

 'I took the TV evangelist persona and created a holy man who thought God had spoken to him. He believed God had told him, "I need many followers, and I need a vehicle to spread my word throughout the universe." . . . the Enterprise . . . but gradually . . . God . . . begins to show his true colours, which are those of the devil . . . So essentially that was my story: that man conceives of God in his own image . . .'

The irony that Gene Roddenberry protested confuses commentators: 'I didn't object to it being an alien claiming to be God, but there was too much in it that an audience could have thought was really God or really the devil, and I very strongly resist believing in either.'[3]

That says it all: the drama is not the point; making sure belief in God is eliminated is. But *The Nine* shows that his atheism led to superstition.

• 7 •
Who Made God?

It is one thing to suggest that it makes better sense to believe in one God than many gods, and that such belief – in God as the Creator of Sun, Moon and stars – works better with a scientific attitude to the material universe than beliefs in astrology. But what most of us ask is about belief in one God versus belief in no God. One striking if defiant way of expressing this is to ask, 'Who made God?' Gene Roddenberry's *The God Thing* is one script suggesting 'God' is an alien. Others have suggested that SF idea for real.

Erich von Däniken: 'God was an astronaut'

In the space age, some writers have used science fiction ideas to reinterpret real history. Most high profile was Erich von Däniken, but he was followed by others. The idea is that religious experiences, particularly the most momentous ones in history, were caused not by God in the conventional sense, but by some advanced astronaut, who was winding us up. *Star Trek* has 'Apollo' as an astronaut god; in *Stargate* Osiris and Thor were alien visitors to Earth, and *Doctor Who* regularly has Exxilons in Peru, Daleks on the *Marie Celeste*, etc., giving a 'von Däniken' spin on history. Douglas Adams' *The Hitch-hiker's Guide to the Galaxy* has the funniest version: immature aliens called 'teasers' who deliberately appear in obscure places to tease the only person seeing them.

But von Däniken says he is not writing fiction when he tells us: 'The past teemed with unknown gods who visited the primeval Earth in manned space-ships.'[1] Von Däniken popularised his ideas in tabloid newspapers and large book sales from the late 1960s, in *Chariots of the Gods: Was God an Astronaut?* and *Gold of the Gods*, etc. He claimed that many artefacts showed pictures of astronauts visiting ancient civilisations (biblical and other), and argued that ancient stories and pictures were really accounts of alien spacemen at work: beliefs in all-powerful beings, angels, demons, gods and God were really caused by alien astronauts. As many have written about him, and his findings have been seriously undermined by evidence that he made up many of them, and was provably wrong on hundreds of statements, I would like, for a change, to explore another, even more colourful, example.

R. L. Dione: 'God drives a flying saucer'

Even von Däniken draws the line at the idea that Jesus was a spaceman. But that did not stop R. L. Dione in 1974 in his *God Drives a Flying Saucer*. The book argues that the many UFO sightings can't all be wrong, and cites a few; and that the language of biblical and other ancient stories sounds like UFO sightings of long ago.

Dione's book is all about UFOs. He is convinced they're real, and he relates episodes of contact with them. In one example, he believes that one couple's 'story of abduction by a crew of saucerians and their subsequent adventure defies any system of logic to refute it. Their story, told under hypnosis to a reputable psychiatrist, is undoubtedly true, incredible as it may seem.'[2] There are, however, several elements to this story that surely defy logic: UFO sighting, abduction and telepathic contact – with a bit of hypnosis added!

UFOs and famous monsters

Claims of UFO sightings are like those of seeing implausible but not impossible things: the Yeti, the Loch Ness Monster, etc. They've been 'seen' but not found. Here are some comparisons.

Yeti/Bigfoot

▶ Evidence: Sightings, droppings and footprints.
▶ Questions: Photo of Bigfoot, but not of Yeti.
▶ Interpretation: The Yeti could exist, but the evidence is not strong enough to be certain.

The Kraken

▶ Evidence: Many Norwegian sailors told of seeing a sea monster they called the Kraken.
▶ Question: Was it drink, dementia or truth?
▶ Interpretation: They probably saw a giant squid.

The Loch Ness Monster

▶ Evidence: Many alleged sightings, with some photographs – most notably the 1934 surgeon's picture of a brontosaurus-like head in the water.
▶ Questions: The 1934 picture was recently shown, by relatives of the men who made the photo, to have been a forgery. Many underwater searches have failed to find the monster.
▶ Interpretation: Fakes weaken but don't end the case. But the longer they look and find nothing, the more probable it is Nessie doesn't exist. If someone actually finds and retrieves a loch creature, its existence would be proved.

No doubt it would be a little different from the popular picture of imagination.

Dragons

▶ Evidence: There were many reports of dragons in the Middle Ages. Famous knights fought them and won. And some even brought their trophies home.

▶ Questions: Are tales of long ago exaggerations, or is that just modern prejudice?

▶ Interpretation: There is a factual basis behind such beliefs: the crocodile. In the castle at Karlštejn, near Prague, there is the head of a 'dragon' slain by a fearless medieval knight, and the skull is indeed that of a crocodile. Similar Indonesian tales were shown to be based on reality when the Komodo dragon, a lizard larger than people, was found in 1912.

Today we can photograph all sorts of reclusive animals repeatedly at will, and indeed capture them. So a Nessie or Yeti could theoretically be located, repeatedly photographed, and even captured. If it were, the principles of science would not be overthrown! But it's unscientific to say that since an awful lot of people claim to have seen Nessie, it *must* exist. All we can say is that it's conceivable but unlikely that Nessie exists. Until harder evidence that we can return to is found, like fossilised or fleshy remains, or a lair in which we can repeatedly film the fabled creature, that's all that can be said scientifically. More sightings for Bigfoot make it a little more probable. But on the ambiguous evidence, to say that Nessie exists or doesn't exist is a belief. Eye-witness accounts, alleged photographs, confessions of forging photographs, and all the underwater searches for Nessie that failed to sight it, add to the reasonableness or unreasonableness of such beliefs.

And the same is broadly true for evidence about UFOs. Some people believe fervently in the sightings – particularly if they were the ones who made them! Of course it is possible that they are real, and the aliens that go with them. And if one day an ET is stranded and, as in the Spielberg film, a bunch of scientists get their hands on it, then the clinching evidence would be there (so long as there's no cover-up!). But so far all we have is reports of unconfirmed sightings, no clinching evidence. Instead, the US government tells us that many earlier 'sightings' were top secret stealth bombers, which they reported as alien crashes or UFOs. Such new evidence, new sightings and evidence of cover-up only tilts the reasonableness or unreasonableness of this belief.

What about telepathic contact? I think it's quite revealing that so many tales tell of telepathic and hypnotic contact with aliens. Meetings with aliens, alien abductions and the like have the flavour of the language of vision, of supernatural encounter. What is really going on here? Unseen entities reply to our questions, claiming to be aliens. It's more than coincidentally like seances, channelling, ouija board experiences, or indeed like the beliefs of many in earlier times that they had been contacted by fairies. You contact 'something'. Maybe in the sixteenth century it would claim to be a fairy. In more recent times it might claim to be your late grandmother, and surprise you by using that secret name that only she and you knew. At that point you might be hooked – or back off in fear. Either way, it is likely you have been affected spiritually. Today that 'something' will often claim to be an alien.

Dione backed up his example of alien abduction and telepathy with evidence through hypnosis. In relating how 'contact' was initiated, he comments: 'The saucerian in this incident was not only receiving and interpreting brain waves from Barney Hill, but also sending the subject an intelligible signal. He was in fact using a form of telepathy . . . and furthermore, it is evident that the creature was inducing a hypnotic state in the subject.'[3]

What is going on with 'telepathic encounters with aliens' is a sort of religious experience. It is important to set this in a spiritual context, and ask about the nature of the experience. After all, those involved in freeing people from evil spirits report that the classic 'alien' looks rather too similar to visions some people have had of demons. I personally have spent time with people who have been unhelpfully affected by spirits posing as aliens – both people for whom the idea of telepathically contacting (i.e. praying to) aliens pops into their minds, and those who have been affected by seeing a vision of an alien, which goes on to manifest itself as spiritual evil.

As for Dione's mention of hypnosis (which he thinks acts as a lie detector!), that actually strengthens the spiritual concern. Hypnosis, particularly by entertainers, can affect people spiritually, like occult activity does. As Francis MacNutt says: 'There are dangers in being hypnotised, when your will is unprotected and you can be exposed to something invading your soul.'[4] To seek psychic contact with aliens, and then seek hypnosis to confirm and entrench that, doubles the spiritual dangers of openness to spirits in disguise. This is clear when we hear that Dione says this telepathic contact with aliens will achieve 'a new era in our culture. The barrier presented by language differences will be swept away . . . The blind will see, and the deaf will hear. Crime will be a thing of the past . . . Communication with animals and insects will be possible.'[5] This is the language of the believer: my new religious experience (psychic contact with aliens) will bring salvation and paradise.

So it is right to be cautious about suggestions of making telepathic contact with unseen powers. A far greater problem than getting abducted by aliens is getting affected by an evil presence that can masquerade as an alien just as easily as it can pretend to be your late grandmother, secret knowledge and all.

Are religious experiences caused by aliens?

Dione recasts the history of religious experience in the Bible and in history as the effect of various alien interventions. A massive problem with his account, like so many others, is a painfully wooden literalism in relation to the biblical text. The old saying about biblical texts is true: 'A text without a context is a pretext for mistakes.' Read it without taking it in its original cultural time and space, without feeling properly how the people of those days thought, how they described things, and you'll get it wrong. If you read a sentence from the Bible or any ancient writing as if plain old Joe Bloggs from next door said it, then all sorts of comic mistakes will abound. You won't get any of the jokes. Nor will you feel what's really important to the writer. You'll treat what they say as a quarry to mine for what *you* want to hear rather than what they want to say. And instead of a quarry, you'll enter a minefield. The Old Testament in Ezekiel 10 tells of angels, fiery shields, heavenly firmaments and wheels within wheels. Dione says that these verses show how 'not only were saucers sighted in biblical times but their occupants actually made contact with earthlings'. With this outlook, it quickly becomes a matter of ease to suggest that the star of Bethlehem was an event that today would be a 'flying saucer report'.

It's not just the Bible. Dione also tosses in a claim that the famous apparitions of Mary to the Catholic faithful – mainly children – especially at Fatima in 1917, with the elements of angels and balls of light, were contacts by aliens instead. Whatever else the visions at Fatima were, it is clear they were a religious experience. Dione sees religious visions as created by what he will call 'God', but 'God' is his name for the chief alien.

Dione tells us his 'saucerians' made a bid to ensure the fulfilment of their Fatima prophecies of the Second World War and Russia's conversion: 'The responsibility for World War II rests solely on one man, Adolf Hitler . . . Is it a coincidence that Hitler, while confined in a prison cell (where electromagnetic signals could be beamed at him), wrote *Mein Kampf* outlining his plans for world conquest, in which the territory of communistic, atheistic Russia was the prime target?'[6]

He adds that inspiring biblical writers by 'beaming signals' was easier for the aliens if the writers were 'incarcerated or otherwise immobilized'!

Dione's biblical stories of alien intervention

Old Testament

▶ The creation of Eve.

▶ The angels whom the Sodomites wanted to abuse.

▶ The cloud through which God speaks in Exodus 13.

▶ Manna and quail.

▶ Thunder and lightning attending the Ten Commandments.

▶ Ezekiel's vision.

▶ Elijah's prophecies of drought and rain.

▶ All references to the glory of the Lord.

▶ Prophecies of the Messiah coming true because the 'God'
alien made them happen.

▶ All visions.

New Testament

▶ Peter's vision at Joppa (the Spirit, we are told, 'is the electro-magnetic signal beamed from a UFO by God').

▶ The transfiguration.

▶ All the miracles, including casting out of demons, which
is put down to 'the effectiveness of . . . the brain-
manipulating device'.

▶ The virgin birth: 'We can be reasonably certain, however,
that a biological specialist, the angel Gabriel, used the
hypnotising device prior to and during the artificial
insemination of Mary; and to insure that she retained her
badge of virginity, Gabriel undoubtedly used a hypoder-
mic needle.'

And so on. If all visions and freeing of people from evil spirits is done by aliens, that leaves me in a quandary. Having prayed with people, and seen them freed from evil and radically changed as a result, that must make me an alien too! Or is some alien forced to act every time I pray 'in the name of Jesus'? Clearly, Dione has no experience of God at work in this way today. His theory makes every Pentecostal and charismatic an alien in disguise, not to mention many Catholics, Orthodox, Anglicans and Protestants who receive answers to prayer.

Dione, von Däniken and in his own way Gene Roddenberry illustrate how people who remove God from the picture can surprise us by filling the gap with the occult and superstition. I'm reminded of G. K. Chesterton's comment that people who stop believing in God don't believe in nothing, they believe in anything! Making a similar point, but more positively, is Michael White in his 'Afterword' in *The Science of The X-Files*:

'So why does the subject of the paranormal intrigue and captivate us so? Why do we tune into the *X-Files*, buy the novels, wear the T-shirts? In each of us there is a yearning for something larger than life, something beyond the mundane. Perhaps, as life becomes more comfortable, we need to find something extra, something beyond ourselves. Most of us cannot find this extra element in our "real" lives so we look for it elsewhere – we escape.'[7]

But the real question that returns every time such a writer as Dione claims that God was really an alien in disguise is: Who made God? Who made this God-alien? Sometimes Christians and other believers in one God are asked: 'You say God made everything, but who made God?' It's a confused question. The standard answer to this is to remind the questioner that 'God' means the one who made *everything*, therefore no one can have made God. Another way is to answer the question as if it made sense: 'An entity called God made everything, but if anything made him, he would *really* be God! Call him the "God-above-God" if you like!' If our questioner then asks, 'And who made the "God-above-God"?' the answer is: 'The God above the "God-above-God".' Of course this could go on *ad infinitum*. Where do you stop? Because the traditional word for the end point in the line, the 'first cause' who was uncaused by anything else, is 'God'. So this question confronts Dione, von Däniken, the *Star Trek* script of 1975, and all others who suggest that 'God' is a powerful alien: 'And who made this "God"?' All the questions about life, the universe and everything remain unanswered by ideas of alien plots.

As philosopher Martin Heidegger once asked, 'Why beings at all, rather than just nothing?'[8] Aliens dressed up as God only defer the question: Does God exist?

• 8 •
That About Wraps It up for God

As we saw earlier, SF in the late 1970s tried to become more realistic in many ways, including the need to understand alien languages. The best and most amusing version of these is the Babel fish in Douglas Adams' *The Hitch-hiker's Guide to the Galaxy* (Pan, 1979), which is supposedly placed in the ear of the traveller. The radio show starred 'the Book', a repository of information for the galactic hitch-hiker. It tells us:

The Babel fish is small, yellow, leech-like and probably the oddest thing in the Universe. It feeds on brainwave energy, absorbing all unconscious frequencies and then excreting telepathically a matrix formed from the conscious frequencies and nerve signals picked up from the speech centres of the brain. The practical upshot of which is that if you stick one in your ear, you can instantly understand anything being said to you in any form of language. The speech you hear decodes the brainwave matrix.

Now it is such a bizarrely improbable coincidence that anything so mind-bogglingly useful could evolve purely by chance that some thinkers have chosen to see it as a final clinching proof of the non-existence of God. The argument goes like this: 'I refuse to prove that I exist,' says God. 'For proof denies faith, and without faith I am nothing.' 'But,' says man, 'the Babel fish is a dead giveaway, isn't it? It proves you exist, and so therefore you don't. Q.E.D.' 'Oh dear,' says God, 'I hadn't thought of that' – and promptly vanishes in a puff of logic. 'Oh, that was easy,' says man, and for an encore proves that black is white – and gets killed at the next zebra crossing.

Most leading theologians claim that this argument is a load of dingoes' kidneys. But that didn't stop Oolon Colluphid making a small fortune, when he used it as the central theme of his best-selling book, *Well That About Wraps It Up For God*.

The argument, wonderfully lampooned here, is John Hick's approach. In *Faith and Knowledge* (Cornell, 1957 and Fontana, 1974), he saw faith as the flipside of freedom. And in *Christianity at the Centre* (SCM, 1968), he talked of the 'epistemic distance' between people and God (from the Greek word for knowledge, *episteme*). We are not given strong proof of God's existence, said Hick, because that removes freedom to believe or doubt, and so cancels the need for faith. If God forced knowledge of himself on us, we could not grow in a searching relationship, and could not develop faith. So God, said Hick, created an 'epistemic distance' – a space between humanity and certainty about God, so faith could grow.

It is this approach that the Babel fish teasingly questions. What if something were discovered that really was a 'dead giveaway'? If faith is so important, then such a discovery would be at least paradoxical. This is connected with the whole question of whether God exists, and whether it can be proved that he does. The old, medieval theology said it could be proved. Philosophers since Kant[1] have said these proofs fail. In response, Hick's theology said forget proof, indeed forgo it, as it prevents faith, which is essential.

105 ●

The fault lies in Hick's idea, which is put too strongly. The problem with the idea of the existence of God, and the various proofs, is that they have been increasingly set up to demonstrate God's existence to those who don't want to believe. Can you prove his existence to a philosopher dead set on maintaining he is unreal? Hick's answer is an attempt to side-step that requirement, by saying the need for faith prevents the possibility of proof. But 'dead giveaways' then become the enemies of faith! In practice, 'dead giveaways' – like seeing people changed after conversion, or answers to prayers for healing – do not prevent faith! But they don't force it either.

Actually, belief in God – not just the philosopher's empty question, but the fuller condition of real, life-changing faith in God – can never arise for the person determined to disbelieve. Jesus himself was once asked to prove not simply the existence of God but the presence of God and God's authority in his life. The Pharisees and Sadducees came to Jesus and tested him by asking him to show them a sign from heaven. Jesus replied, 'A wicked and adulterous generation looks for a miraculous sign, but none will be given it except the sign of Jonah' (Matthew 16:4). So Jesus refused to give proof. That did not mean he would not perform miracles, but it did stop him performing them in order to convince doubters. They were done out of compassion.

Jesus raised Lazarus several days after his death, commanding the dead man from the tomb, in front of many people standing there. We are told that many of the Jews who had seen what Jesus did put their faith in him. What's surprising is that of those who saw this miracle, some of them went to the Pharisees and told them what Jesus had done. And they responded with exasperation, anger, fear and disbelief. This may seem odd, but in practice people with strong disbelief (in God or in Jesus) will be able to reject even so striking an event as someone being raised from the dead in front of their eyes. The ability to disbelieve, even in face of such a thing happening, is still found today, where the prejudice against belief, or the fear of the consequences of being known as a believer, is strong enough. 'Epistemic distance', in the full sense of a kind of screen precluding doubters from seeing strong evidences of God, is not needed to prevent people with no freely expressed faith from having to enter a relationship with God; prejudice is quite sufficient.

So how do people discover whether God is real? How do we find the ultimate answer to the question of whether we are ultimately alone in the universe, or, by knowing God, can know the partnership for which we were made, for ever? Disbelievers don't usually find the answer by pressing intellectual arguments until they are convinced against their wills. More commonly it comes when something else they have believed in, which acts as a barrier to belief in God, starts to become doubtful. One large-scale example is how, following the collapse of the atheistic communist regimes of eastern Europe, people now feel more able to ask questions again, instead of accepting the atheistic propaganda; so active faith in God has been strongly on the increase, and churches have been growing at a rapid rate. Most people are not party-line disbelievers, however. Opinion polls in the UK suggest that 70 to 80 per cent of people believe in some sort of God or Ultimate Reality behind and beyond the material universe. But only 15 per cent pursue this in the form of active religious commitment.

What helps such people to believe in God, not simply as the answer to the opinion poll question, but in the strong sense of the development of a real relationship with God, a life-changing faith in him, is when reasonable questions receive realistic and helpful answers. This usually takes years rather than months. God is not like an idea to be followed at a remote distance, 'epistemic' or otherwise. He is seen to be relevant, to make a difference first in the lives of others with whom we come into contact, and then, as we dare to take the first faltering steps of faith, in our own lives.

The traditional question 'Does God exist?' is the wrong question. And the answer 'Yes' is pretty near meaningless for most people. Not because of hypocrisy, but because it is remote and irrelevant. For many people the question is a bit like someone asking, 'Do you believe in the existence of the planet Saturn; that out there in deep outer space there is this planet with rings?' They will say 'Yes', but if one day someone were to prove that it was all a strange trick of lights, and the planet doesn't exist, what difference would it make to them? Not the slightest! And for many people the question 'Do you believe in God' translates as 'Do you believe that out there in deep metaphysical outer space there is this being called God?' And if they were to be told that someone had proved God didn't exist, it would make no difference to them.

So the big question is not 'Does God exist?' but 'If God is real, can he make a vital difference in our lives?' And that is part of the question 'Are we ultimately alone in the universe?' No discovery of human or non-human life-forms, however scientifically and culturally interesting, will form an ultimate answer, any more than the discovery of so many new cultures on earth over the past 500 years has. The discovery of life elsewhere – or the lack of it – is good for its own reasons, but not to solve the problem of aloneness in the universe. The discovery of, say, something like the Ferengi (the 'filthy capitalist pigs' of the *Star Trek* world) would not satisfy our need to answer the question of whether we are alone in the universe. It would just prolong the question.

The real question is: 'Can we find companionship in the universe to overcome that aloneness; one to accompany our inner selves?' And the answer to that was put in a prayer to God by Augustine of Hippo many centuries ago: 'You have made us for yourself, and our hearts are restless till they find their rest in you.'[2]

Part Three:
Faith in the Future

• 9 •
The Prime Directive

Guiding *TNG* and the other stories of *Star Trek*'s twenty-fourth century is a strong commitment to 'the Prime Directive'. In the future, the Ten Commandments have been largely reduced to one: 'Thou shalt not interfere with more primitive cultures'. This is a kind of post-colonial angst. In *First Contact*, Vulcans had also pursued the Prime Directive before 'first contact' with Earth in 2063, implying that twenty-first-century humans may learn such non-interference from Vulcans. There is a logic here – that advanced cultures can be contacted by other advanced races without losing their integrity, while more primitive ones will be swamped. (The trigger in *Star Trek* to allow first contact – warp drive and easy interstellar travel – shows the programme's faith in technology – a later theme.)

Such an outlook of non-interference was not common in the nineteenth century! But the mid-twentieth-century abandonment of military conquest of empires in the Third World has led many people today to conclude that such disruption of the 'natural' development of cultures has been detrimental to their progress. A disaster like the Rwandan holocaust is attributed by many to the colonial policy of the Belgian Empire (in pitting Hutu and Tutsi against each other with a divide and conquer policy). Collective repentance has led many to promote a 'Prime Directive' towards the Third World. In practice, however, such virtue is easier to promise than to implement. There is a new form of interference – Coca-Colanisation or McDonaldisation – and far from leaving cultures to develop, free of exploitation, we trade, abusing our economic power rather than military might.

Star Trek reflects this post-colonial repentance in its Prime Directive. So the same questions may be asked. If Federation ships avoid 'first contact' because that might lead to exploitation, can we really believe they would leave the field solely to the Ferengi to trade with future 'backward' planets? Or do even the Ferengi abide by the Prime Directive?! The Prime Directive is at the heart of *TNG*. But one of the surprises in going back to the original series is to find the Prime Directive there also. Funny, as Kirk is one of the most interfering people . . .

Language: diversity and harmony

Star Trek has moved on from everyone speaking English, to the presumption of universal translators and the development of Klingon. However, it seems that by the twenty-fourth century all human languages have been eclipsed by English – including French! Jean-Luc Picard, Captain of the *Enterprise* in *The Next Generation*, not only speaks English with an English accent, but in the episode *Family* so do all his French relatives. French words that he speaks seem to be mere colloquialisms, odd words from a dead language like Latin phrases today! This idea that English is the only human language of the future is also assumed in the *Conversational Klingon* audio cassettes, as they contrast Klingon sounds not with English, but with 'Federation standard' sounds, implying that that is the same as English.

There is an interesting parable here of the way to Utopia: everyone will defeat hunger and war, and even Klingons,

Romulans, Cardassians, the Borg and Q will be friends. There will be complete freedom, and everyone will see their culture flourish. But the hidden assumption is that it will be assimilated to the Federation (US) model: your culture is welcome to join, so long as it becomes Federation (US) first. It all seems so post-colonial and anti-racist, but actually the Federation, and the US culture it presumes, relies on a hidden presumption of cultural superiority.

A further striking feature of this is how other cultures are portrayed as largely unified (whatever political battles there may be within them). Thus all Klingons speak Klingon (with mild divergences in dialect). Similarly all Bajorans, Romulans, Vulcans and Cardassians, it seems, speak one language on their planets. And it's not just language. The whole culture on each world seems unified. Klingons have one system of honour – there are not several different Klingon races with different languages, values or religions.

Religion

It seems that Vulcans, Klingons and Bajorans each have just one religion. Apparently, all Vulcans pursue the culture of logic and mysticism, and all affirm the existence of the *katra* ('What some would call the soul,' as Tuvok explains). The only exceptions are maverick individuals, like Sybok in *The Final Frontier*.

In *Emanations*, an Uhnori woman, Ptera, is beamed (accidentally) and revived aboard *Voyager*, shortly after her death. Confused by not being in the after-life, she is disorientated. Kes, an Ocampan, tries to help Ptera in her disorientation. She explains how in her religion they believe the soul is released into the after-life. Another crew-member, half-Klingon B'Elanna Torres, doesn't console her by saying, '*Some* Klingon religions . . .' but, 'The Klingons believe in the after-life.' Ptera's own people all believe that in the after-life they move physically to another plane: a kind of bodily resurrection. We are presented with hermetically sealed cultures and religions; there are no other religions on the Klingon homeworld, no atheists or unbelievers. And the same is true for every planet (except Earth, where religion seems dead). Even the religious Bajorans, who reflect different tendencies, as between the more militant Vedek (later Kai) Winn and the more moderate Vedek Bereil, all turn out to be members of the same culture and of the same religion. All honour the same prophets and traditions (*pagh wraiths* notwithstanding).

Taken as a metaphor of the future, this is illuminating. The *Star Trek* future is Utopian; it is a world where poverty and war have been long gone, back on Earth. In fact, as in John Lennon's song 'Imagine', it is also a society 'with no religion too'. In Gene Roddenberry's story *Return of the Archons* (1967), the crew discovers an imposed 'paradise' and Kirk saves the people from a dominating computer. As Joel Engel puts it: 'This was the first of what would be several *Star Trek* episodes in which man searches for God, finds Him, debunks Him, and lives more happily afterward – or kills Him off metaphorically, thus improving mankind's well-being.'[1]

So how is human culture going to be enriched and united in *Star Trek*'s future? By all humans losing their own languages and adopting English, and by losing their cultures and religions and being assimilated into Federation (US) standard mono-cultural humanism? Rather Borg-like. . . . Theoretically, people are 'allowed' their religions – as hobbies. But they must make no real impact on society or life! Society is not governed by the principles of the faiths it thinks it is guided by, but by a more secular set of values.

Let's look at *Bread and Circuses, Star Trek*'s story of a planet paralleling Earth's struggle between Roman power and Christian values, but prolonged into the TV era.

Bread and Circuses

SPOCK: Sun-worship is usually a primitive superstition-religion.

UHURA: You're wrong, Mr Spock, all of you. It's not the sun in the sky. They worship the Son of God.

KIRK: Caesar and Christ – they had them both! And the Word is only spreading now.

MCCOY: A philosophy of love and total brotherhood.

The rebel leader says, 'There is only one true belief.' This matches the Christian outlook, an exclusive claim to truth. In the *Star Trek* world that makes it but an interim 'stage' towards future Utopia, where many beliefs all promoting love and brotherhood will be equal. Christianity is pictured as an evolutionary phase. *Star Trek*'s future religion is shown in McCoy's words: 'Well, if you are speaking of a worship of sorts, we represent many beliefs . . .' In fact this philosophy is far from futuristic: it was already vogue in the 1850s and is widespread today. The same evolutionary model also continued with *TNG*.

The Emissary

It's no coincidence that a more positive approach is found in *DS9* and *Voyager*, which assume that there is something real going on in religious experience, as these two series also reflect a Federation that is no longer perfect after all. *DS9* presents an advanced religious society in the Bajorans, and one of the crew, the Bajoran Major Kira, is shown as a mature, practising, religious believer.

Ira Steven Behr, who has been an executive director of *Deep Space Nine* since its fifth season, and a writer from its start, believes that part of what has happened is that both the original series and *TNG* could not explore alien religions in any depth because the crew would be off to another planet in the next episode. However, *DS9* would be more continuity-intensive, with much of the action centred on a space station not far from a planet, Bajor. That has contributed to the change, but I do not believe it is the only element, as we see other changes in *Voyager* that follow the 'new planet each week' pattern.

As for religion it was the original executive producers and creators of *DS9*, Rick Berman and Michael Piller, who pressed for it to be dealt with more strongly: 'They ran into this whole Emissary thing. They gave us the Prophets of the wormhole, and. . . . There's only so much Bajoran politics you can do! So we inevitably turned to religion.'[2]

The main religious focus in *DS9* has been the Bajoran religion. We have been shown its positive side, as a means of cultural and social strength for the Bajoran people, including for Sisko's deputy, Major Kira. We have also seen a more questionable aspect, where, in common with societies where a religion is taken seriously by its people, the possibility of corrupting religion for political ends emerges. And there has also been the personal angle. First for Benjamin Sisko, the African American, who right at the start becomes captain of the station, and also something of a religious icon for the Bajorans. And he is not too keen on that. He wants to keep his distance. But as the seven years of the show unfold he begins to wrestle with the role of Emissary with more acceptance.

 Behr describes the difference between the earlier approach in *Star Trek*, and *DS9*:

'Going back to my year on ST:TNG, according to Gene Roddenberry, there was no religion on Earth anymore. God was a concept that had kind of grown out of favour and was replaced by technology and man's basic goodness. This was never written on any piece of paper I ever saw, but at the time you couldn't even say "Good God, what are we going to do?" You couldn't even use the word God.

'Then ST:DS9 came along, and by the second season we were questioning the basic foundations of the 24th Century as extrapolated from the *Star Trek* franchise. For myself, it all started early on in the show's evolution, with [Producer] Peter Allan Fields coming over to me and saying "What are we using for money? We have a bar, and everyone is gambling. What are they gambling with?"'[3]

Similarly, Kira Nerys, the Bajoran major who is Sisko's deputy in the command structure on the station, shows a development from her more 'fundamentalist' or militant Bajoran attitudes – where she is originally not convinced

about the Federation, and where she supports the hard-line
Vedek Winn in her campaign to become Kai (supreme religious leader among Bajorans) – through working practically
with Sisko, as he becomes this almost messianic figure in
Bajoran faith. Says Behr: 'There is an amazing and difficult
underpinning to her relationship with Sisko. She really does
believe that he is the Emissary. She truly believes that he is
there for a religious purpose, aside from the job that the
Federation has sent him there to do.'[4]

In a sense, that softening of approach follows the broaden-
ing of the team behind *DS9*. The last episode of Season 1, *In
the Hands of the Prophets*, which deals with this rivalry
between Vedek Winn and Vedek Bereil, really shows the transition. Michael Piller comments:

'This episode is really the show-down
between the humanist ideals of the Federation
and the religious spiritual philosophy of Bajor.
It provides a bookend to the season that has a
confrontation that seems to have been coming all along
when we met these people and found out what their lives
were like. You start to deal with religion in school, the
Scopes Monkey Trial, and fundamentalism, and it's very
thought provoking.'[5]

In *DS9*, Bajoran religion is most visible. There is also further
exploration of Klingon culture and religion. In *The Sword of
Kahless*, Worf can even say, 'Kahless appeared to me in a
vision,' and later, 'When I held the sword, I felt the spirit of
Kahless himself had guided me to it.' Even so, not many
clues are given about other alien religions, apart from the

general unified picture of the cultures. *DS9* continues the earlier absence of any living faith that you and I have heard of and might meet here on Earth today. O'Brien is Irish, but there's no mention of Catholicism. His wife, Keiko, is Japanese, but there's no Buddhism shown. Maybe the Federation is still uniformly humanist, even in *DS9*.

Federation faith in the Delta Quadrant

Voyager goes further in that its crew includes religious believers not only among aliens like Kes and B'Elanna, but also in Chakotay we have the first human crew member with a personal, religious faith – which is explored rather more closely. He is a Native American, who, as in *Initiations* (1995), engages with his cultural and religious traditions with a mixture of faith and disengagement caused by being in the modern world (i.e. in space far away from his roots). This exploration of Native American spirituality fits in neatly with the mildly New Age feel of the newer Treks. New Age spirituality on this side of the Atlantic is sometimes taken up with Druidic and Norse religions, but in the US the corresponding pre-Christian pagan focus is on the religions of the indigenous people.

At the end of *Emanations*, the story about Uhnoris and their after-life, Captain Janeway rather strikingly allows an element of objective, even physical, truth in the Uhnori belief in the after-life to be held open:

KIM: All those people think they know what happens after death . . . But the truth is, none of it's real.

JANEWAY: I wouldn't be so sure of that if I were you. That neural energy their bodies release, it becomes part of the ambient electro-magnetic field surrounding the planet. Our readings also indicate the energy is unusually dynamic. There is a great deal of variation in pattern complexity, quantum density.

KIM: Are you saying, you think they do have an after-life? That the energy field is where they exist on a higher plane of consciousness, just like they believe?

JANEWAY: I'm not certain. But I am certain about this: what we don't know about death is far, far greater than what we do know.

While there are many differences between such faiths (or Eastern religious practices and experiences) and mainstream Christianity, it is a new context. The strange new worlds, new life and new civilisations now include faiths, which sustain these people, no longer as make-believe nonsense. What's more, those who venture out where no one has gone before also have a faith of their own – sometimes a religious faith. But what faith will help us explore and make sense of these worlds? What faith will sustain us for the future?

Star Trek: modern or postmodern?

Star Trek, both the original series and *TNG*, presents a 'modern' outlook on life in the future, one in which scientific humanism wins through clearly. But *DS9* and *Voyager* tilt matters a bit more in the direction of a 'postmodern' outlook.

Modern view	Postmodern view
▶ One truth: scientific humanism. ▶ *TNG: Who Watches the Watchers?* Renewed belief in gods renews 'dark ages of superstition'.	▶ Allows contradictions, because it sees the truth as elusive. ▶ *Voyager: Emanations*: 'What we don't know about death is greater than what we do know.'
▶ Religious people believe 'God' to be real. No scientific facts point to this – they reveal an 'illusion'. ▶ *TOS: Return of the Archons*: 'God' is discovered, proved false, and people are set free.	▶ 'God' is the name for religious experience, which can be valid for the believer. ▶ *Star Trek V*: God is not 'out there', but is 'in the human heart'.
▶ Religion will die out. By the twenty-third century it will be a museum piece. ▶ *TOS* and *TNG*: No crew member is a religious believer.	▶ Religion is part of human experience, which will continue. ▶ Believers: Major Kira and Worf in *DS9*; Chakotay, Kes, B'Elanna and Tuvok in *Voyager*.
▶ Mistaken beliefs should be shunned; cultures shunning them are evolving positively. ▶ *TOS: Bread and Circuses*: 'Sun worship is a primitive superstition religion.' ▶ *Errand of Mercy*: Klingon culture dismissed as aggressive.	▶ All beliefs and cultures should be affirmed, whether Klingon, human or Ferengi. ▶ *DS9*: All episodes focusing on Klingon or Ferengi culture. ▶ *Voyager: Initiations*: Chakotay's spirit beliefs affirmed.

▶ 'Spirituality' humanist.
▶ *TOS: Bread and Circuses*: 'We represent many beliefs.'
▶ *This Side of Paradise*: 'We were never meant for Paradise . . .'

▶ Spirituality more New Age.
▶ *DS9: Emissary*: Sisko is urged to seek his *pagh*, his spiritual centre.
▶ *Voyager*: Chakotay's vogue Native American spirituality.

Of course it's too simple to say that all later stories are postmodern. But such postmodern ideas about faith imply that we should just accept that all religions with all their major differences of belief and practice are 'true'; that 'the truth is out there', i.e. all the religions have their truth in them, however flatly they contradict one another. Error in religion is raised by the Ferengi religious lies. Let's consider the following two stories:

TNG: The Price. Two Ferengi competing with the *Enterprise* for acquisition rights to the Barzan wormhole through to the other end of the galaxy, fail to accept Geordi's warning that the far end of the wormhole is unstable, so any crew remaining there will be trapped there. The Ferengi assume it's Federation lies, and end up stuck in the Delta Quadrant.

Voyager: False Profits. Janeway's stranded crew encounters both wormhole and Ferengi. They plan to take the Ferengi home via the wormhole. But the Ferengi argue that would corrupt the Prime Directive, by affecting local beliefs. However, a solution re-enacting the local poem of the 'Holy Pilgrim' results in the dispatch of the Ferengi back into the

Alpha Quadrant, while *Voyager*'s crew remains stranded as the wormhole moves again.

Between the two stories our interest is in what the Ferengi did in their seven years in the Delta Quadrant. Nothing if not resourceful, the Ferengi adapt themselves to the local culture. They pass themselves off as 'Holy Sages' using their advanced technology to transform the cultural and religious beliefs and mislead the locals, who now sing a chant: 'Greed is eternal'. The Ferengi, Arridor and Kol, live in a palatial 'temple'. They exploit the Takarans, selling them copies of 'the rules of acquisition', enslaving the impoverished locals, who adulate the Ferengi. As Scully says in *The X-Files* story (1:17) *E.B.E.*, 'The truth is out there, but so are lies.' The Ferengi religion introduced among the Takarans is lies. It's simply a device for making money, for enslavement. In practice there *is* more truth in some understandings of reality than others. Or, to put it another way, there are more lies in some approaches. The lies of the Ferengi and the shadowy authorities in *The X-Files* are deliberate. The lies of Lenin or Hitler were lies they themselves believed, and were all the more dangerous for that.

Star Trek's error is confusion between the assumption of equality of cultures and the contrary assumption that Federation culture is superior. This matches the current conflict between assuming that all cultural groups should be treated equally, and affirming Western culture as superior (precisely because it treats all equally!). This contradiction forms the heart of Daniel Leonard Bernardi's *Star Trek and History Race-ing Toward a White Future*. The basic comparison here is with the typical western film, which glorified the frontier of the white man against the 'Indian'. Bernardi comments: 'Perhaps the clearest example of the frontier myth in Hollywood cinema occurs in the western, a genre that has consistently retold the story of a white hero who domesticates or obliterates "wild" Indians, "dirty" Mexicans, and "heathen" Chinese in his quest to tame the West.'[6]

 Gene Roddenberry first sold the idea of *Star Trek* as a 'wagon train to the stars'. For all its progressiveness, the problems in Westerns with racial stereotyping recur in its treatment of aliens. Bernardi again: 'Not unlike Tonto in *The Lone Ranger*, Spock is an Other that is depicted as stoically and loyally withstanding the prejudice of others in the interest of serving the manifest destiny of the Federation.'[7]

The Prime Directive, initially so post-colonial in appearance, so tolerant and affirming of all cultures, is actually a statement that the Federation (and the liberal humanism of the West it exemplifies) is morally superior to all other cultures. Differences in culture are affirmed, only to be absorbed. This leaves a tension between saying that all views, all religions, all cultures are equal, and that one is better. We are reminded of the revised slogan of *Animal Farm*: 'All animals are equal, but some are more equal than others.'

One story that illustrates this tension is *Unification* in *TNG*, which explores the difficulties in bridging the cultural gap between Vulcans and Romulans. (This turned out to be the swan song for Mr Spock, who is revealed to be involved in the clandestine struggle to promote reunification with Vulcan for Romulans.) The clash between them is not ethnic.

It's openness and logic versus secrecy and power. Which is best? Which is true?

The Federation model affirms cultural differences in order to assimilate and transform them, and even Ferengi, like Quark, under their influence become kinder and gentler in *Business as Usual*. Harmony is achieved by assimilation disguised as tolerance. Tolerance need not be cultural assimilation. It can affirm difference in basic faith on the basis of an open faith.

The tension in *Star Trek* is the tension in the modern West. In moving on from the old humanism with its debunking of all gods towards a tolerant welcome to all faiths, it tries to picture all beliefs as equal. But that is also a belief. The belief that all religious beliefs are equally true and valid is a belief, and a truth claim, and as such a strikingly self-contradictory thing for people to believe! The result is an unconscious colonial attitude, where all cultures are to be assimilated by the spread of Federation values.

Is this unique to *Star Trek*, or does that other interstellar epic, *Babylon 5*, hit similar problems? That is the next topic.

• 10 •
The Parliament of Dreams

Religion and realism

Arguably, *Babylon 5* has shown a sharper realism than any other TV science fiction series. In addition to the technical realism in assumptions about science in a possible future which is characteristic of *Star Trek*, *Babylon 5* has developed a stronger realism in its characters and societies, including the way it shows religion in human and alien cultures. In some ways, religion pervades the whole series. It is part of the realism of *B5*'s creator, Joe Straczynski, to assume that religion will not simply vanish in the future. Straczynski is not guided by a personal commitment but a fascination about religion:

 'I'm not sure if I'm fascinated by religion or religious impulse. The religious impulse is the flipside of science. Both are attempts to find out where we came from, how we got here, who we are, where we're going. They both use different methodologies, but the impulse is the same. And I use the show to explore the sense of wonder, the exploration, the scientific parts of science fiction and my feeling is "Why not give voice to, or explore the other side as well?" I am an atheist, I have no religious interest personally at all, but as a writer it can lead to some very compelling drama.'[1]

Compared to Gene Roddenberry, this 'atheist' has a massively different attitude to religion. Even after Roddenberry, the later *Star Trek* series and films only explore alien religions (apart from Chakotay's Native American roots). But *B5* also shows humans following the major religions and denominations we are familiar with: Buddhists and Jews, Catholics and Baptists, as well as atheists, agnostics and those who are just uncertain among the heroes.

Straczynski is not afraid of religious humour. As Season 2 opens (*Points of Departure*), Garibaldi is comatose, after an assassination attempt earlier:

IVANOVA: Well I'll say a prayer for him tonight.
FRANKLIN: He's agnostic.
IVANOVA: Well I'll say half a prayer.

Foundationism

The future of *B5* assumes there will be change and development in religion as in other areas of life. Over the five years the series is set in (2257–62) one major developing story concerns change in religion among the Narn. Closer to the heart of the programme's outlook is a future human/alien religion called 'Foundationism', or simply 'the Foundation'. Dr Franklin is a Foundationist (see 2:17 *In the Shadow of Z'ha'Dum* and 3:18 *Walkabout*). Straczynski explains:

'One thing I did for Franklin was to create a new Earth religion which basically came up in the last 150 years or so [before 2260]. He's a Foundationist, and what the Foundationists have done is looked at all Human belief systems with the notion that there are so many alien cultures and alien beliefs. Maybe what defines our religions and our beliefs is not denominations, but what is the core of our beliefs. That makes us Human. I looked at a variety of Earth religions and went down to the core of the foundation of that belief and said "Let us incorporate this, let us draw upon the root of our beliefs rather than the schisms or the dogma or the doctrines that were overlaid on top of that." So they'd looked into everything from Aboriginal beliefs, to Muslim beliefs to Buddhism and sort of stitched together this quilt. Consequently Franklin's beliefs have a wide number of beliefs that spring into it, including the Aborigine notion [of "Walkabout"].[2]

Straczynski may call himself an atheist, but his openness seems far from straight atheism. Instead, the view implied by *B5* as a whole is nearer Franklin's Foundationism. The episode *The Parliament of Dreams* (1:6) shows this. *B5*'s Commander Sinclair wants to promote greater understanding and peace between races on the station, and inaugurates a week-long festival in which each race will share something of their religious and cultural traditions. Minbari meditations, Narn holy readings and the Centauri binge are true to their cultures! But what could express human religion? In the end Sinclair finds a whole load of religious dignitaries of different religions and denominations, and has them all in a line to greet the alien ambassadors. This is the 'parliament of dreams', and it is in line with the 'parliament of faiths' first assembled in 1893 with the same message that, despite differences, all religions have a common purpose, etc.

Straczynski remembers this scene with 160 extras: 'Some

of the Warners executives came down to be there on that day, and even they were moved by it.' He comments: 'My belief is that we profit from a diversity of voices and a multiplicity of opinions. At our best we embrace our differences and [I wanted] to show that through that last ceremony. Some of the people who were there [playing the religious representatives] were who they appeared to be, and some were not.'[3]

This is the message of Foundationism. But it contains a fundamental problem for orthodox Christian faith (and some other faiths); a problem that goes right back to the beginning. In the time of the Roman Empire, religions were allowed to flourish, so long as their gods were made compatible. Roman, Greek, Egyptian, Persian and other gods were reshaped a little to become equivalent to each other – an ancient Foundationism. All religions had their gods, and affirming them in this broad way meant religion helped people to belong to the empire. One exception was mostly tolerated: Judaism. To the ancients their rejection of the gods made them 'atheists', but they were allowed to persist with their religion because it was seen as restricted to their race (by circumcision, etc.).

At first, Christianity was tolerated as a Jewish sect. Later, its universal message was seen: it proclaimed the God of Abraham, but without circumcision – a God for *all* people. This challenged the Roman Empire: the call to reject other gods was for everyone, not just one race. That is why Christians were so heavily persecuted from 64 on and off until 313, when Emperor Constantine accepted the Christian faith.

Unification by Foundationism

Religion in the *Star Trek* world moved from being a museum piece to a showcase of tolerant acceptance and affirmation of all faiths and cultures. The picture changes from the good Federation in a world of hostile Klingons, to a more cosmopolitan affirmation. In *DS9* (*Melora*) we even have a Klingon restaurant. This reflects the shift from modern to postmodern and New Age mindset.

In the last chapter we saw how *Star Trek* envisages the interstellar culture of the day (and, by reflection, our global culture today), developing unification by a gradual assimilation of the Federation values of respect for all cultures and faiths. We also noted the contradiction between such ideas and the particular ideas of believers, for example Bajorans. The idea of a planet, or galaxy, where all the people of whatever religion or none get on without fighting is a great one. But the issue of whether people fight over religion is different from the choice between acknowledging real divergence in faith and seeing all faiths as just different versions of the same thing. After all, let's take the Hindus and Sikhs: they have a track record in affirming all religions as different paths to the truth, but that has not meant the end of all political hostility between them in the Punjab.

The secular answer to religious conflict and war is to quit religion. The postmodern answer is to kill it by kindness: by affirming all the competing beliefs and values as 'true', their individual claims are suffocated. Individual religions, beliefs and values get replaced by the belief and value that all beliefs and values are OK, and by a consumerist, pick 'n' mix spirituality and religion to suit the tastes of each individual.

This leaves a self-centred faith where it works, and confusion, insecurity or a spiritual vacuum where it doesn't. The big need here is to distinguish between toleration and indifference.

 The first Baptist in England, Thomas Helwys, made this, the first plea in the English language for universal religious toleration, in 1612:
'. . . if the King's people be obedient & true subjects obeying all human laws made by the King, our Lord the King can require no more. For men's religion is betwixt God and themselves; the King shall not answer for it, neither may the King be judge between God and man. Let them be heretics, Turks [i.e. Muslims], Jews, or whatsoever, it appertains not to the earthly power to punish them in the least measure.'[4]

(Vintage spellings have been modernised)

He was sent to the Tower of London for his impertinence, for this was just six years after Guy Fawkes attempted to blow up Parliament to turn England into a Catholic state.

Helwys's plea for political toleration of all religions (including 'them of the Romish religion') was not because he was *indifferent* to religious beliefs. He did not think that the beliefs of Catholics, Jews and Muslims were as equally valid and true as his own dissenting beliefs. Instead, he believed that genuine faith could not be forced out of the barrel of a gun. True Christian faith could only happen where people genuinely, freely believed in Jesus as Lord. This led to the idea of a gathered church of believers, and a corresponding baptism of believers. All religions should be freely tolerated so that people can follow the true faith without political compulsion. That is a completely different approach to what Matthew Arnold 100 years ago dubbed as 'indifferentism': the idea that all religions should be given equal toleration and civil rights because they are seen as equally true (or false).

Franklin tries to express his feelings about working with many Narn patients close to death in *Points of Departure* (2:1). He asks Ivanova, 'Do you believe in God, Susan?' She replies falteringly, and asks him, so he explains his faith:

> FRANKLIN: I am Foundationist.
> IVANOVA: I've never heard of that one.
> FRANKLIN: It's fairly new. It's only been around about a hundred years.
>
> One of a bunch that sprouted after we made contact with aliens. You see the idea that God is too big to be defined by words – sort of like Zeno's paradox? You never really get anywhere because there's an infinite number of dots between you and the object. The closer we get to defining God, the further away It gets.

Foundationism is pictured as a response to the discovery of alien cultures, beliefs and religions. It tries to isolate the underlying elements of faith, and stitches them together in a new pattern. It's likely that if aliens with religious beliefs were discovered, someone would dream up a new system including them, because such an approach is already common. Moonies teach that Mr Moon's Divine Principle includes and transcends all other religions, giving the new definitive version for our time. Moonies call their sect the Unification Church because it unifies all religions. This gives us the hard-edged, sectarian version.

With Baha'i, we have the softer, tolerant, inclusive model, much closer in spirit to Foundationism. Here all religions and religious experiences are affirmed positively, but reinterpreted in the process. You can have your Christian, Buddhist or Muslim experiences, but they are only part of the Baha'i experience. Baha'i arose in a Muslim context in Iran (where it continues to be persecuted). But Foundationism is more like the post-Christian model that John Hick presents. In 1974, Hick wrote a book called *God and the Universe of Faiths* in which he argued that the truth (about God) is out there, but unobtainable. In a way, it was an extension of his earlier idea of the so-called 'epistemic distance' – the space between faith and knowledge in our experience of God. What's at the centre of the known universe, spiritually? What are we orbiting around, spiritually? Christians say that it is God as we know him through Jesus; that Jesus is 'the way and the truth and the life' (John 14:6). But Hick stopped believing Jesus' exclusive claim that 'No-one comes to the Father except through me.' He said we needed a 'Copernican revolution' in religious faith. In astronomy, Copernicus changed the picture of the universe. He said that people must not see the Earth as the centre of the universe. Instead, the Sun is the centre, and the Earth is just one of the planets in orbit around it. Hick says that the truth of God is similar: belief in the truth of any faith like Christianity must go; instead, the unknowable God is the centre, and Christianity is just one of the approximations to the truth. Nor will Hick allow that Christianity is the best approximation, because that implies we have an independent and superior means of proving what is true.

This is similar in spirit to Foundationism. It is also similar in some ways to the views of Weston, the villain of C. S. Lewis's *Voyage to Venus*, when he claims that nothing divides his own view of Spirit as the goal of evolutionary biology from Ransom's orthodox Christianity, 'except a few outworn theological technicalities'. Weston adds, 'The Meaning beneath it is as true and living as ever.'

David Bassom's *The A to Z of Babylon 5* (Boxtree, 1996) defines the Foundation as 'a multi-alien religion started in the mid twenty-second century which believes in the concept of God, but does not attempt to define it'. But there's a big problem with this, as with Hick's ideas. If God is so unknowable that all religions are equally false in their claims about him, how can we say anything at all about him? How, especially, can we say what Hick says? In the end, people believe particular things.

Foundationism accepts the root experience of all religions. But when push comes to shove, Franklin acts against the core experience of the 'Children of Time' in *Believers* (1:10). They value being 'born of the egg' and reject surgery as only appropriate for animals, believing they would lose their soul if operated on. Humans and other races that accept surgery are soulless 'animals'. Without any consent, Franklin operates to save the child's life. The operation succeeds, but the aliens, believing the child's soul destroyed, sacrifice him anyway. This story shows that a religious system with an affirmation of all religions, like Foundationism, has its limits. When Franklin sacrifices both his own supposed theology *and* that of the parents in order to save the child, he shows the real faith he has: a medic, driven to save life, whatever.

What a free society needs is not the 'indifferentism' of trying to say that all religions are equally true. We need equal freedom, equal toleration. Society doesn't require the odd belief that all views are equally true; such an attempt is doomed to confusion. In practice, societies depend on actual beliefs and values, of which the Christian approach is one. What's needed is toleration: a society in which, while one set of values may be more affirmed than the others, according to those values all other faiths should be given free rein to function, within the law.

One early attempt at this was the act of toleration in Britain in 1689: Anglicans were the official church in England and Wales (and Presbyterians the official Scottish church), but others like Baptists were allowed to practise their faith, though with fewer political rights. The US constitution is another attempt. Rooted in the flight from European religious wars and persecution, it separated church and state, permitting all faiths to operate, with no favoured established church. In practice, however, this permission was not made on the basis of indifference to belief, but from a strong belief in the rights of 'life, liberty and the pursuit of happiness'.

Where did these beliefs come from? At the time, people said that these truths were self-evident, written into nature, to be read off by all. The US constitution states that we are *created* with equal rights, and that these rights are endowed by our *creator*. It is less secularised than the French constitution. Theologian Karl Barth wryly commented on this: 'The Calvinism gone to seed still distinguishes itself favourably from the Catholicism gone to seed of the French one.'[5] But either way, the beliefs we assume today don't come from nowhere. If we carefully investigate people in radically different cultures, we find that the things *we* take for granted are often disputed elsewhere.

The idea that all religions are somehow equal, and even that it's wrong to say one is more true than another, is actually a religious belief. Where did that word 'wrong' come from? It assumes one belief (i.e. religious equality) is more true and appropriate than its competitors. What's more, the hidden assumption in the relativist idea that different faiths are identically true just doesn't make sense. Whether it's called Foundationism, Baha'i or John Hick's 'myth of Christian uniqueness', this view claims that the truth in all faith is only as a part of the truth of *their* faith. This Foundationist approach may affirm all views, but it is itself a claim to be right. It says that the traditional Christian claim of Jesus to be the way, the truth and the life, *the* way to God, is wrong, and that the Foundationist claim that the truth about God is not knowable is right.

Meanwhile, there will still be conflict about what is true in religion. A recent row over *Xena: Warrior Princess* flared up as angry American Hindus complained that their god Krishna was treated as a fictional character, and the episode was withdrawn. That's nothing compared to the trouble Salman Rushdie got into . . . Interestingly, there was no such campaign when an earlier episode of *Xena* had her replacing God and helping David defeat Goliath! The conventional 'Foundationist' view today can get rather confused, as it's based on a hidden assumption that all religions are equally false. However, Christian positive tolerance of the right of non-Christians to promote such views does not mean acceptance of those views.

Close encounters of the spiritual kind

It is interesting to consider what the impact on faith and life might be for Christians or others if we really did make contact with alien races capable of experience of God. The *B5* story *TKO* (1:14) raises the question of Jewish orientation nicely. While Judaism has no mission to convert aliens, questions about the faith would be raised. Rabbi Yossel Koslov is on *B5* to try to encourage Susan Ivanova to achieve reconciliation with her father posthumously, by sitting Shivah, the appropriate Jewish ritual. He succeeds – just. Meanwhile, he is about to eat a fish raised by the Centauri and asks, whimsically, if it is Kosher.

If Foundationism is one very imaginable way in which people might respond to the discovery of alien races that have their own religions, it is not the only one. The *B5* episode *Convictions* (3:2) introduces Brother Theo, the leader of an order of talented Catholic monks, who are skilled in computer research, physics, biogenetics, chemistry and engineering and detective skills, helping a surprised, sceptical but ultimately grateful Commander Ivanova track down a mad bomber on the station. The monks also appear briefly in the background, with Baptist minister the Revd Will Dexter and his team of gospel singers in *And the Rock Cried Out 'No Hiding Place'* (3:20).

In *Passing through Gethsemane* (3:4) a monk had been the subject of a futuristic punishment – sentenced to the death of his personality, in which his mind was wiped – in a moving and challenging treatment of the subject of forgiveness. Brother Edward has to face his personal Gethsemane when he is reminded of earlier crimes by a Centauri telepath overriding his mindwipe, and is then lynched by his victim's sur-vivors. The episode ends with Sheridan having to greet and try to forgive a new member of Brother Theo's order – the killer, freshly mindwiped.

First contact

But it is why Brother Theo and his monks are there that's interesting. Theo explains that they want to be allowed to set up semi-permanent residence on *Babylon 5*, as it's the ideal place to meet aliens and find out about their religions. They want to learn about alien experiences of God more than to convert.

 Straczynski comments: 'In reality, if we were to make contact with aliens who had their own belief structures, after the scientists and researchers and the archaeologists and the builders left to go there, the next bus would have the evangelists and the religious folk. To find out what they believe, in case they might have a better grasp of, or a recognition of, the almighty than we have. Or, on the flipside, to take these poor heathens and convert them to our ways. There are a number of religious folk who are big believers in inter-faith research and studies, particularly Jesuits. I thought, let's take this and deal with this, bring in these characters and have them there.'[6]

Broadly, that's how we've seen it in human history, except that some – especially the evangelists – have often been there on the *first* bus, ahead of all others, especially where the cul-tures are isolated and technologically backward. A well-known case in point is of the Auca Indians, with whom 'first contact' was fatally made by a group of evangelistic missionaries. They landed by plane on a beach nearby, but their initial attempts at contact resulted in the tribesmen killing them. Undeterred, the wives of the murdered men went to the Aucas, and helped them to accept Christian faith. These men and their widows preceded the scientists and anthropologists!

That's just a detail compared to the main point that religious people, particularly Christians, would be among the first to visit alien people whose experience included the possibility of religious experience. Why Christians? Because that's the way it's always been. Christianity more than any other human religion has this inner drive to 'go into all the world' – even 'to boldly go where no one has gone before'. As a result, while the world's second most translated book, the Qur'an, has been translated into 128 languages, the Bible has been translated into over 2,000 languages. There is this drive to ensure that *all* people, however insignificant politically, shall hear the Christian message.

Evangelists on Mars

The debate is already starting. *B5* has Baptist churches on Mars in *Objects in Motion* (5:20). Garibaldi plans to marry his love, Lise, and arranges for a minister: 'I've got it right, haven't I? – First Baptist Church, Mars (Reformed)?' Kim Stanley Robinson's *Red Mars* trilogy tells of mankind terraforming Mars. This could become science fact with Robert Zubrin's feasibility proposal for just such a colonisation of Mars. In *The Case for Mars*, he flags up the case for 'Mars

Direct', arguing it could start as soon as ten years' time for as 'little' as $20 billion (small by comparison in real terms to the Lunar programme of the 1960s). And at the Mars Society's Founding Convention in August 1998 Lutheran minister the Revd James D. Heiser argued that such colonisation should learn from the colonisation of America, where military and economic colonies failed, but those that started with genuine community, the Pilgrim Fathers, succeeded. And the March 1999 issue of *Christianity* discusses whether Christians would be motivated to a mission to the people who colonise Mars.

In practice, the first evangelists on Mars would not be those sent by a mission board spending the billions needed for a team on Mars, but the ordinary Christians who were part of the expedition, and any progress would depend on the quality of their Christian faith and life, as in Kim Stanley Robinson's original 100 colonists. But what about missions to *aliens* capable of experience of God? What would Christian responses be?

▶ There would be those who assume that because the Bible only mentions the human race, aliens should largely be ignored, spiritually. Whether that approach could be sustained would depend on what happened to the other two most likely responses.

▶ There would, as Joe Straczynski said, no doubt be those like Brother Theo who would be intrigued by the concept of aliens with their own religion, and who would expect it to be beneficial to learn from them. Some would have a fully fledged interfaith attitude. Others would simply be curious.

▶ And the third group, as Straczynski rightly said, would be the evangelists.

Actually no evangelists appear within *Babylon 5*, *Star Trek* or any other sci-fi series so far. But Straczynski is right to assume that if the sort of imaginary universe he pictures were anything like right, somebody would be likely to begin to share their faith with aliens. The nearest we get is where Brother Edward visits Delenn and Lennier to find out about Minbari religion, and in turn Delenn proves keen to discover from him the emotional core of his faith – his personal faith. He answers that it is the story of the Garden of Gethsemane, where he confesses he doesn't know if he would be as brave as Jesus when asked to stay put, when soldiers ready to kill him are on their way.

All evangelism begins with such words – and actions. The real clash of cultures would come further down the line. What would happen if a Narn, a Centauri or a Minbari became a Christian? How would Delenn react if Lennier started to show a greater respect for Christian beliefs than for traditional Minbari ways? Or what would the Grey Council do if Delenn herself, in part of openness to humanity, opened herself to this human faith and accepted it? Christian faith has often spread in new cultures fastest and strongest in the underclass. What if a Minbari in the worker caste, rather than religious caste, started to believe and act this way?

In the *Star Trek* universe, you can imagine the reaction of Klingons to a Klingon who rejected the idol of honour, blood and glory in favour of the God of love, as shown in Jesus. Or try Ferengi responses to one of their race who ditched the rules of acquisition in favour of Jesus' commands to love God and love your neighbour! A slightly larger leap of imagination is required to picture the monsters of *Doctor Who*, like Daleks, giving up extermination for the gospel of love! And consider the Time Lords themselves: what would be the response of others if one of their number allowed human influence to lead to Christian conversion? A conflict with those who don't agree is rather likely – a bit of persecution from those who think their traditional ways are being threatened.

But what would persuade a Minbari, or a Klingon, or a Time Lord to accept Christian faith – to see Jesus of Nazareth, a human born in Palestine, a remote and primitive part of Earth, 2,000 years ago as the embodiment of the fullness of God? If we go beyond where Christian traditions are known and think of more parallel situations, where Christian faith is new to a community or is new to an individual in our modern world here on Earth, what happens is that the proof of the pudding is in the eating. A culture pits its traditions against the new idea, the new contender, Jesus, and sometimes concludes that Jesus is after all Lord. So, in response to missionaries a tribe may make a battle ground with healing. In one case, following prayer in the name of Jesus, a person is publicly healed, and the tribe turns to Jesus. In another situation, conventional medicine is presented and offered to the people, and the healing received there is persuasive.

In our society, what people notice may be where a relative or friend becomes a Christian, and they see that person change notably for the better. Then they might accept that there may be something in it after all. At that point of recognition, the questions about Christian faith and life are asked with a greater sense of engagement. Statistically, far more people find the impact of a partner or close friend to be the main trigger for turning to Jesus as Lord and Saviour than any of the more conventional avenues, like services, clergy and evangelistic events.

And with real or realistic aliens that had the same self-awareness as us, and the same interest in 'the meaning of life, the universe and everything', it seems likely that the same pattern would follow. After a period of curiosity coupled with maintaining distance, eventually there would be situations where people tried out other cultures – not just their cuisine, poetry or mating rituals, but their beliefs and religious practices too. And the proof of the pudding would be in the eating.

Christian faith and life means accepting Jesus as Lord and Saviour, so that the way we live, pray and act towards God and others shows openness to Christ above all else. And this has been tried in different ways by over two billion people in our time. People have taken on this faith by starting to accept it and trying to live according to it in practice. And whether it's Minbari in the twenty-third century, Klingons in the twenty-fourth or humans in the twenty-first century, an individual can enter what has previously been 'undiscovered country' by trying it out, by living and being committed on the basis of seeking and seeing Jesus as Lord.

The challenge would be radical, and an interesting and so far untried dramatic situation for any such alien in the future. But no less radical and challenging for any of us right now.

Seven of Nine, Data and the Transporter

Technological Utopia or the nightmare from hell?

Seven of Nine, the female Borg drone who becomes a crew member aboard *Voyager*, embodies the question sharply. The March 1998 *Star Trek Monthly* article about her quotes Bertrand Russell's paradoxical comment:

 'Machines are worshipped because they are beautiful and valued because they confer power; they are hated because they are hideous and loathed because they impose slavery.'

While the Borg presents us with a rare glimpse of this dark side – hated hideousness and loathed enslavement – *Star Trek* generally suggests worshipped beauty and valued power. Seven of Nine provides us with all four elements in tension.

What is the future? It is clear that if our culture keeps on its current path, there will be new technological developments, new inventions and many changes. But will these changes make life increasingly easier, or will there come a point when technology takes over, and our worst nightmares of enslavement to machines follow? One of the ways science fiction can develop the issues of our time better than other forms of drama is in addressing such questions.

What futures are envisaged – Utopia or dystopia?

Blake's 7: a 'dystopian' nightmare

Terry Nation's *Blake's 7* has a future fascist Federation with virtually uncheckable power. With military control over the slightest dissidence, and mental control over the population by drugged water and air, and the use of mind-altering drugs and other technologies to delete any memories of independent thinking, all hope for free humanity seems to be lost. The 52 episodes tell an extraordinary tale of a group of 'criminals' (Blake and his unlikely assembled crew) gaining an alien super-advanced craft. But in the end all the heroes die, and the dystopian nightmare wins. Is this the future: technology providing unlimited power to an individual or clique? Does it mean that democracy, hope and human freedom will die?

Doctor Who: far more ambiguous

Terry Nation's *Dalek Invasion of Earth* pushed *Doctor Who* in the same direction, but the many different strands within *Doctor Who* present a far more ambiguous picture. Many of the sharpest themes present the more pessimistic view. With the Cybermen, we see visions of technological medicine gone catastrophically wrong. With Davros, inventor of the Daleks, we have the best example of a whole string of mad scientists, whose desire for the success of their project would, if unchecked, lead to the destruction of the planet or even the universe.

Stahlmann, the magma geologist of *Inferno,* is another example. If we look at such cases, the message of the series would seem to be beware all science and technology! However, the Doctor himself is a scientist, and constantly affirms the scientist's search for truth. And while he normally eschews weaponry, he often uses gadgets like his sonic screwdriver, and even more often turns the technology of those who plot evil against them, to rescue those threatened each week.

2001: graceful yet lethal

Another common plot is the sentient computer that threatens people, supremely with the friendly HAL 9000 in *2001: A Space Odyssey*, whose ill-thought programming leads 'him' to kill. Technology in this influential film was graceful, yet proved lethal. This is also a favourite *Doctor Who* theme (WOTAN in *The War Machines*, 1966; BOSS in *The Green Death*, 1973). In a world where even the world chess champion loses to a computer, the fear is of a computer somehow able to cross a threshold into self-awareness and make independent decisions – decisions that we would no longer be clever enough to defeat.

Babylon 5: rare technical quick fixes

While *Babylon 5* assumes major technological advances – easy interstellar travel in particular – technology only plays an incidental role (unlike in *Star Trek*). Its medicine is closer to our own than the *Star Trek* assumption of gadgets that a doctor waves at a patient while injuries and diseases vanish before their eyes. Plot lines rarely depend on technical quick fixes, and such uses of technology are rare plot devices, and are not part of the underlying philosophy of *B5*. The assumption is that technological advances will be used by humans and others for varying mixtures of improvement and attempts at abuse of power. An example of a rare quick fix in *B5* occurs in *Messages from Earth* (3:8). Sheridan escapes the revived, all-powerful Shadow vessel by flying into Jupiter and pulling out at the last moment, leading his pursuers to buckle under the planet's terrific pressure. Straight after, he must escape without attacking a hostile Earthforce craft. The 'it's never been done before' trick works, opening up a jump gate *within* the upper reaches of Jupiter's atmosphere.

Blade Runner: negative potential

The influential film *Blade Runner* shows a more negative potential in technological change, especially in the 1991 Director's Cut version (expressing the director's original vision). It shows the potential and dangers of future city life. The year is 2019. It is a world not far off our own in some ways, but with androids, 'replicants', in revolution against humanity. Such androids are intended to serve – to be a slave labour market. In the most advanced cases, where they are conned into believing the false identity and false memories given them, the truth about their identity is hidden from them. Technology, or at least the way it's used, has gone a step too far, and led to an unstable nightmare world. But the clue is in the exploitation of and lies towards these increasingly self-aware manufactured humanoids. They are strong, clever and have major grievances. Their threat to humanity leads to a policy that any replicant leaving the off-worlds to go to Earth must be killed – a job for the 'blade runner'.

Star Trek: Utopia with no poverty or war

All this is a massive contrast with Data, the friendly android of *Star Trek*, whose Pinocchio-like innocence, and even sweetness, is famous. Perhaps no character so firmly shows the series' faith that the future use of technology will be an unmitigated blessing for humanity as this vision of a sentient superbrain, with intellectual and physical power far in excess of all humans, working so loyally and happily with and for humanity. Data is a vital part of the Utopian vision of *Star Trek*. What is the Utopia of *Star Trek*? It is a world where poverty and war are long gone, back on Earth. It is a world of harmony. Gene Roddenberry, the 'great bird', the visionary behind *Star Trek*, famously believed that by the twenty-fourth century, people, humans at least, will have grown out of the petty squabbles that currently dominate. And it is a Utopia brought about by the beneficial development and use of technology.

But this takes us back to the tensions between technology's hated hideousness/loathed enslavement and its worshipped beauty/valued power. *Star Trek* generally suggests you can have the benefits and avoid the pitfalls. But the history of technology, as used by human beings, is that both elements go together. Every technical advance has brought both benefits and dangers. Fire brings cookery and arson; the wheel brings transport and chariots; iron and bronze bring pans and swords; rockets bring TV satellites and intercontinental ballistic missiles; and so on. The idea that a bit more technology will abolish greed and violence is an odd saviour to believe in. Indeed many technological advances now seen as beneficial, with numerous applications, first saw the light of day in military conflicts, like nuclear, rocket and computer technology. In practice, in *Babylon 5* this is the slant behind the Shadows' destructive philosophy. They promote conflict and war, because they argue that will actually help species evolve quickly.

A brief history of perfection

Star Trek's vision is part of a long dream in Western thought: the ideal of a future perfecting of society.

▶ **Before c. 1650** people assumed that the great writers and thinkers of the ancient world were better than their modern equivalents.

▶ **During 1650–1700**, as science progressed, the belief began to emerge that we know more now than people did in antiquity. So the idea began that modern culture was progressing.

▶ **By 1700–1800** this became the notion that modern ideas of philosophy and religion were better than ancient ones.

▶ **In the modern era, especially 1800–50**, this led many influential writers to argue that Christian ideas were now also out of date. Famously, Karl Marx said that religion was an 'opiate'. But even within the church many 'modern' writers suggested that progress meant adopting all the latest ideas, and changing beliefs to suit.

▶ **By 1850** the growing theory of evolution (for which Darwin merely provided the best argued example) was now seen as a model for what was happening to society. Progress and evolution were seen as one. As time marched on, the human race would not only progress in science but also in morality and religion. The present was better than the past, and the future would be better still. In the colonial era, people simply assumed Europeans were not only technologically ahead of all others, but also far ahead of all other races in culture, morality, religion and even biology (or genes, as we would call it now). It was assumed we had nothing important to learn from other cultures, but everything to teach them.

▶ **By 1900** the Perfect World was just around the corner. The only question was, which European vision would produce it?

▶ **In 1908** Henry Ford launched his 'Model T', the mass-produced car. Many people assumed capitalism, through its channelling of market forces, would propel us towards the future where poverty and war would fade – an idea resurgent in the US and here.

▶ **In 1910** European Christians were presuming that they would bring about the conversion of the entire world within one generation, assuming world Christianity would imitate Europe.

▶ **In 1911** Francis Galton died. He was a cousin of Charles Darwin and foremost in his generation in promoting 'eugenics': the programme to advance progress by restricting reproduction to more skilled classes. This social Darwinism went out of fashion, as its development into racism and fascism has led to its eclipse since the Holocaust.

▶ **In 1914** various imperial nationalists, especially British, German and French, assumed that theirs was the destiny to produce the perfect culture for the world.

▶ **In 1917** atheistic Marxism, in its new Bolshevist form, promised its proletarian revolution would permanently end all exploitation. It proclaimed itself alone truly 'scientific'.

▶ **By 1918** in Europe (including Britain!) people's belief in inevitable moral progress was shaken to its foundations by the First World War. A generation became embittered and

disillusioned. They no longer believed in what their leaders told them. And the idea that people were bound to
get better as technology increased died, for in this war
technology had meant systematised, mechanical slaughter.

▶ **In 1966**, when *Star Trek* first appeared, the belief in
progress moved back to centre-stage. It was strongest in
America, but also revived in Britain and the rest of
Europe, with the impact of the 'baby boom' generation
(vast numbers of affluent youth) and technological inno-
vation, with domestic appliances, cars and, most fantastic
of all, the space race. It was also a decade when people
expected to make a difference and make that difference
for the better.

▶ **During 1968–75**, America's descent into national self-
doubt about war only seems to have hit fully on the same
epochal scale as Europe with its failure in the Vietnam
War. It had not been so severely affected by the earlier
alienation, only entering the World War in 1917, and has-
tening its end.

▶ **After 2063** 1960's-style optimism, continued indefinitely,
is the vision for *Star Trek*. Utopia has arrived in *Star Trek*.

Jean-Luc Picard tells us that on Earth war is over, and no one
is hungry any more. Indeed, in films like *First Contact*
(1996) and *The Voyage Home* (1986), we are told that in this
future world there is no longer any money. Burglary is a
thing of the past, perhaps because anything a burglar wants
can be replicated! It is above all an age full of confidence in
technology. How many stories depend on a piece of technological wizardry for their resolution? How often does Scotty
say, 'But Captain, I canna break the laws of physics,' to be

told, 'Scotty, you've got to!' – and then succeed?

But what is the basis for this Utopia? More to the point, what sort of society is this Utopia? How are differences resolved? How are the conflicts we know as the stuff of life solved in the future – things like deceit, lack of loyalty, petty (and serious) crime, fear, jealousy, envy and rivalry? How are differences between people, which lead to challenges and arguments now, smoothed away? How do people rise above such things in the future? How, in short, is the great mass of sin to be overcome, with everyone emerging a hero? Actually *Star Trek*'s answer is clear: the basis for Utopia is technology. Scotty's 'But I canna change the laws of physics, Captain' or Geordi's patient explanation as to why the alterations are impossible, or they'll take six hours while there's two hours before destruction, sets the scene. Kirk (or Picard) will then order him to succeed. Scotty will meekly reply, 'Well, I'll do my best. But I canna promise miracles.' Kirk will answer, 'You've got to, Scotty. We're relying on you. Two hours.'

And what happens? It's certainly not as in the world you and I know. In just under the 'two hours' Scotty will have contrived a new solution (or Geordi says, 'I've transversed the technobabble conduit'), firmly warning, 'It's the best I can do. It's never been tried before . . .' But of course it succeeds. In fact, wherever there's a problem it is solved most times by such technology, and where that's not enough, a rousing speech by Kirk/Picard unlocks the door to the crew's freedom, survival, etc.

This is not just a scriptwriter's *deus ex machina*. It is a statement of belief. How will mankind achieve perfection? By technological progress. Medicine paves the way: Bones waves his medical tricorder at a problem and it vanishes. But more significantly, the development of replicator technology at the turn of the twenty-fourth century removes the need for burglary. If anything can be replicated at will, then every burglar can replicate a zillion gold bars, TV sets, hamburgers, baseball games or whatever.

Perfection is here; sin is gone. The eighth commandment (Do not steal) is not going to be broken, and the tenth (Do not covet) goes with it. Technology and the bias of most people towards the good means that most sin has been abolished by the twenty-fourth century. One exception, however, is adultery! Indeed Roddenberry gloried in it. Joel Engel's biography of Roddenberry is revealing, and shows how his sex obsession made its impact on *Star Trek*, but was also limited within the show. For example Roddenberry originally had Betazoid females, including Lieutenant Deanna Troi, as four-breasted women who 'engage in almost constant sexual activity'. Otherwise, sin is over. Mankind is close to perfection. And the vital element that has made it possible is technology.

But is this true to experience, or just whistling in the dark? Even Gene Roddenberry did not really believe this vision. In 1953, when he was a police officer, he commented in his police papers, 'Despite the work of the world's religions, self-interest is still the paramount consideration of the individual.' The Roddenberry-based *Earth: Final Conflict* is far less optimistic than *Star Trek*, and his unsuccessful 1973 scripts, *Genesis II* and *Planet Earth*, were the opposite of *Star Trek* with a ghastly post-nuclear catastrophe, and slaves, savages and mutant tyrants. Even William Shatner, whose appetite for *Star Trek* continues after playing Captain Kirk, as he now writes *Star Trek* and *TekWar* novels and TV scripts, doubts the benefits in the future development of technology, as his violent world in *Tek War* shows. He once said that he thinks it unlikely we will make it to the twenty-fourth century, still less achieve virtual paradise:

'There is impending doom because we have destroyed this natural world. It's no accident we have viruses like Ebola, HIV and others even more dangerous.'

William Shatner

Star Trek presents salvation by technology, in a far stronger and more consistent fashion. As we've seen, its technobabble is worth analysing, unlike that of *Fireball XL5* or indeed *Doctor Who*, where science is far nearer fantasy. In *Star Trek*, it's far more important. The technology *is* the plot. That technology saves us *is* the storyline.

Transporter technology: good guy, bad guy

Ah, the transporter! Invented to save production costs, it is now part of the charm of the show. But is the technology of transporters, replicators and holosuites our great hope or fear?

Technology-based plots: a small sample	
Star Trek: TOS – early plots	*Star Trek: TNG* – early plots
The Enemy Within (5) **Plot**: Transporter malfunction splits Kirk into two halves, a 'good' but bland Kirk and a 'bad' Kirk. **Resolution**: Scotty bypasses the faulty transporter through the impulse engines, beaming both Kirks down, and one reunified Kirk back up.	*Encounter at Farpoint* (1–2) **Plot**: Q condemns humanity for barbarism. Picard's crew must die. **Resolution**: Picard proves their honour by the way they handle the next mission, where they discover the basis of the Bandis' rapid technical advance: in enslaving an advanced alien at Farpoint Station, which they save.
The Naked Time (7) **Plot**: The crew is taken over by a virus affecting their deepest emotional conflicts and desires. It threatens to render them so out of control they cannot stop the ship losing its orbit and crashing. **Resolution**: They regain control and manage to hurl the ship back in time.	*The Naked Now* (3) **Plot**: The crew is incapacitated by the virus that attacked the original crew in *The Naked Time*, including disabling the computer, so the crew drifts towards death. **Resolution**: The android Data works at superhuman speed to restore the computer, save the craft, and as the antidote is discovered, everyone is cured.
What are Little Girls Made of? (10) **Plot**: Exoite technology of androids revived by Dr Korby, who replicates Kirk and aims to replace life with androids. **Resolution**: Kirk gets the androids to work against Korby, who dies with his androids.	*Where No One Has Gone Before* (6) **Plot**: The attempt to use new warp theories sends the ship into another galaxy, then at the edge of physical and mental reality. **Resolution**: The cause is a Traveller, and child prodigy Wesley steadies him, and they return.

Dagger of the Mind (11)	*The Last Outpost* (7)
Plot: Dr Adams has abused the technology of a 'neural neutralizer' to control penal colony Tantalus Five, and tries to control Kirk with it. **Resolution**: He perishes in his own machine.	**Plot**: Confrontation with the Ferengi leads to both ships being immobilised by the guard of an extinct advanced race. **Resolution**: Riker's exposition of Federation philosophy wins the day.
Miri (12)	*Star Trek: VOY*
Plot: Disastrous life-prolongation experiment kills all at puberty, so only long-living children survive, leaving a kind of extended *Lord of the Flies* type of society. Captain Kirk is attacked and he and his landing party are infected. **Resolution**: McCoy synthesises an antidote, which saves both crew and inhabitants.	*Tuvix* (2:20) **Plot**: Tuvok and Neelix are fused together in a transporter accident, and their separation becomes a moral quandary, as he asserts the right to exist in this new form. **Resolution**: Captain Janeway overrides Tuvix's protests, reverses the transporter event, thus bringing Tuvok and Neelix back.

Many of the plots (see table) start with a technical fault and are resolved by one – or else by a rousing speech from Riker, Kirk or Picard, etc. This pattern is common in *Voyager* (as in *Tuvix*) and in *DS9*, as for example in *The Way of a Warrior*, where the need to de-cloak to beam people aboard to safety would leave our heroes defenceless. This is solved by a novel use of tractor beams. The use of technology to save the day is virtually assured in every single story, often several times. This is because in the *Star Trek* world, salvation of the human race is achieved by technology. Hunger, poverty, war, violence, even rivalry have been overcome – by technology.

It is precisely this element of *Star Trek* that is most far removed from science. This is a far bigger hole than any nit-picker's gaffe. This is where *Star Trek* moves out of science fiction and into fantasy, and quite deliberately so. And in a way this is the charm of the programme. It is a fantasy about the future in which we have solved all our really big problems. Or to be more precise, technology has solved them for us. Technology is God, Lord and Saviour. And while there is plenty of room for adventure and discovery, we are safe in the future. Money, conflict and evil are over – at least as human problems. And in Roddenberry's Utopian universe, even the aliens are heading towards this paradise. All this is supplied at no apparent cost. Huge starships can travel vast distances, and whatever damage they suffer, they seem able to repair themselves (with a helpful tweak from Scotty).

'Technology is my shepherd, I shall lack nothing. He gives me a holodeck of green pastures, he transports me beside still waters, he provides Rest and Recreation. He guides me in the Prime Directive for the Federation's sake. Even though I warp through the event horizon of a black hole, I will fear no evil, for you are with me; your sensor array, tractor beam, phasers and photon torpedoes, they comfort me. You replicate a table full before me in the presence of my enemies. You anoint my head with pleasure; my cup overflows. Surely goodness and technology will follow me all the days of my life, and I will dwell in the Federation for ever.'

Anthony Thacker

● FAITH IN THE FUTURE

Is technology our salvation? Is it our ultimate hope for heaven on Earth? In a way, *Star Trek* homes in more on the ultimate hope that a day is coming when we shall have broken free from our present sufferings; the day pictured in the Bible, when 'there will be no more death or mourning or crying or pain, for the old order of things has passed away' (Revelation 21:4). Of course death continues in the *Star Trek* universe, but the end of much human misery is certainly said to be achieved in the future by a combination of technology, human goodness and, it seems, our learning to work together with alien species. The future pictured in *Star Trek VIII: First Contact* suggests war and other evils continue until 5 April 2063, when following the discovery of warp speed and the arrival of the Vulcans, the future paradise finally begins to take hold.

Is this all a stirring prophecy of a world with no suffering, and no sin either? Is it an inspiring vision of one possibility we know we'll never achieve, but consider worth striving towards? Or is it a naïve yet grand delusion, promoting false gods of technological power and pleasure, which will corrupt and destroy our civilisation? 'Time will tell. It always does.'

● 160

• 12 •
Doctor Who, *Davros and Science*

Education, education, education – or entertainment?

Star Trek considers the development of technology, and especially space travel, to be the gateway to Utopia. But as we have already mentioned, *Doctor Who* is rather more ambiguous.

'*Doctor Who* was spelled out to me as a children's programme.'[1]

William Hartnell

'I had been briefed that *Doctor Who* was to be aimed at children from the ages of 9 to 14.'[2]

Verity Lambert

The programme's creator, Sydney Newman, intended the series to provide a wonderful education for children, as William Hartnell and Verity Lambert remembered, both in terms of the historical stories and the science fiction tales, where cultural diversity and the problems of surviving in an alien environment could be stretched further. In practice, it changed with the second story, *The Daleks*.

In the main, *Doctor Who* is a space fantasy with time travel. The hallmark of most stories is a battle with monsters. That, incidentally, may be a reason why the 1996 film did not rekindle the fire, as the nearest we got to anything to do with monsters was a few seconds of the seventh Doctor mentioning the Daleks. In *Doctor Who* the monsters still form the strongest appeal to younger children, while the adventure element appeals to older children. *Doctor Who* took off for this reason, as the second story – now called *The Daleks* (1963–64) – stimulated the imagination of a generation of children because of these exterminating aliens. *The Tomb of the Cybermen* (1967) excited viewers because of its chilling sequences where the supposedly dead post-human Cybermen were revived and took over, and where one was killed, and died realistically. Similarly, the highpoint in *Spearhead from Space* (1970) was when shop window dummies sprang to life as 'Auton' killers.

As *Doctor Who* succeeded far beyond the original dreams of its inventors, it attracted a growing number of teenagers and adults who needed extra depth to the storylines and characterisation. The final Peter Davison story, *The Caves of Androzani* (1984), presents an example of the result: one of the best ever *Doctor Who* stories in terms of genuinely believable villains, motives, plot developments and storylines; at the same time, however, it is baffling to young children. At its best, as in the Hinchcliffe and Holmes 'Gothic Era' with the fourth Doctor and Sarah, we had classic battles with memorable monsters, gripping adventures, credible characters, mystery, science and fun. It was intellectually stretching, without convoluted confusion. What is the secret of *Doctor Who*? To misquote: 'It's the monsters, stupid!'

Daleks, Cybermen and Sontarans: losing humanity

Daleks, Cybermen and Sontarans, notorious *Doctor Who* monsters, threaten not just extermination, but a 'post-human' catastrophe: the collapse of our essential humanity, everything we hold dear about ourselves. Unlike other monsters, which simply attack externally, Daleks and Cybermen (Cyborgs) and Sontarans (clones) present an additional chilling threat: that we might become like them, and become the monsters they are. This threat was made explicit in that all-time classic *The Tomb of the Cybermen* (1967). The apparently long-dead Cybermen, revived by mad logician Erich Klieg, have assembled obediently around their Cyber-controller, who addresses the captive archaeologists, the Doctor and his companions with the chilling words: 'We will survive. You will become like us!'

Who are the Daleks?

▶ They were originally trapped in their travel machines because their humanoid form was grotesquely mutated by radiation from a neutron bomb (in *The Daleks*, 1963–64).

▶ Later, they were pictured as deliberate ultimate genetic mutations, GM humans, intended by Davros, their Kaled creator, to become dependent killing machines (in *Genesis of the Daleks*, 1975).

▶ They are a parody of the Nazis, a warning that war if pressed indefinitely could lead us to lose our essential humanity in the desperate desire to win at all costs. This is one of the stock features of SF – the fear that some mad scientist with a terrible invention will permanently destroy our humanity.

Who are the Cybermen?

▶ Their threat comes through our desire for medicine to ensure longevity and approximate immortality, such that we allow our bodies to be altered to the loss of our very selves, our souls. What does it mean to be human, or to lose our humanity? This lies at the heart of many SF horror stories, especially of the Cyborg variety.

▶ They are also cybernetic, telepathic creatures, whose mechanical, electric brains interact by some form of radio waves. They use gadgetry to control humans cybernetically. In this, the chilling idea of the Cybermen is presented, especially as worked through in the early stories, where the cybernetic side is strong.

Who are the Sontarans?

▶ A race who allowed cloning of soldiers, fuelling endless wars. Since they are cloned, they have lost their race and any humanity.

The Doctor as scientist

The Doctor faces, and defeats, such monsters in every story. The Doctor's outlook is well expressed at the end of his first encounter with the Daleks. In episode 7 (*The Rescue*, 1964) he says to Alydon: 'You wanted advice, you said. I never give it, never . . . but I might just say this to you. Always search for truth . . . My truth is . . . in the stars. And yours . . . is here.' A few episodes later, the main villain in *The Aztecs* (1964), Tlotoxl, questions the Doctor: 'In whose service are you?' and he replies, 'I serve the truth. Help me, Tlotoxl, and I promise you, you will find it.'

It is an outlook not paraded, but one implying the scientific method as the true way through life. It implies you should avoid all dogmas, all received beliefs, and create them yourself, by your own (scientific) discoveries. Really, despite half-hearted Buddhism in the Pertwee era, this sort of view continues throughout the series. In it, as we have seen, the Doctor relies on science, mathematics and experience to defeat evil, not the raw power of fists or weaponry. Meanwhile, Hartnell himself saw the Doctor as 'a cross between the Wizard of Oz and Father Christmas'. Hartnell's Doctor, for me, was utterly credible as this advanced time traveller. To me, as a child, he came over as a kind of cross between Bertrand Russell and Albert Einstein, and fitted their Edwardian manners well, as an eccentric philosopher-scientist and humanist or, as the Doctor says in *The Daleks' Masterplan*, 'a Citizen of the Universe, and a Gentleman to boot'! Even his forgetfulness (Hartnell's) added charm to his elderly character.

So here we have the paradox: *Doctor Who* has as its hero a lover of science, who relies on science and the use of technology to outwit his foes, yet he is pitted against the degeneration of science in a succession of mad scientists. This paradox is pressed to the point of perversity on occasion, where the Doctor seems to decry the very science of the scientists. In *Inferno*, he seems to oppose geological investigation. In *The Daemons*, the Doctor protests his scientific beliefs, but also uses 'an old magical defence', and explains magic in the florid technobabble that crops up frequently in that tale. Yet the implication is that he is only against more primitive science, or the misuse of science for evil ends or by those who are blinkered by their prejudices and over-confidence. Such tensions are increasingly at the heart of public debate. However, the fault-lines may be placed slightly differently in debates today.

The GM debate

One aspect is how the focus of controversy has shifted somewhat from physics (e.g. the nuclear debate, the space race) to biology (the battle against diseases, the rise of new viruses, genetic advances like cloning, etc.). The GM debate is a good example. Here we have a suggestion that a new biotechnology is emerging, and needs to be tested scientifically. The battle about GM crops, coming into the arena of food after BSE, has been largely framed in terms of distrust of scientists. So much so that when a suggestion for genetically modified medicines was made, the scientists were surprised by the initial positive response. But medicine is a different area. With food, Joe Public thinks he is alive and healthy, and doesn't want any new-fangled idea threatening that. But with illness, disease and genetic abnormality, Joe Public is not well, and wants to be free of all these problems, so all new-fangled ideas are welcome.

Doctor Who doesn't usually tackle issues this complex. In a story like *Planet of Giants*, we have a morality tale of a businessman prepared to murder in order to foster a dangerous pesticide to protect his investment in the product. The Doctor and companions, despite being an inch high, succeed in securing his arrest, ending the risk.

But the debate about whether technology is friend or foe not only includes the issue of how it is used, and by whom, but also the more complex one of what it is used for. Genetic modification may be popular where it saves life, but the debate about the genetic modification of people must also press things beyond the immediate effects to foreseeable and credibly possible developments further down the line. That was the undoubted genius of the *Star Trek: TOS* story *Space Seed* and its film sequel, *Star Trek II: The Wrath of Khan*, where GM people like Khan had tried to take over the world (in the 1990s!).

But *Doctor Who*'s GM people – Daleks and Sontarans – add to that danger the context of biological warfare. Imagine GM or cloning in a context of all-out war, and humanity is threatened. We must be aware of the ways new scientific and technological breakthroughs could work out and affect us. The Daleks and Cybermen are a warning that the price of complacency about powerful developments could be high.

Part Four:
Return of the Myth Makers

 IN THIS SECTION

▶ **The Jedi**

Star Wars and the Force – is it a spiritual power?

▶ **The Lone Ranger from Gallifrey**

'How to save the universe', by the Doctor.

▶ **The Babylon Project**

Vorlons and Shadows, those mythic cosmic powers: will they leave us alone? And what can help us in our daily struggles (like with Dr Franklin's problem of addiction to 'stims')?

▶ **Vader and Palpatine**

Star Wars and the struggle between good and evil.

▶ **The Myth Makers**

A guided tour of the creative myths in science fiction. Is fantasy a no-go area for Christians, or is it a mission field?

• 13 •
May the Force Be with You!

Religion in *The Phantom Menace*

If we look for direct religious elements in the *Star Wars* series, we find there were none in the first two films. In *Return of the Jedi*, there was the comic scene where the Ewoks mistake C-3PO for a god. *The Phantom Menace* attempts to push things further in the direction of a kind of realism, both in the supposed science behind the Force, and the more direct religious elements. The Gungan, Jar Jar Binks, occasionally comments, 'May da guds be kind, mesa palo' (May the gods be kind, my pal). Meanwhile Shmi Skywalker suggests her son, Anakin (Darth Vader), was born by virgin birth, and Jedi, Qui-Gon Jinn, is asked if he means that Anakin is the fulfilment of 'the prophecy of the one who will bring balance to the Force'.

In the *Star Wars* films, director George Lucas expresses his hope for the Force, and its effect on viewers. Commenting on *The Phantom Menace* he said, 'I put the Force into the movie to try to awaken a certain kind of spirituality in young people.' On another occasion he was even more explicit: 'I would hesitate to call the Force "God". It's designed primarily to make young people think about mystery . . . to say "Think about this for a second. Is there a God? . . . How do we relate to God?" '[1]

Surprisingly, perhaps, C. S. Lewis also talked of 'the Force' in his *Voyage to Venus*. But here, the Force has guided the villain, Weston, who tells hero Ransom:

'Call it a Force. A great, inscrutable Force, pouring up into us from the dark bases of being. A Force that can choose its instruments. It is only lately, Ransom, that I've learned from actual experience something which you've believed all your life as part of your religion. Guided. Chosen. Guided. I've become conscious that I'm a man set apart. Why did I do physics? Why did I discover the Weston rays? Why did I go to Malacandra [Mars]? It – the Force – has pushed me on all the time. I'm being guided. I know now that I'm the greatest scientist the world has ever produced.'[2]

This pride in the Force does not bode well – Weston concludes the argument with Ransom with something like a demonic fit.

Allegory

Far more important, spiritually, is the allegorical, almost mythic, feel in the series. While allegories of myth and religion can lie beneath the surface of much science fiction and fantasy, whether deliberately (as in C. S. Lewis's Narnia stories) or more accidentally or incidentally (as in *Doctor Who*), such allegory seems more at the heart of *Star Wars*. And like Narnia, it has been seen as reflecting something of the Christian story allegorically. Indeed, when *Battlestar Galactica* appeared the year after the first *Star Wars* film, in what seemed massive copying, and was inundated with lawsuits, its creator Glen Larson claimed in defence to have lifted the plot not from *Star Wars* but straight from the Bible, without the need of intermediaries!

In *Star Wars*, the key allegory concerns the battle between good and evil, light and darkness, with suggestively named villain, Darth Vader ('Dark Invader'), and hero Luke Skywalker. There is a further dimension in the invisible (quasi-spiritual) powers of each. Luke develops the powers of a Jedi, the use of mental powers similar to telepathy, hypnosis and telekinesis, to de-cloak and defeat evil, and the corresponding telepathic awareness of evil. Meanwhile, ex-Jedi Darth Vader is able to detect Jedi presence. If we add to this the corrective note that the Jedi is not supposed to use his powers for evil, while the dark power of the Evil Empire seeks power for its own sake and is determined to do evil to achieve its selfish ends, then the moral allegory is clearer.

The prayer 'May the Force be with you!' has the implication of wishing a blessing on the Jedi, that their 'spiritual' sensitivity shall be effective. Meanwhile, Darth Vader has tried to use the Force (telepathically sensed Jedi power) for evil, selfish purposes. That is the warning in the Force: beware the dark side! Furthermore, the element of forgiveness and of the redemptive power of suffering that emerges especially in *Return of the Jedi* presses the significance of this allegory further in a more explicitly Christian direction. Luke completes his training to become a Jedi Knight, and is able to defeat Darth Vader without violent anger and revenge, thereby breaking the hold of the dark side of the Force, and saving the galaxy from the Evil Empire.

While there is much of the typical science fiction world of starship chases and battles, and personal combat with armed light-sabres, the ultimate victory turns out not simply to be by fisticuffs, superior weaponry and technology, as so often in *Buck Rogers* and *Star Trek*, nor by superior intellect, ingenuity and a heavy dose of luck, as in *Doctor Who, Blake's 7* and *Star Trek* again, but by facing down the evil within, in this case the temptation to abuse the power of the dark side of the Force. Although it is painted in the simple primary colours of fantasy, this puts it closer to *Babylon 5*, where the heroes have flaws and the villains have their redeeming aspect, and where the hardest battles are inner ones, both those faced by Garibaldi and Franklin against addictions, and that by Sheridan in needing to hold out against torture. Here, as Straczynski says, the victory by the hero is not 'a victory over massive forces, it's a win over yourself'.

May the Force be with you!

Ah yes, but what force? The almost mystical feel of the Force of *Star Wars* has led many to suggest a parallel with Christianity. Are we not dealing here with something akin to the power of prayer or to the Holy Spirit? But is this idea particularly *Christian*? David Pringle's *The Ultimate Encyclopedia of Science Fiction* (Carlton, 1996) comments, 'the Force [is] a sort of spiritual substrate to the Universe, into which human beings can plug themselves in order to perform amazing mental feats – or, to be honest, magic.' However, the *Star Wars Encyclopedia* (Virgin, 1998) offers this definition: 'The Force: Both a natural and mystical presence, it is an energy field that both suffuses and binds the entire galaxy.' Is the Force spiritual, or magic, or a scientifically plausible energy field? After all, in the January 1975 stage of George Lucas's screenplay for *Star Wars: A New Hope*, the original focus for the Force was 'the Kilber Crystal, a powerful energy source that controlled the Force of Others', as Ted

Edwards described it in *The Unauthorized Star Wars Compendium* (Boxtree, 1999). That points to a physical Force. Of course in New Age circles crystals are sometimes believed to have mystical powers. On the spiritual side, interestingly, this same early screenplay would have concluded the initial roll up scroll introducing the film with these prophetic sounding words: 'In times of greatest despair there shall come a savior, and he shall be known as "The Son of Suns".'

Meanwhile, *The Phantom Menace* gives a biological explanation. Qui-Gon says that Anakin has a high reading of a lifeform called 'midi-chlorians' in his body, and explains, 'Midichlorians are a microscopic life form that resides within all living cells and communicates with the Force.' Without them, 'we would have no knowledge of the Force'.

So the Force is:

▶ spiritual
▶ natural
▶ magic
▶ an energy field
▶ physical crystal power
▶ messianic salvation
▶ or a biological capacity.

Physics of the Force

Is the Force physical? Are telepathy and telekinesis possible in physics? This is the question Lawrence Krauss tackles. His sequel to *The Physics of Star Trek* (not, after all, *Star Trek II: The Wrath of Krauss!*) was *Beyond Star Trek*. In three chapters he discusses the Force, and looks at whether ESP could be a physical, measurable force like electro-magnetism, and concludes that no known force, or even the unknown 'fifth force', could achieve the result of providing a mechanism for telepathy. Krauss concludes:

'The Force in *Star Wars*, which led off this discussion, is in fact much closer in spirit to a notion originally at the basis of astrology, which in turn had its roots in ancient Greece.'[3]

While Greece alone did not invent astrology (it is common to many ancient cultures), what Krauss means is the belief in aether, a fifth essence beyond air, earth, fire and water, which somehow was thought to inhabit space and connect all things. He then notes the famous Michelson-Morley experiment of 1887, which showed the non-existence of aether. Krauss later adds, 'When Obi Wan Kenobi exhorts Luke to "use the Force", he is clearly implying that there exists some energy available in the ambient space and that you can learn how to tap into it.' He even compares this to the 'yogic flying' claims of the Natural Law Party and its Transcendental Meditation devotees, who claim the ability momentarily to fly, and who argue that this power is based on accessing a force by tapping the energy from the vacuum of the universe! Krauss shows we should forget thinking of the Force as a scientifically measurable physical energy field. Instead it's nearer magic and astrology.

Spirituality of the Force

One capacity of a Jedi presses its spiritual side further: the visions Luke has of Obi-Wan Kenobi, and, at the end of *Return of the Jedi*, also of Yoda and of a third, apparently Anakin Skywalker. Each of those seen is already dead. What's more, the ghostly figure gives Luke correct information he could not have gained independently. Somehow, the Force seems to include communication from the dead. It also includes guidance: Qui-Gon says his meeting with Anakin 'was not a coincidence. Nothing happens by accident.' He explains to Anakin, 'You are strong with the Force . . .'

Is the Force of *Star Wars* more the force of astrological belief in aether than Christian belief in prayer? Perhaps. For if it is taken as a physical possibility achieved by spiritual (telepathic) techniques, it seems closer to magic than prayerful dependence on God. The key difference is that the idea of tapping into a hidden invisible force is closer to magic (even if in the disguise of science) than it is to prayer. For magic is the idea of a *human* technique or ability, and its difference to science is not that it is simple nonsense or arbitrary belief, but a set of practical techniques with a mystical basis, while science operates (with increasing complexity) on the basis of practical techniques with a mechanical basis, i.e. cause and effect. Prayer is different from both: it is based on the idea of openness to God. Its benefit, if it does not degenerate into a human, magical technique, comes from a relationship with God; a sense of being guided and inspired by God.

Having said that, *Star Wars* is not designed like *Star Trek* to provide an imagined future, with attempted scientific credibility. It is both a fantasy and a parable, a story, which though it is not a strict allegory, parallels human drama against its cosmic backcloth. So the Force is better *not* taken as a 'physical possibility achieved by spiritual (telepathic) techniques' but as a picture of the energy that comes from moral and immoral actions. The Force is in no sense just an odd name for God, but it could be seen as an equivalent, in the sense of our depending on the invisible power of goodness in our struggles with the equally unmeasurable but real powers of evil. For some things are beyond scientific measurement, yet they are still real. Neither love nor humour nor evil can be measured in a test-tube or in another physical way, but we reckon there is a real difference between a good joke and a weak one; between genuine love and sham; and between good and evil. We reckon to be able to distinguish, morally, between Holocaust victims, like martyr Maximilian Kolbe, and 'final solution' architect Adolf Hitler.

When Tim Henman and Greg Rusedski battled it out in the 1999 Davis Cup for tennis glory, in a very tight and close contest, the impact of their 9,000 fans was real enough. They would have been buoyed up, and arguably played better for it, but no physicist could have detected the 'energy field' between players and supporters. Nevertheless it was still real: the force of 9,000 fans is emotional and psychological. Meanwhile, the force felt in Hitler's Nuremberg rallies – a kind of dark side of the force – was an emotional rallying for evil. This force would also have failed to show up on any physical, electromagnetic detector. Unfortunately, it too was real. Hitler's almost mesmerising ability was legendary. Commentator Kimberly Cornish says, 'With Germany facing utter ruin, front-line officers who entered Hitler's presence determined to tell him that the military situation was hopeless, emerged from the bunker with complete confidence in ultimate victory.'[4]

So the Force – whether of goodness or of evil – is real,

though in the real world it does not depend on a physically measurable energy field, like aether, for its operation. If we think of emotions in sport or nationalism, we can recognise that they operate via awareness. Jedi power, however, is not dependent on consciousness, as the surprising impact on the Ewoks of Luke's powers of levitation shows. The same is also true for the power of prayer and the power of the Holy Spirit: though much of the impact comes through obvious channels, like changing the way people think and feel, some of the more dramatic examples in my experience involve situations with no possible conscious 'interference'.

While the Force is simply a pleasant fantasy, and perhaps a reflection of our real struggles with good and evil, it reminds us that the effects of moral, emotional and indeed spiritual forces, though not physical, are a real and vital part of our human experience.

• 14 •
Man and Superman

Saving life, the universe and everything

Deep out on the planet Krypton, so the story goes, a little baby, a *wunderkind*, was packaged and sent to a far-off planet: Earth. Having been brought up well, he goes around saving those he comes across, fighting 'for truth, and justice, and the American way', and especially Lois Lane. Disguised as the innocuous Clark Kent, to safeguard his Superman *persona* (or to get near Lois?), our hero is a model messianic myth for our time. Superman is a saviour-figure. When all seems lost, Superman will suddenly appear and miraculously save all concerned.

Science fiction profoundly taps into this whole question of salvation in a wonderful variety of ways. *Superman* gives us the simplest model – the Lone Ranger of space, the 'masked man' who appears from nowhere, whose only goal in life, it seems, is to act miraculously to get people out of trouble. *Doctor Who* follows this pattern in a different way. The 'saviour' is other-worldly, but his way of saving the day, especially in the earlier regenerations, is to rely solely on using his wits, his unparalleled time-travelling experience and his scientific skills. He spurns military technology, or (originally) psi powers.

But what kind of 'salvation' is on offer here? I'm reminded of the account of a man who had been helped by Gamblers Anonymous to break free from his gambling addiction. His comment was, 'I have been saved,' but on seeing the

Methodist minister who had founded the group he added in his confusion, 'I don't mean that word in any religious sense. I mean I've been *really* saved.'[1] 'Being saved' has become a religious cliché, and as saving 'life, the universe and everything' is a common feature in SF, we'll need to be careful.

A hundred years ago the cliché was up and running, when B. F. Westcott, the New Testament lecturer, was stopped in the street by an earnest young man with the question, 'Sir, have you been saved?' With New Testament Greek nuances in mind, Bishop Westcott silenced the man with, 'Do you mean, "Have I been saved?" "Am I being saved?" or "Will I be saved?"?' This reminds us that this deceptively simple question hides a richness of experience, which in the Christian tradition includes the historic event of Christ's atoning death (Romans 5:10), the personal experience of salvation (Romans 8:11) and the cosmic hope of the restoration of all things (Acts 3:21).

As we have seen, the Doctor saves people by using his wits, not weapons. The first Doctor made the character's general attitude to guns clear in an underground scene in *The Dalek Invasion of Earth*: 'No. I never take life. Only when my own is reasonably threatened.' There is a model of salvation here: we will be saved, not by military might, but by intellect and wisdom. We have seen this side of the Doctor's philosophy: we rely on truth, science and experience. This remains the norm, though later Doctors relax it, and in *The Seeds of Doom* we even see the fourth Doctor carrying a gun around. As for psi powers, neither of the first two Doctors has anything to do with them, but the third Doctor is not beyond 'hypnotising' a monster with 'Venusian nursery rhymes', and using a bit of 'Venusian karate' (a 'Vulcan neck pinch' by another name!), and the seventh Doctor can even be seen hypnotising someone to get himself out of a sticky situation, just like the Master would do, in *Battlefield*. But these are aberrations from the Doctor's normal way of saving the day.

This Superman saviour can also be a superfamily, as Gerry Anderson's *Thunderbirds* showed. Here a futuristic family have a mission to turn up in the most intractable disasters and save the potential victims in the nick of time. *Thunderbirds* has salvation based on technology plus basic human goodness, just like *Star Trek*.

How to save the universe

In any story of salvation, there are a number of different factors involved: those being saved; those saving; the method of saving; and so on. In a typical *Doctor Who* story, like *The Daleks*, once any uncertainty is removed, and it is clear who the 'goodies' are (the Thals) and who the 'baddies' are (the Daleks), then the Doctor saves the goodies. At first he is reluctant. The first Doctor starts off as an anti-hero and part-time fatalist. But later he is a deliberate saviour. The second Doctor presents the settled pattern:

'There are some corners of the Universe which have bred the most terrible things — things which are against everything we have ever believed in. They must be fought.'

The Doctor in *The Moonbase*

How do you defeat evil like the Daleks? The battle with these evils will go back and forth. But the decisive move is usually made by the Doctor – a canny move, as often as not using the intended evil of the monsters against them.

Four simple ways to defeat the Daleks

1. Switch them off (*The Daleks, The Dalek Invasion of Earth, The Power of the Daleks*).
2. Switch their own, exterminating attack against them (*The Daleks' Masterplan, The Evil of the Daleks, The Day of the Daleks, The Five Doctors, Remembrance of the Daleks*).
3. Use handy technology against them (*Planet of the Daleks, Death to the Daleks, Genesis of the Daleks, Resurrection of the Daleks*).
4. Involve another set of baddies against them (*The Chase, Destiny of the Daleks, Revelation of the Daleks*).

The same pattern can be seen with the Cybermen and other evil attackers. Most other races are stopped in the tracks of their attempt to invade or destroy Earth, the whole universe or whoever. So we see a similar pattern of switching off, mirrored-back attack, handy weapon or other baddies thwarting their plans, coupled of course with the Doctor's brilliant use of the ploy. What does this say about salvation? That we will be saved by two things. First, evil will in the end defeat itself by over-reaching itself. There is indeed something in this observation. Hitler's attempt to wipe out all his enemies – to the east, the west and within – eventually over-stretched Nazi evil to the point where it could be completely overthrown. But it is not always true. The two greatest evils of the postwar period have been seen as Stalinism (hated by the right) and apartheid (hated by the left). However, neither collapsed by over-reaching itself in the conventional sense. Instead, both declined because a new leadership emerged that no longer believed in the exclusive truth of the propaganda. Gorbachev and de Klerk were moderate centrists, whose attempts to reform the evils they inherited led comparatively painlessly to their abolition. They were neither extremists, whose evil galvanised opposition, nor revolutionary crusaders.

Second, salvation will come mainly through intellectual skill – a clear picture in most stories of *Doctor Who*. That's a 1960s faith in the 'white heat of the scientific revolution', the last expression of the belief in rational science and techno-logy, even in the midst of a series of worlds where science (Davros) and technology (Cybermen) have gone wrong.

But is it the universe that's being saved – and if so, how? With the Doctor, it is sometimes the group he's with, but more usually it's the whole race, planet or universe, or all space and time! In the case of *Superman*, like the Lone Ranger, it is mainly a string of individuals who happen to be in a position for Superman to save them.

'So long, and thanks for all the fish'

Douglas Adams's dolphins are supposed to have said this on fleeing the doomed Earth. Westcott's comment, 'What does it mean to be saved – what difference does it make?', reminds us that 'being saved' has many different dimensions: the his-toric event, the day-to-day experience, and the ultimate hope. But *Doctor Who* centres on the historic event side of salvation alone. Life, the universe and everything is about to be destroyed, but the Doctor switches the deadly machine off, just in time!

Batman gives us yet another (wacky) example of the hero-outsider who saves us. Why is SF so replete with aliens and other outsiders who save us? Perhaps it's because of a recognition that as humans we get ourselves into difficult situations, and sometimes we need outside help, even superhuman help, to sort things out. The *Superman* model reminds us that aspects of this salvation are beyond us: we need supernatural help. However, some things are beyond even Superman and the Doctor. Eternal life is often promised to people within science fiction: Q promises as much to Riker in *Hide and Q*, and pretends to Picard that he governs the after-life. But it is never really delivered. Nonetheless, the treatment of salvation in SF reminds us that this is part of the human condition, part of the human quest.

Monsters

The monster is pretty near essential for most *Doctor Who* stories, though of course the monster may dress up as the most suave, respectable, sophisticated and intelligent foe, as with the Master. But whether alien, human or an angel in disguise, the character reveals monstrous intentions in the end, and our superhuman hero is necessary to save us from evil. Why is *Doctor Who* so full of monsters? More broadly, why are monsters such a recurring theme in fiction? They are a mythic representation of the downside of experience. In a world where we might be undone by betrayal and other evils, they express the monstrous side of humanity, and of experience generally. And the Doctor neatly poises a tension in our assumptions. Can we solve such problems by human ingenuity alone or do we need help beyond human resources – divine help? The Doctor, by providing unique help from a super-advanced culture, provides the only escape from certain death in almost every story. That seems to picture help coming from outside. But the way he does it is not by superior magical powers of technology; it is far more often by application of scientific skills, common sense and decency – and a slice of luck!

Doctor Who is a fantasy, so it is incongruous to criticise it as untrue to experience of how frequently we might be saved from impossible situations in the nick of time. We know it is untrue to experience. Even more so with *Superman* and *Batman*! The point of these stories of survival in face of impossible odds has a different rationale: it is to express the human desire for survival. To that extent such stories are often criticised as escapist. And of course at one level they are. But at another, they simply represent the mythic extremes of more common experience. They are symbols, and the images function more like those in dreams than in real life. But even dreams and images need to match up to life in their own way: do they help us to face life problems, or do they provide the worst sort of escapism – that of the ostrich with its head in the sand?

At its best, *Doctor Who* goes well beyond pretence. It enables us to name, in symbolic terms, some of the evils and more ambiguous challenges of our time; to face them, and to declare that they are against everything we have ever believed in, and must be fought (like the Cybermen in *The Moonbase*). Of course, the *Doctor Who* style of monster drama is quite different from some others, particularly those that press matters as far as they are able in the gruesome, in the 'horror' genre. Here, the monster is not always domesticated or defeated. The sheer terror is increased as it becomes clear, gradually or suddenly, that the nightmare is not going to end; that the bestial destroyer is going to end the heroes' lives. But that issue, both the drama and the psychology of it, is another theme.

The alien monster that successfully destroys the human race (or a large slice of it) in an orgy of destruction, evoking terror, expresses the hidden evils we feel, not far beneath the surface of humanity's shared memories. With all fears, the first steps towards overcoming them are naming them and facing them. The problem with such fictional horror is that being fictional, there is a tendency towards the extreme, the absurd, even the laughable. This fosters a phoney response to horror; a cavalier disregard that in no way helps develop appropriate responses to real terrors.

· 15 ·
Our Last Best Hope

J. Michael Straczynski, the creator and author of most of the stories of *Babylon 5*, gives us naturalistic realism without pessimism. He once commented that Roberta Leigh's puppet show *Space Patrol* was, for him, 'the best show from my childhood, bar none'.[1] As Leigh said, about Gerry Anderson's space puppet fantasy, '*Fireball XL5* was quite different from mine because it didn't have any reality about it. All the things that I say about space are actual facts.'[2] She was advised by Colin Ronan, Vice-President of the British Astronomical Society, to check relevant facts. The other feature that separated this series from its main competitor was its stronger moral tone, as it eschewed violence and nonsense to resolve plots.

Strikingly, it is this greater realism that characterises *Babylon 5*, not just in the science, but in the assumptions about humanity, and how we would be likely to react to interaction with alien powers, if one day we actually encountered them. Like *DS9* the action in *B5* is centred on a space station where many human and alien characters meet. However, while *Star Trek* expresses a faith that humanity by the twenty-fourth century will have given up fighting one another, in *Babylon 5* the backdrop is of developing war, Armageddon even. (Although *DS9*'s later seasons have been influenced by *B5*, with its story of war with the Dominion.)

Joe Straczynski's *Babylon 5* is a universe like the one we know, where humans can behave awfully, and where true heroism can arise despite this. It is a world where even the heroes are flawed; a universe where people (and aliens) can change radically, and the hero of one season can be the flawed or even villainous character of the next, while yesterday's Machiavellian can be converted, repent and change.

A checklist of flawed heroes and reformed villains

▶ **Captain Jeffrey Sinclair** is an all-American hero, who is reckless because of living on the edge. Is this the only way he can gain a sense of meaning in life? He has no real answer. He changes by 'becoming' Minbari legend Valen.

▶ **Security chief Michael Garibaldi** is a 'reformed' alcoholic with a continuing weakness. Despite earlier failure, he is mainly a hero on *B5* from 2257 to 2260. Then Shadow and Psi Cop intervention helps him change into a traitor. When Psi control is lifted, he saves the day, but falls back on alcohol for a while.

▶ **Commander Susan Ivanova** is more consistent, but suppresses the instability arising from a distant father and a mother who committed suicide, by showing a brittle exterior, an acerbic wit and a semi-agnostic wrestling with her Jewish faith.

▶ **Dr Stephen Franklin** is the typical idealistic, hardworking medic of SF, but his very workaholic virtue tempts him to abuse 'stims' (powerful stimulants that enable him to work 36-hour shifts) at cost to his health. He is out of action for several months.

▶ **Captain John Sheridan** begins as the *bête noire* of the Minbaris (he uniquely destroyed their flagship in the earlier war), but he ends up being the first and only person to marry a Minbari.

▶ **Elizabeth Lochley**, third captain of *B5*, had years earlier married Sheridan in a brief relationship that failed. She supported EarthGov against Sheridan, but afterwards is his choice to lead *B5*.

▶ **Zack** eventually becomes security chief, but first went in with the SS-like 'Nightwatch', taking time to decide between it and Sheridan.

▶ **Marcus** has lost all family, and signs up with the Minbari/human Rangers. His love for Ivanova proves fatal.

▶ In anger, **Minbari ambassador Delenn** cast the deciding vote that led to the war to wipe out humanity, before repenting and working to unite humans and Minbaris spiritually. She believes herself called to fulfil a 900-year-old prophecy to secure that unity in person, and – with many twists and turns – achieves that.

▶ **Lennier** is Delenn's good-natured, deferential assistant and he protects Delenn and others. But a 'noble' love for Delenn leads to jealousy and a moment of madness where he would have left Sheridan to die.

▶ **Narn ambassador, G'Kar** is haughty, angry and vengeful, and a womaniser, lusting after alien females. His religiosity turns to a real conversion experience and a long-lasting change, as he enables his people to break from the cycle of mutual vendettas.

▶ **Na'Toth**, G'Kar's trusty aide, is assumed dead by all for three seasons, only to have been a prisoner.

▶ **Centauri Londo Mollari** starts as more of a victim, and a colourful buffoon, gambler and womaniser, but his nostalgia for the glory days of the Centauri empire sees him become a tragic figure. The Shadows exploit this, and he instigates genocide, before a growing recognition of how terrible the regime he has fostered is, and later there is a recognition of his injustice, and acceptance of his tragic fate.

▶ **Vir Cotto** is Londo's bumbling assistant, who gains the courage to save Narn lives, assassinates the mad emperor, saving Londo at the same time, and eventually becomes Emperor.

▶ **Vorlon ambassadors (both called 'Kosh')** are reclusive and ambiguous, but apparently the most powerful if reluctant force for good until Season 4, where their authoritarian and destructive nature leads them to genocide – to foster goodness, of course! In rapid turn they shift from long-term ally to most terrifying foe.

▶ Even **the Shadows**, who are presented as the main evil (quasi-demonic powers) throughout the series, who threaten not just Earth but thousands of races across the galaxy, are shown not just to be evil crazies who want to destroy the universe 'for no good reason' (to quote Douglas Adams). Rather they are creatures with their own ideological logic – a Hegelian/Darwinian philosophy that races need provoking into all-out wars to promote fast evolutionary advance.

▶ **Bester**, top telepath, is head of the Psi Cops, and a key villain. A creep loathed by all, his slightly charming, bland exterior hides a schemer who is quite at ease killing face to face in cold blood. But even he shows a more sympathetic, family side. He is played by Walter Koenig, famous as *Star Trek*'s Chekov. They're both major parts.

'When I was in *Star Trek* my role on the show was expository, to give information about the plot and in that regard, there's very little opportunity for character, it's simply you are a device, you are a tool. But Joe writes for the character so you get to be a human being.'[3]

Walter Koenig

▶ **Talia Winters** is resident telepath on *B5* for two years, during which time she seems positive and wins confidence, only to turn out to be a subconsciously programmed ('sleeper') spy and traitor.

▶ **Lyta Alexander**, a normal telepath, uncovers the 'sleeper', and is greatly enhanced in power by the Vorlons, enough to withstand Bester. She helps liberate Mars and Earth, but later teams up with rogue telepaths and goes off with G'Kar in a solo mission and almost Vorlon-like power.

Triumph or tragedy?

Star Trek, even *DS9* and *Voyager*, can't resist the sentimental ending. In the *DS9* story *Paradise*, a deliberate skit on isolationist cults, its members all vote to stay in the technophobic cult because that is the sentimental ending. Straczynski resists this, preferring realism. In *No Surrender, No Retreat*, G'Kar reluctantly agrees to sign a document with his enemy, Mollari – 'but not on the same page'! Just like Ulster! ('But not in the same room!') If we are at best flawed heroes, how does

Straczynski's realism answer the question of whether technology can destroy the human spirit or whether, more optimistically, we can survive it? Will it be more like *Star Trek*, where Jim Kirk will always win through, or more like *Nineteen Eighty-Four*, where the torturers and their technology are destined to triumph?

The key episode is *Intersections in Real Time* (4:18), where key hero, John Sheridan, has been captured by the fascistic Earth Alliance and is being tortured in order to force him to appear on TV speaking the lies the EarthGov wants him to. In practice, though, the difficulties for him are portrayed realistically – especially in the use of mind-bending drugs in the following episode, *Between the Darkness and the Light*. Sheridan somehow manages to hold off from betrayal. Straczynski comments:

'The reality is that not everyone does break. Fundamentally the show is about – and I've always said this about the series – the fact that hope exists in the darkest of rooms, it exists in the voice that says "I will not break and I will not bend". That he doesn't break is, to my mind, a statement that no matter how terrible the odds, no matter how alone we are, we can still persevere. If he were to break then it would send the other message that in the end the state will always win. No, you can fight the state and you can win and it isn't a win in terms of a victory over massive forces, it's a win over yourself.'[4]

As for salvation in *B5*, that is achieved despite the heavy-handed interference of Shadows and Vorlons. The freeing of Earth from its clandestine coup and cleverly but sinisterly imposed fascist and xenophobic dictatorship is achieved by the painstaking development of the widest alliance of support, single-minded determination, and perseverance against the odds by those who have come to believe in this goal. This is a rather more realistic model of the way such a saving of Earth from futuristic tyranny might happen. Technology would not be saviour, but used as effectively as possible by all sides.

Angels and demons?

What do we make of the Vorlons and Shadows, those apparent angels and demons? Where does that experience fit in? Shadows are the ultimate plotters, promoting evil 'that good may come'. The picture is revealingly close to the demonic, to the forces of spiritual evil, though even this is not as simple as it looks. But what about the Vorlons, those creatures of light that prove so destructive? Actually, Straczynski's picture here is powerfully insightful. The light shines in the darkness and so overcomes it, but as we hide in the darkness, in evil, we get destroyed. A biblical picture arguably nearer to Vorlon destruction of evil is not so much angels – even recognising that they can be destructive (Revelation 15–16) – but the wrath of God (see, for example, Romans 2:8–9; 9:22). Even so, the wrath of God has more the idea that as people opt for selfishness and other expressions of sin, God allows us to stew in our own juice, to be free to see the folly of our own evil run its course to our detriment, as in Romans 1. Wrath against evil is more impersonal and passive. But Vorlon anger against evil is far more personal and active. Vorlons picture a vengeful, vindictive wrath.

Meanwhile, in our world, the Shadows' type of evil (genocidal chaos by the ambitious) and the Vorlons' type (geno-cide of the ambitious) does not just go away. In *B5*, Sheridan ends the problem by ordering them to 'get the hell out of our galaxy!'. But that doesn't work for our experience of cosmic suffering or evil. In the end, Straczynski follows Roddenberry after all, in implying that mankind finds a god (the Vorlons), debunks it and gets on with life, supposedly the better for it. It is another mythology of 'man come of age'; another mythic expression of the atheist hope that if only people would throw off all gods all would be right with the human race. But evil doesn't have the habit of getting out of our galaxy, our world or our own experience. What is needed is one who can absorb all the evil *and* all the wrath, which, of course, is right at the heart of Christian claims about Jesus' death for sin.

The long, twilight struggle

The other side thrown up so well in *B5* is how life-changing events can play their role. G'Kar's conversion experience is the most obvious and sudden. But just as striking, if far slower, is Londo Mollari's reluctant recognition that his nostalgia for the great days of empire, together with the insidious action offered by the Shadows through Morden, has caused potentially fatal disaster for his planet. So he must take great risks to save his people, even, extraordinarily for him though believably, the possible sacrifice of his own life (in 4:6, *Into the Fire*). Other events in Season 2 bring about the key change – the belief of Sheridan and Delenn in each other – without which there would have been no independent *B5* freeing Earth.

Babylon 5 is an epic, recording the historic event of the saving of mankind for what is proclaimed 90 episodes earlier in the pilot, 'the dawn of the third age of mankind' – the age when humanity comes of age in the galaxy, able to set up the first galactic alliance. But salvation also shows a day-to-day dimension which is reflected in *B5*. G'Kar has his conversion experience; Dr Franklin comes to terms with his workaholic behaviour, which led him into addiction to 'stims'; Susan Ivanova is able to sit 'Shivah' for her late father, and in so doing become reconciled to him. These are not cosmic events, but 'saving events' in the life of an individual, episodes in which we shift from destructive (or self-destructive) behaviour towards healthier, more fulfilled patterns. For Christians this shift from destruction to life in all its fullness is a key part of the work of Christ (see John 10:10).

So this personal dimension is very much a Christian insight and perspective. The idea of being saved has a very different resonance in other religious traditions, where such a concept can be located meaningfully. It's very clear that Western and Eastern attitudes vary strongly, with a contrast between the Western personal, individualistic aspects, and Eastern approaches, which see salvation in terms of being lost (if that's not putting it too paradoxically).

In Hinduism, there is the picture of a drop getting immersed in an ocean, as the soul, finding fulfilment (or what we might call salvation), loses itself in the 'ocean of being'. The traditional Buddhist picture of salvation as nirvana, often translated 'extinguishedness', can be illustrated by the Buddha's question, 'Where does the flame go when it goes out?' This concept is rather different to Western ears. These pictures of salvation are not about *individual* salvation. Now the New Age movement, which modestly influences *DS9* and *Voyager*, as well as the pictures of Foundationism and Minbari religion in *B5*, borrows heavily from Eastern religious experience. But it finds this impersonal element the hardest part to swallow, so the Eastern picture is recast with Western goals of individual, personal fulfilment. Eastern religions emphasise that there is something of God in each one of us. That is why they urge their followers to lose their personal individuality, their desires, their craving, by realising their unity with ultimate reality. But New Age salvation makes a Western version of this belief, that each of us in a sense *is* God, personally. And it says: 'If I am God, I can and should do whatever helps me to realise personal fulfilment, and no one has the right to stop me.'

Eastern religions You are God/Spirit: lose your self in God!	**New Age religion** You are God/Spirit: find your self, fulfil your self!	**Western religions** You are personal: know God personally!

Western culture and religion has emphasised the more personal, individual side of salvation and faith generally. This can be seen not only in the three main faiths that began in the Middle East – Judaism, Christianity and Islam – but also in the earlier religions of the Middle East and Europe, where gods of the old Saxons, Vikings, Greeks or Egyptians were all too personal. However, Christian faith promotes the more transcendent side to God, which might seem conducive to Eastern faiths, while also presenting the personal angle very strongly. For the heart of the Christian faith is the belief that we meet God personally and truly in the person Jesus. And the same duality is also there in the experience of salvation: it's both personal relationship and transcendent glory, a taste of eternity.

This makes a difference to the day-to-day side of salvation. In practice, salvation is not only the major world events, not simply the ultimate hope; it is also life-changing experiences of the sort we see in the lives of some of the main characters of *B5*. In Christian experience, there is a tie-up between both sides, the cosmic and the personal. Christ's death on the cross expresses God's love and overcomes the barriers to our experience of that love. And we know that love, both in the everyday factors of life and those life-changing experiences; and we know it in the ultimate unbroken experience of that same love in heaven:

 'Love never fails . . . when perfection comes, the imperfect disappears . . . Now we see but a poor reflection . . . then we shall see face to face. Now I know in part; then I shall know fully, even as I am fully known. And now these three remain: faith, hope and love. But the greatest of these is love.'

I Corinthians 13:8–13

Salvation is not only a faith that God has acted decisively for us in Christ, nor only that he will act comprehensively for us in that eternal future we know as heaven; it is also part of our daily experience. Salvation is not cosmic, not just eternal; it starts now. And that is our evidence for it.

What is it that can help Franklin come off stims? Or Ivanova face her inner turmoil about her father? What helps

Garibaldi break with alcoholism (even if he periodically fails)? What leads Vir to break with Londo and the Centauri oppression of Narns by secretly smuggling Narns from danger of execution into safety? These are everyday issues (even if some, like Vir's, are the product of extreme situations), and the characters try to deal with them with whatever resources lie to hand. Part of the Christian claim is that God has increased the resources available to those who are open to receiving them, by receiving him. A lot of the time this is a simple enhancing of well-known resources. For what helps Franklin? A moment of self-recognition where he comes to terms with himself. What helps Ivanova? The personal touch of her rabbi. What helps Garibaldi? Shame and what might be called repentance – the attempt, the determination, to stay off the drug even if he sometimes fails. What inspires Vir? Belief, matched by opportunity – and courage. Indeed his help of Narns is reminiscent of those Gentiles, like the family of Corrie ten Boom, who risked their lives to help local Jews escape the Holocaust in the last war.

And what happens, as God's work of salvation strengthens in our day-to-day lives through the personal work of Jesus, in the power of the Holy Spirit, is that these everyday features are enhanced. Moments of self-recognition, the help of other believers, the conviction that leads to repentance, moments of sheer inspiration and courage: they are all part of life. And they are the ways God is at work in people's lives. This is the foretaste of salvation: to know God already at work in revelation, fellowship, conviction and inspiration; and to realise this is just the beginning of what God has in store for us. For the Christian, this day-to-day experience of salvation is a work of the Spirit, God himself personally at work, helping us sort out the issues life throws at us.

Babylon 5 proves to illustrate how human problems may operate in the distant future. Some problems we now know will continue, like addiction to alcohol or to work, not to mention many human struggles with conflicts and pressures. But technological change will certainly open up other new challenges, like stims or indeed the largely underplayed possibility of holosuite addiction. (I have a question: How come *TNG* heroes can actually get into the holosuites? Surely they would always be filled with teenagers – unless they were restricted to over-18s!) As a mirror on today's problems, such SF (unlike *Red Dwarf* in its comic way) has skated optimistically over the effect of this technology. But when it comes to the upside, 'our last best hope' turns out not to be the humanist hope that we can win through on our own, but that God himself, the basis of all hope, enables us to face life's challenges with the increased resources we need, which are rooted in his love. So it is not only true that *eternal* salvation comes through Christ alone, but also that even in *everyday* saving moments or redemptive experiences which are common to humanity (like liberation from addiction) we Christians experience Christ powerfully at work, helping us gain such hope, enabling us to 'have life, and have it to the full' (John 10:10).

• 16 •
A Long Time Ago, in a Galaxy Far, Far Away

The Empire and the Jedi

The world of *Star Wars* is very different from that of *Star Trek* (or indeed *Babylon 5*) in many ways. First, while Trekkers have over 500 episodes and nine films to savour, together with many books, and *B5* fans have over 100 episodes and four films, until recently *Star Wars* fans were limited to just three films, though also a competing number of magazines and books. However, the appearance of *The Phantom Menace*, as the first of a preceding new trilogy of films, is generating massive new interest. The introduction of a trilogy that is set *before* the existing stories, rather like the film *In the Beginning*, set before the events of *Babylon 5*, reminds me of Passolini's quip that a good story needs a good beginning, middle and end – though not necessarily in that order! Gene Roddenberry himself once commented on how *Star Wars* was different to his vision. He said that *Star Wars* 'was not about humanity. *Star Wars* . . . is really about princesses and kingdoms and knights and things in another galaxy. *Star Trek*, on the other hand, is about humanity, about us, about our children's children.'[1] It contrasts with *Star Trek*'s highly optimistic prophecy of technological glory.

In many ways, *Star Wars* is a space fantasy that operates not simply as a yarn set in space but more as an allegory of the struggle between good and evil. As such it not only reflects the feel of a traditional fairy tale, though one set in space; it allegorises our struggle for goodness. And that says something that lies at the heart of what it means to be truly human. Meanwhile, just as *Star Trek* has dominated SF on TV, *Star Wars* has increasingly dominated SF on film. The critics may have panned *The Phantom Menace*, but it did not stop it breaking many records. Perhaps that's because it works for its young target audience. *Star Wars* presents the nature of the struggle to avoid the good side being overtaken by the temptation to the dark side of our characters, not as a prophetic dream but a space fantasy, a fantastic world of the imagination that pictures in lush colours of adventure our inner struggles. Not for nothing does *Star Wars* deliberately avoid being set in the future, but, like all fairy tales, talks of the mythic past: 'A long time ago, in a galaxy far, far away . . .'

It seems Lucas deliberately set out to produce a film mythology. He was struck by a comment that Westerns were the *last* American mythology, and by the way in which space was the next frontier. Seeing the way heroes in the 1970s were now 'killer cops', he wanted to combine space as the context with adventure, and stimulate the imagination and develop a new mythology, a classic fairy tale, but set in space. The way Lucas developed his characters has given *Star Wars* even more of this legendary fantasy feel. Lucas studied ancient legends, like those of Arthur, as well as a wide range of fantasy and SF, including Tolkien's famous *Lord of the Rings* trilogy, to help him craft his characters. For example, Princess Leia was originally an amalgamation of Dejah Thoris (from *A Princess of Mars*), Lady Galadriel of Lothlorien (from *Lord of the Rings*) and Dorothy Gale (from *The Wizard of Oz*).

When *Star Wars* first appeared, it was widely regarded as a landmark in SF. Its special effects awed viewers. Its subtitles for alien talk set a new trend, and its wide range of alien species stimulated imagination beyond alien humanoids. But its pulse is the combination of science fiction with a rounded morality tale, coupled with elements of romance, comedy, action (including action in space) and a degree of character-isation. It has to be said that its appeal far outstripped all expectations, and those among the original reviews that dis-missed it as 'totally inept' and with 'no sense of wonder or magic' are widely regarded by SF fans and film buffs gener-ally as examples of historic ineptitude, on a par with those predicting cars would never catch on. As we have seen, *Star Wars* goes beyond its simple primary colours of fantasy, with its main characters, who combine clear stylisation as goodies and baddies, but with surprises.

'What is there about it that has created this hysteria? It can only be its marriage of sci-fi knowingness with something it is hard to resist calling religious nostalgia.'

The Listener (1977)

This takes *Star Wars* beyond simple escapist entertainment, where evil is always outside the heroes. Such escapism shows a simple, terrifying and totally unmitigated evil: *The Daleks*; the 'nDs' of *Invasion Earth*; or the hostile invaders of the three *Alien* movies – not to mention monsters in countless other horror films. Instead, as in classical fiction, *Star Wars* shows a more three- or four-dimensional approach to the struggle. It recognises, with Christians (along with most philosophers and other religious traditions), that we only really come to terms with the struggle with evil when we stop blaming others for everything, and learn to face our own inner struggles.

Characterisation: good and evil

The central moral and religious theme is the struggle between good and evil. Some characters are less developed and simply emerge as wise heroes, like Yoda; brave, if head-strong, heroes like Princess Leia and Han Solo; or straight-forward villains like Darth Maul and Darth Sidious. But in the key characters, particularly Luke Skywalker, Anakin Skywalker/Darth Vader and the Emperor Palpatine, we have the tensions worked out most dramatically.

Darth Maul and Darth Sidious

In *The Phantom Menace*, the new villain, Darth Maul, simply emerges as a highly skilful and murderous enemy of the Jedi. With red and black face, and several stumpy horns, one of my sons, on seeing the picture, immediately exclaimed, 'Satan!' Certainly dark and satanic, evil and every bit as ruthless as Darth Vader. His master is another suggestively named villain, Darth Sidious (Dark Insidious). Who he is, is not revealed.

Luke Skywalker

Luke may be the hero, but he is not beyond corruption by the dark side. Indeed, much of the dramatic tension depends on the possibility that he is able to fall as his father did before him. The old Jedi Yoda, in his death-bed speech in *Return of the Jedi,* warns him of this, having seen danger in the reck-lessness Luke had expressed earlier: 'Remember, a Jedi's strength flows from the Force. When you rescued your friends, you had revenge in your heart. Beware of anger, fear and aggression. The dark side are they. Easily they flow, quick to join you in a fight. Once you start down the dark path, for ever will it dominate your destiny.' Here we see a hero cap-able of falling.

Palpatine

A senator in *The Phantom Menace*, Palpatine managed to hide his desire for power in the years of decline and corrup-tion of the Old Empire. What is his relationship to Darth Sidious? Presumably the second or third 'prequel' film will show how Palpatine gains such power from the dark side of the Force. In due course, Palpatine gained almost absolute power throughout the Empire, first becoming head of the Senatorial Council, then President of the Republic, then declaring himself as Emperor. At some stage, Palpatine's use of the dark side of the Force overwhelmed him, and he became the most absolute and unmitigated embodiment of evil, a man who would destroy everyone and everything necessary to achieve power. In particular, he hunted down and killed most of the Jedi and their children, as those most committed and able among his opponents. He plotted to lure Luke to a final clash with Darth Vader, his dark side father. However, in the twists and turns of that struggle, Luke first shows forgiveness to his father, who would receive absolution if he reverted to the light side, then, as his con-nection with Leia is uncovered, and Vader and Palpatine hope to seduce her into the dark side, Luke loses his cool, and attacks Vader, cutting off his hand in a light-sabre attack. Even then, Luke declares to Palpatine that he refuses the dark side. Palpatine then unleashes the full power of his fury against him, and he seems doomed, until Vader interrupts on his son's behalf, throwing his master into the power core shaft, where he disintegrates.

Darth Vader

Vader is the most complex of the characters. Originally (as seen in *The Phantom Menace*), he was Anakin Skywalker, a potential Jedi hero. But further down the track, his training is advanced too quickly. For him the adage of Lord Acton holds true: 'Power tends to corrupt; absolute power corrupts absolutely.' However, as we have seen, right at the end – after years of dedication to the dark side and of actively massacring all who got in his way – it seems that he was not quite so absolutely lost as Palpatine, and a faint trace of humanity in his concern for his son enabled him to act to save him, even at the cost of the Emperor and the Empire. *Doctor Who* fans will see a similarity to perhaps its most well-drawn villain, the similarly masked Sharaz Jek – a manic yet (unlike Morgus) not totally lost man (in *The Caves of Androzani*, 1984).

When we reflect on the challenge of evil, these two characters (Vader and Palpatine) represent two types of experience. The first is where people have so actively sought power that evil seems to have penetrated their souls to the very depths. It seems as if no event or concern could ever shock them into repentance. Such evil is truly pathological. The phrase 'demonic' crops up when we meet such evil. Those craving power, like dictators and child abusers, seem among the more likely to resist all repentance. The other type is where people are seduced by evil, but in the deepest and most hidden places in their souls there remains the possibility of recognising their wrongdoing and repenting of it, i.e. actively turning away from it and towards the good instead. In principle all are redeemable (that is the verdict with Vader and Sharaz Jek), but not all would ever want redemption (that is the verdict with Palpatine and Morgus).

Meanwhile, even where as humans we do good, we remain capable of corruption by evil. The idea that we will simply rise above temptation and always do good, as implied in Roddenberry's universe, is far more of a fantasy than any of Lucas's creatures. Lucas's *Star Wars* world, despite its mythic structure, is more true to human experience of the conflict between good and evil, the problems of temptation and the struggle to resist it.

Christ and Culture: Is Fantasy Christian?

Christ and culture: five relationships

The American theologian H. Richard Niebuhr specialised in issues of society, and in his classic book *Christ and Culture*[1] he presented five typical pictures of the relationship between Christians and the world around us, or 'Christ' and 'culture' as he put it.

Christ against culture

▶ Attitude: the ghetto approach – 'Christ is Lord, culture is evil'.
▶ Biblical: keep yourself, unspotted, from the world (James 1:27; 1 John 5:4, 21).
▶ Historical: Tertullian, hermits, Tolstoy, exclusive Brethren.

Christ the hero of culture

▶ Attitude: pro-world and culture – 'Let the cultured critics of religion see in it the cream of culture'.
▶ Biblical: no obvious text, but Judaisers and Gnostics tried to make a cultural Christ.
▶ Historical: Gnostics like Basilides; Abélard; Liberal 'Culture-Protestants' like Ritschl and Schleiermacher.

Christ above culture

▶ Attitude: mixes both, but with religion as boss – 'The church as the guardian of society'.
▶ Biblical: give Caesar what is Caesar's and God what is

God's (Matthew 5:17–19; 22:21; Romans 13:1–7).

▶ Historical: Justin Martyr, Clement, Aquinas, Leo XIII, Joseph Butler.

Christ and culture in tension and paradox

▶ Attitude: a degree of uncertain dialogue – 'God is right, culture sinful, but we must live positively in this sinful culture'.

▶ Biblical: Paul, especially his attitude to Old Testament law – all have sinned and we deserve wrath but receive mercy (Romans 1–3).

▶ Historical: Marcion, Luther, Kierkegaard, Barth.

Christ the converter of culture

▶ Attitude: promoting change amid ups and downs – 'Society is sinful, and needs transforming'.

▶ Biblical: God sent his Son into the world, not to condemn but to save it (John 3:16–17).

▶ Historical: Diognetus, Augustine, Calvin, Edwards, Wesley, Maurice.

Christians sometimes have different agendas, which lead to different ways of operating, and Niebuhr showed how these five approaches could be seen as cropping up at various times in history, and could with one exception be seen as having some basis in Scripture. (The exception is the tradition promoting culture among nineteenth-century Liberals, whose roots are closer to the way the Gnostics reshaped faith in Christ to fit their neo-Platonist culture, than to particular biblical writers.) As these five express different attitudes to culture, we can also see how a cultural phenomenon like science fiction and fantasy is approached with different attitudes by people. Christians who take the ghetto approach reject SF and fantasy. The accommodating approach uncritically accepts whatever is on offer. The medieval synthesis is nearest in Tolkien and C. S. Lewis. The paradoxical tension is maintained by those who read or watch SF but also reject its values. Stephen May's *Stardust and Ashes*[2] shows an avid SF fan whose theological critique rejects the humanistic values implied in much SF. This tension expresses a great spiritual truth, but my inclination is more with the conversionist approach, which sees Christians engaging with culture with a view to a healthy transformation of cultural life. In relation to SF, this would mean that Christians should engage creatively and critically within the genre of SF, while seeking to express Christian values.

Myth, fantasy and Christian imagination

So some have argued that the fantasy and unbridled imagination of science fiction and fantasy are not compatible with Christianity. Others have seen the rise of science fiction this century as the emergence of a kind of substitute myth or even replacement religion, in a world which may be secularised outwardly, but still needs a mythic dimension to its inner life. However, others have written fantasies while professing Christian faith, whether orthodox or less mainstream. What are we to make of all this? Should Christians consider the whole of science fiction in much the same way that Plato considered the study of philosophy, and others the biblical erotic poem cycle 'The Song of Solomon' (i.e. something so advanced and potentially difficult to understand properly, it should be left only to experts over the age of 30)?

SF as creative myths for our time

Science fiction may have a long pre-history, but it is in our century that it has become widespread, and since the space age its fantasies have gained a greater air of reality. With its pictures of cultures, worlds, universes and even pluriverses, it has a cosmic, universal feel. These provide a number of over-all pictures of reality. Some may be what postmodernist writers like to call 'meta-narratives': big picture stories of the direction of the whole of history. Others, like many post-modernists, assume such pictures have come to an end, and work with more ambiguous representations. We're going to call all these approaches 'myths' and talk of 'mythic' pictures, and as the word 'myth' is taken in very different ways, a definition is in order. When we talk of a mythic picture, we are not commenting on whether it is true or not. In the most direct sense of literal realism, all of them are obviously false, as they are all fiction! Instead, such mythic pictures express an overall outlook, whether consistently or not, with certain implied beliefs and values. And it is these assumptions, whether obvious and deliberate or accidental and hidden, that are interesting here.

C. S. Lewis: SF and fantasy in Christian mythic mode

Lewis provides a clear and well-known example of how SF and fantasy can express an orthodox Christian outlook. For those who strongly doubt if science fiction can ever be acceptable for Christians, Lewis gives a clear reply. In his Narnia stories, most famously in *The Lion, the Witch and the*

Wardrobe, we have a classic children's fantasy, which is also a Christian allegory. Furthermore, the Christian 'meaning' is sufficiently subtle in presentation that the book stands up for readers unaware of its Christian symbolism.

Lewis's Christian substructure is worked through in a different way in his SF trilogy. Here we are (unlike beyond the wardrobe) apparently in the real world, where a scientist megalomaniac (Weston) can use his amazing inventions (rocketry) to colonise other planets. At the same time, the creatures met on Mars and Venus turn out to be fully aware of the Son of God (called Maleldil), and seem spiritually in a far better state than humans. Indeed they also seem aware of the fallen state of humanity, and of the great transformation in cosmic affairs since Christ died for our sins 2,000 years ago. As a result, the Venusians, who have come into being *after* Christ, are unfallen creatures.

Lewis presents deliberate allegories of clearly Christian ideas: the atonement in *The Lion, the Witch and the Wardrobe*, and creation and fall in *Voyage to Venus (Perelandra)*. Even so, this is not without its problems. The resolution of *Perelandra* is problematic, if taken as straight SF, as hero Ransom prevents the fall on Venus by killing the possessed Weston. It is clear Lewis sees this murder in mythological terms (like pictures of Satan and the archangel Michael locked in combat). However, if taken as straight SF, this resolution is disturbing, with its implied approval of murder of the possessed! Later, Lewis repudiated medieval writers for adopting pagan ideas in their cosmology. This outlook was conducive to him as a historical romantic, and apparently suited Christians generally.

But it . . . 'is not eminently Christian. The Pagan elements embedded in it involved a conception of God, and of man's place in the universe, which, if not in logical contradiction to Christianity, were subtly out of harmony with it.'

C. S. Lewis[3]

However, the talk at the end of *Perelandra* on feminine Venus and masculine Mars, supposedly echoed in the ancient gods, also reveals that despite the outward form of SF, Lewis is writing a mythological fantasy set in space, and shows him arguably overstepping this mark.

J. R. R. Tolkien: fantasy in Christian/pagan mythic guise

What is borderline in Lewis is centre stage in Tolkien. His Middle Earth is no allegory, but is widely regarded as the most extraordinary, complete fantasy culture – an inspiration for many – and it would take us well beyond our theme to discuss his approach in any breadth or depth. We must restrict ourselves to a modest observation. Tolkien himself was a practising Christian, a Catholic. It is therefore of interest to see how much and in what way his faith interacts with his fantasy culture.

When he wrote about his fantasy interests, he did it under the title 'On Fairy-Stories', published in his book *Tree and Leaf*. There, he distinguishes the fairy story as a tale set in imagined real worlds of magic from travellers' tales (Gulliver), dream tales (Alice) and 'beast-fables' (Peter Rabbit, etc., where the animals are humans in disguise). Fairy stories are more than tales about fairies, they are an entry into the Realm of 'Faërie', the world of magic. As for its origins, Tolkien is less interested in speculations about its pre-history; instead he notes its creativity and inventiveness. As people learn the art of description, so fantasy becomes possible: 'But in such "fantasy" as it is called, new form is made; Faërie begins; Man becomes a sub-creator.'[4] As for history, the interest actually starts when the historical elements are left and the transformation into legend begins. So Arthur will have had some historical elements that are probably not that interesting, but it is only when he is added to the developing imagination that he becomes interesting, indeed 'a King of Faërie'.

Tolkien is dismissive of the general assumption promoted by Andrew Lang in the nineteenth century that fairy tales are principally for children. Those children who like such stories tend to do so as adults too. Such tales, like all other writing, should be written for adults, with children introduced to them, as they are to other fiction and fact. As for fantasy, it is the expression of imagination: Tolkien is scathing towards those whose severe lack of imagination leads them to confuse fantasy with dreaming or mental illness. Unlike these, fantasy exercises a degree of rational control. More surprisingly he differentiates fantasy from drama. This is because he sees visualisation as limiting imagination. His point can be made by comparing the radio and TV versions of *The Hitch-hiker's Guide to the Galaxy*. Those who listened to the radio scripts will have found their imaginations running wild, while visualisation had to restrict all possibilities to one. Try this line: 'In those days spirits were brave, the stakes were high, men were real men, women were real women, and small furry creatures from Alpha Centauri were real small furry creatures from Alpha Centauri.' Witty, verbal humour, which can have a thousand imagined versions, is reduced to one by TV – which has to choose only one version of what a real man and real woman look like (*Gladiator* style!), and even more ridiculously only one creature, looking more like a cute prize won by a small child. There is no doubt that Tolkien would have considered TV SF inferior, and loathed the attempts to visualise his works (in animations and the like). Nonetheless the best of contemporary special effects has been employed for the film version due out in autumn 2001. Tolkien even criticises Shakespeare as an inferior writer because he wrote *Macbeth* as drama not as a story: '*Macbeth* is indeed a work by a playwright who ought, at least on this occasion, to have written a story, if he had the skill or patience for that art.' Here his delight in the art of writing stories becomes prejudice against visual drama.

Tolkien argues that fantasy aids 'recovery', i.e. seeing natural things better – having the benefit of seeing the familiar from an unfamiliar angle. It also provides escape from the imprisoning of the imagination, without being escapist in the derogatory sense of providing a means of avoiding life's challenges: '. . . critics . . . are confusing . . . the Escape of the Prisoner with the Flight of the deserter.' However, he sees SF itself as escapist, with its yearning for a technological future, over against fantasy, rooted in the mythic past. And in a rare, directly theological aside, he suggests that fantasy also provides consolation, through its traditional happy ending; indeed its sudden twist, its 'good catastrophe' denies 'universal final defeat and in so far is *evangelium* [gospel], giving a fleeting glimpse of Joy'.

In the epilogue to this essay, he then presses this point home. The gospel story of Christ, though not invented by the gospel writers, contains the essence of all fairy stories in that it presents, not as fiction but as truth in the 'Primary world', the greatest 'good catastrophe': the human story ends not in defeat but in God becoming man in Christ; the story of Christ ends not in the defeat of his death, but in the sudden twist of his resurrection. Tolkien does not mean that the event of Christ is fictional, but that what all fairy stories aim at, it achieves for real. Thus he expresses his credo. The gospel does not end but inspires his work: 'Story, fantasy, still go on and should go on. The Evangelium has not abrogated legends; it has hallowed them, especially the "happy ending". The Christian has still to work, with mind as well as body, to suffer, hope, and die . . . So . . . in fantasy he may actually assist in the effoliation and multiple enrichment of creation.'

If we consider Tolkien's fantasy, unlike with Lewis his characters cannot be seen as direct religious allegories. Gandalf is not Jesus in disguise. However, the actions of the heroes reflect Christian values like humility, forgiveness, peaceableness and spiritual strength as the clue to success. Meanwhile Gandalf's transformation of the Grey into the White has resonances with Jesus' resurrection. Tolkien himself commented:

'*The Lord of the Rings* is of course a fundamentally religious and Catholic work; unconsciously so at first, but consciously in the revision. That is why I have not put in, or have cut out, practically all references to anything like "religion," to cults or practices, in the imaginary world. For the religious element is absorbed into the story and the symbolism.'[5]

In practice, as commentator Patrick Curry has argued, Tolkien's 'Christian' mythic picture is seriously compromised by pagan elements. There is by implication not just one God, but a series of lesser gods, and an implied animism (spirit worship) and reincarnation. Meanwhile Gandalf shares characteristics with Woden/Odin, the god of the pagan Saxons and Vikings. Also, traditional pagan virtues like courage are promoted alongside Christian virtues. Tolkien's myth is not simple paganism, but a broadly Christian picture with many pagan elements.

Star Wars: another Christian/pagan mythic picture

As we have already seen, *Star Wars*, despite its very different setting in space, in many ways pursues a similar picture to Tolkien. There is a Christian element in its mythic picture – of the struggle with evil, the importance of forgiveness and redemption – but there is also a more astrological, vaguely pagan side to the Force.

Star Trek: a myth of scientific perfection

The mythic picture in *Star Trek* – particularly *TOS* and *TNG* – is a humanist myth. Consistently, it gives a picture of the march of progress through science and technology, in which human goodness and ingenuity will triumph over all. The final frontier, space, goes on for ever, and so does this human triumph over adversity and alien contact. Humanity will be defeated neither physically nor spiritually. Instead, Federation humanism will, by the assumed perfection and assumed undeniable attractiveness of its scientific reasonableness, win over all species in the unending encounter with strange new worlds and civilisations: the alien will become human, and join in the forthcoming humanist Utopia.

It is for this reason that the departures of *DS9* and *Voyager* are so significant. Thomas Richards, in one of the best books on the series, *Star Trek in Myth and Legend*, comments on this:

'*Deep Space Nine* and *Voyager* usher in a world in which the Federation's confidence in its own mission is undermined by a changed political situation. . . In a great many ways space in *Deep Space Nine* and *Voyager* is a far more uncertain and insecure place than it was in *The Next Generation*. . .

'In some ways *Deep Space Nine* shows the breakdown of the *Star Trek* balance of power. The Klingons are on the move again and may not remain Federation allies for long . . . Unquestionably *Deep Space Nine* is the most urban of the *Star Trek* series and the space station itself is often an unruly place requiring the police services of Constable Odo. . .

'Like *Deep Space Nine*, the crew of Voyager is thrust into a world in which none of the old rules seem to apply . . . Captain Katherine [sic] Janeway is presented with the task of upholding Federation values in a universe in which those values no longer apply. She finds she must form an alliance with the Maquis, Federation enemies. . .'[6]

Richards suggests that the episode *Tuvix* illustrates this shift powerfully. Despite the protests of Tuvix (the accidentally formed humanoid fusion of Tuvok and Neelix) and the holographic doctor, Janeway performs what is a sort of execution of Tuvix to retrieve Tuvok and Neelix. There is, as Richards notes, far more moral uncertainty presented here than in any episode of the first two series. The struggles Janeway faces are seen in today's confusion in medical ethics bodies, whose members wrestle over whether siamese twins are two people who must be separated, or one person who must not be split.

This all shows that the original myth of *Star Trek* is under severe strain in the more recent series. The naïve assumption that human goodness and technology will solve every problem, the naïve myth of scientific perfectionism in *Star Trek* has died. The myth showed the bride and groom of humanity and science living happily ever after. But the myth has not survived the spotlight on this fairy-tale marriage.

Doctor Who: moral certainty in the face of scientific uncertainty

The world of TV *Doctor Who*, despite its hundreds of different stories and authors, is more consistent. It presents a straightforward myth of the moral struggle between good and evil, where evil is represented by the monstrous abuses of power, especially the abuse of science and technology, while good is represented by the Doctor who uses science and wit (in both senses) to ensure that right prevails.

The other obvious mythic dimension is the Doctor as other-worldly saviour, like Superman. There is one story where the Doctor actually fails to save the world/universe – *Inferno*. But even here, that doomed world was a parallel, comparatively evil world, and the Doctor still saves the real world! The myth is that the scientific hero will come and save us.

Babylon 5: the third age of mankind

Babylon 5's myth is of the dawn of the third age of mankind. What are the first and second ages supposed to be? The episode that explains all is *Into the Fire*, Season 4's resolution of the Shadow/Vorlon war. At the end, Sheridan and Delenn reflect:

DELENN: It's hard to believe it's really over; the First Ones gone.
SHERIDAN: Hm. We're all alone now. Just the younger races. We can't blame anyone else from now on. It's a new age, Delenn; a third age.
DELENN: Why third?
SHERIDAN: We began in chaos, too primitive to make our

own decisions. Then we were manipulated from outside by forces that thought that they knew what was best for us. And now? Now we're finally standing on our own. Lorien was right: it's a great responsibility. This is ours now.

DELENN: Strange. The galaxy seems somehow smaller now that the First Ones have gone for ever.

SHERIDAN: It feels as if the magic's gone.

DELENN: Not gone. Now we make our own magic. Now we create our own legends. Now we build the future. Now we stop . . .

SHERIDAN: . . . being afraid of 'shadows'.

The idea of a 'third age of mankind' is not so new, however. The idea of three ages – the first age BC, the second AD, and now a third – goes back to Joachim of Fiore. By a strange 'coincidence' (an observation I owe to Anthony Cross) Joachim's third age was expected by his followers to begin in 1260, the most special past year in Straczynski's universe, when the earlier major Shadow war was narrowly won by time-travelling assistance from *Babylon 4*. Joachim's first age was the age of the Father (an age of slavery to law), the second was that of the Son (the beginnings of freedom), and the third would be the age of the Spirit (where the age of spiritual freedom, the future perfection prophesied by Paul in 1 Corinthians 13:9–10, would emerge). Auguste Comte promoted a different sequence 150 years ago, with superstition, then theology but finally science (sociology) – a sequence Gene Roddenberry's *Star Trek* broadly follows. Straczynski's epic picture has a further variation on this myth: primitive chaos; manipulated dependence; and finally humanity come of age, and heading up a galactic alliance.

The X-Files: a postmodern myth

The underlying ambiguity of *The X-Files* stands in stark contrast to the assumption of traditional Christian and scientific modernist thinkers alike, that 'the truth will out'. The mythic picture is of a world where the emotional dynamics of fear and power have overwhelmed both political and scientific stability. But the heroes are (for all their differences) Mulder and Scully. They stand virtually alone against the machinations of the nameless powers against them. We identify with them. It is not clear whether they will fail (tragedy) or succeed (triumph); though it seems it will be a confusing bit of both (pathos). It is the myth of the individual (or pair) who alone might save the world, or at least uncover the truth. But it is also a thoroughly postmodern myth, in that our heroes are frustrated by subterfuge, power games and deceit. The truth is out there = the truth is unknowable = your truth and mine are interchangeable = a confusing mess. It is a myth of confusion.

Conclusion

The mythic pictures vary, and so must any Christian response. While it is far too narrow to permit only Christian allegories like Lewis's, such writing at least reminds us that directly Christian SF exists. Since other pictures reflect assumptions that humanity will thrive without God, consistent Christian writers will need to challenge and modify them.

Part Five:
The Measure of a Man

▶ **Spock, Data, Odo and the Emergency Medical Hologram**

Part of the brilliance of SF, especially of *Star Trek,* is the way it helps us to look again at what it means to be truly human. But big questions remain: creation and evolution; Utopian hope and continuing sin; individuals and families; maturity and spirituality.

▶ **What transporters of delight**

Do humans, or Vulcans, have souls? Check the transporter!

▶ **The devil in the dark**

Is the devil an alien invader? Could he be defeated by science, magic or prayer?

▶ *The Wrath of Khan*, **the Shadows, Daleks and the demonic**

SF pictures the struggle against evil, but is evil always the other guy? And are the heroes always good? Can the real evil be finally defeated? Or is it true that in the battle with evil 'Resistance is futile!'

• 18 •
The Search for Spock

The most human first officer

Spock is the ultimate symbol of *Star Trek* – recognisable across the culture to Trekker and SF-phobe alike. But what is he? Man or machine? Human or alien? At his funeral, Kirk calls him his most 'human' colleague. So many of the nice moments of the series depend on this character. Described as coldly logical and alien, there is something far from cold or even alien about him. 'Curious, Captain.' 'Most interesting.' 'Fascinating.' You can almost see him raising that eyebrow, that Vulcan eyebrow, as he says these words, displaying scientific and dispassionate interest. For an alien he is a recognisable human stereotype – the rational, logical type, stoic and repressed; so lost in science, in the world of ideas, that he feels alienated by the expression of emotion, dismissing it as irrational.

He is the perfect foil for Bones, the full-blooded old timer, whose gutsy common sense leaves him with a sense of irritation that anyone should overlook the obvious. When it comes to Spock's deliberate rejection of what so often feels obvious and right to Bones, this irritation would become frustration and rage were it not for his charm. Spock and Bones: it is part of the genius of the original *Star Trek*, part of its charm and appeal, this sparking – with such fun – of the all-too-human conflict between reason and emotion incarnated in the Vulcan and Dr McCoy.

Modern Western culture is shot through with this tension.

Historically we have the rationality of the eighteenth-century Enlightenment era coming to a head with the 'age of reason', followed by the passion of the romantic era at the start of the nineteenth century. Part of our culture emphasises progress through order, rationality, science and discovery, and suggests the repression of emotion will help in this. The opposing side rejects this as one-sided, as losing the glory of humanity. In education it becomes the rivalry between maths and the sciences over against the humanities and arts. To make Spock an alien enables Roddenberry to go that little bit further with this classic contrast. A human so buttoned-up would easily look two-dimensional; but with an alien, the exclusive commitment to science, rationality and logic can be explored coherently.

Spock, Data, Odo and the Emergency Medical Hologram

What is Spock? In the stories he is of course half-Vulcan and half-human. This enables conflicts between his humanity and his alien nature to be explored. This was such a success that it has been a recurring theme in the succeeding shows, with variations that have often provided the series with equivalent charm, humour and dramatic possibilities.

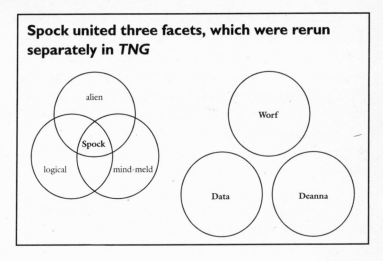

Spock united three facets, which were rerun separately in *TNG*

- *TNG* gave us Data (the android with a programmed desire to become more human), Worf (the Klingon brought up by humans) and Deanna Troi (the half-Betazoid empath).
- *DS9* has Odo (the isolated and distant Changeling, a misfit in human, 'solid' society), Dax (the Trill, whose human body includes a symbiotic, sentient life-form with eight lives' experience), and with Quark, Rom and Nog, the alien surprise, as the odious Ferengi emerge as heroes.
- *Voyager*'s near humans include the Emergency Medical Hologram, who is obliged to develop a personality, B'Elanna (the half-Klingon), the Vulcan Tuvok, and Seven of Nine (a human turned Borg, now regaining her humanity).

Data

The idea that Data should be seen as a kind of Pinocchio is stated explicitly by Riker. But he is more than that; more than a fantasy toy desiring humanity. He is also a brilliantly able robot, and indeed a very-nearly human-looking android. Much of the tension in this character plays on conflicts about his very-nearly human rights – or lack of them. Or again, the possibility of the machine working against us, if his programming is altered – as in stories featuring his malevolent twin, Lore.

But this idea of an increasingly human robot, indeed android, is not new. It formed the centrepiece of the short story that Isaac Asimov considered his own favourite: *The Bicentennial Man*. This is a delightful and moving story of a robot who certainly exceeded the intentions of his programming, and provides an engaging tale of legal arguments about the rights of robots.[1]

This half-humanity is at the centre of *Star Trek*. You never find it in *Doctor Who* (except the 1996 film's dreadfully mistaken attempt to make the Doctor 'half-human' after all these years). In *B5* it's missing, apart from the special cases of Delenn and Sinclair/Valen, who allow themselves to receive complex genetic treatment to combine human or Minbari DNA into their bodies, respectively. What is so creative about *Star Trek* is that it provides a great and very different way to explore what it means to be human. We have already looked at how probable sentient alien life is. *Star Trek*'s aliens paradoxically raise the question of humanity. But it has an even wider context. Men and women, and the myriad life-forms imagined in the *Star Trek* universe and the other SF worlds, are part of the created universe.

The Genesis Project: creation, evolution and supernovae

The word 'created' might raise an eyebrow (even a Vulcan one!) and introduce a discussion about evolution. Both words, 'creation' and 'evolution', are loaded. Evolution, in a *Star Trek* context, is more than a theory about historic development of species over millions of years; it has become a belief in social and religious development. In this context, evolution has become the answer to the riddle about the destiny of creation, and with it the destiny of mankind. It has become the picture to answer everything – and has also been vastly accelerated. In the *Star Trek* world, evolution, social evolution, has become faith in the future: faith in technological Utopia.

Creation, meanwhile, is more a statement about God as the author of the whole of reality than about the precise mechanism he chooses to effect the development of the universe as we know it. Earlier, we homed in on the question of the existence of God. The idea of lots of gods was based on superstitious fears. So long as reality is seen as an unpredictable thing, to be appeased in case it turns against us, science is going to be a hit and miss affair. Science really took off when Christianity reaffirmed its biblical basis in the Reformation era, as a result emphasising consistency, predictability, repeatability, order and so on in the study of the natural world. The world is created by God. That means it can be studied scientifically.

This also gives the context that shows that Christian faith and interest in science and science fiction need not be separate. Christian faith affirms faith in God as Creator, and therefore faith in the world as his creation – something to be discovered and affirmed. The magazine *Astronomy Now* once ran an article about how to hunt for supernovae: those rare explosions that light up a star brighter than its galaxy. It was September 1988, not long after a supernova in the Magellenic Clouds, which are satellites of our Milky Way galaxy, the first 'local' supernova since 1604. In a galaxy, such explosions only happen four or five times each millennium, so it's like looking for a needle in a haystack. The article is an interview with an Australian minister, the Revd Robert Evans, who had discovered far more supernovae than anyone else – 17 in fact. Most of the article follows technical tips on searching for supernovae, but in view of Evans' Christian profile, interviewer Jim Barclay can't resist the question, 'You have been so successful that some people have made remarks about you having a direct line to God . . . What do you say?' Evans' reply is a classic:

 'A Christian has the honour of dedicating everything that he does to God, instead of simply doing things to please himself. So it is possible to pray about every area of life, including our hobbies. I have not prayed for my success at the expense of others who might deserve to be successful. I wanted the efforts of others to [be] recognised, so I was not asking for any special treatment. I have prayed for God's guidance and help in my astronomy.

'I have prayed for various kinds of results – including discoveries – to flow from my observing which would give a true indication of what my search programme was worth. I prayed also that God would show what visual supernova hunting was worth as a means of searching. And I think my prayers have been answered. The result is that my search is being used to make estimates about the appearance rate of supernovae. (See van den Bergh et al. 'The Supernova Rate in Shapley-Arms Galaxies', *Astrophysical Journal*, December 1987, pp. 44–53.)

'An unbeliever could reply that the results would have followed whether God existed or not. All I can say is that events happened as I described them, and the other explanation is hypothetical.'[2]

Evans expresses well a Christian understanding of creation. His words remind us of two things relevant here: scientific study of the universe is a natural part of the Christian attitude to creation; and we should not divide up the world into spiritual, godly bits and worldly, ungodly bits. Psalm 24:1 states: 'The earth is the Lord's, and everything in it, the world, and all who live in it.' So hobbies, whether supernova hunting or indeed science fiction, are a part of life that God is interested in.

'Creation', then, is also a loaded word. Far more than an account of the genesis of the universe, it is a statement of faith in the world – the whole of reality – as ultimately not random, not meaningless, not impersonal. It is a faith in the universe and of our place within it, as held within the love of God.

It is also a statement about human destiny, and the destiny of creation. It says that our future is not dependent on the Vulcans or any other alien first contact, nor on human ingenuity alone, but on a relationship with God that places not only each individual, not even everyone living and dead, but the whole of creation within his loving purposes.

'I am convinced that neither death nor life, neither angels nor demons, neither the present nor the future, nor any powers, neither height nor depth, nor anything else in all creation, will be able to separate us from the love of God that is in Christ Jesus our Lord.'

Romans 8:38–39

Faith in the future

What is the future of humanity? As we have seen, *Star Trek* projects technological Utopia. Roddenberry's vision is full of the atmosphere of the 1960s, the last really optimistic decade. That time was full of a 'can do' mentality. In ordinary domestic life, it was a time of revolutionary change. The appearance of washing machines, fridges and freezers, TVs, cars not as luxuries for the few but normal for most, and a host of gadgets, anticipated an age when technology would be the best friend of all. And it all seemed to be without cost. Robots and mechanisation had long been feared for their potential in producing terrible unemployment, but in the 1960s, with unemployment historically low, Minister of Labour Ray Gunter told us instead to prepare for extra leisure time.

And social changes were afoot. Despite the race riots, and the voices of strident racism, the challenge towards racial integration gathered pace. And as the new feminism began to take shape, challenging the 'truce' since the suffragettes, the demand grew for real equality, and the end of racial and sexist oppression. It was a decade proclaiming new freedoms: the 'permissive society' with sexual experimentation, the mini-skirt, and legal changes loosening censorship, abortion law and decriminalising homosexuality, among others.

To the humanist of the day, like Roddenberry, it looked as if the 'shackles' of religion and tradition were being thrown off, and that in the future we would discover our true selves. Religious wars would be a thing of the past, and rational science tempered by the spirit of 'enterprise' would lead us towards a golden new age, when the things that blotted our past would be removed. The new scientific age would also promote greater racial equality, pictured in Uhura's role, and the first US TV interracial kiss.

Star Trek believers point to the advance of technological gadgetry already here (mobile phones), or not far off becoming generally available (voice-activated computers), and to the moves towards racial integration and sexual equality that have gathered pace, though not without a struggle. This is *Star Trek*'s vision of the future. Now hear its downbeat picture of our own time, in *The Voyage Home*:

'I want you all to be terribly careful. This is *terra incognita*. This is an extremely primitive and paranoid culture.'

(Kirk)

'We're dealing with medievalism, here!'
(Dr McCoy, about a doctor using twentieth-century medicine)

And as we have seen, even the races of alien planets seem to get swept up in this headlong move towards paradise. Klingons, Romulans and Ferengi alike become more humanised. Even the Borg, the most frightening monsters faced on *Star Trek*, get humanised. *Their* menace is not just their emotionless hostility, nor their advanced technology. It is, like the Cybermen of *Doctor Who* before them, the threat of a group of humans or humanoids who have lost their humanity because they let the machine take them over. If Cyborgs take over, then a fate worse than death awaits: losing our humanity, and becoming an unwilling part of the evil, incapable of doing what is right.

But even here, at its darkest point, we find even the Borg are redeemable. It begins in the *TNG* story *I, Borg* (1992): a lone Borg survivor is found at a crash site, and through Geordi's friendship especially, he regains something of his humanity, even an individuality, and so a name, Hugh. Hugh helps foil a plot against the *Enterprise* by Data's jealous 'brother' Lore in *Descent II* (1993). This redemption is pressed much further when Seven of Nine comes aboard *Voyager* as a Borg-female recovering her humanity from Season 4 on (1998).

Even the godlike gadfly Q develops a liking for Federation values. Starting as a threat to the human race, Q teases then wants to join Starfleet (with ambiguous sincerity), later learning a degree of unselfishness from the crew of the *Enterprise*. Eventually, as Q and indeed the whole Continuum learns from Janeway, their almost pantheon-like Q Continuum changes! Even 'gods' must change and grow from meeting Kirk, Picard, Sisko and Janeway! The future of humanity, according to *Star Trek,* is not simply to perfect our own future, but with it that of all other races in the universe, even gods!

Meanwhile, as we have seen, this emerging Utopia pictures humanity largely without sin, where the Ten Commandments have been overcome. The first four (dealing with God) have been ignored, but the rest – good family relationships, lack of interpersonal violence, thieving, dishonesty and coveting or rivalry – seem to have been achieved, and sin is no more. Adultery is the only striking exception! So there will still be heartache caused by relationship failure. Marriage, divorce and illegitimacy still exist in his future. Otherwise human sin is history.

Humanity without sin? I am reminded of theologian H. Richard Niebuhr's comment about the assumptions in much religious liberalism: 'A God without wrath brought men without sin into a kingdom without judgment through the ministrations of a Christ without a cross.'[3] It's without cost, and untrue to life. Indeed the developing years have not seen a decline in sin. Far from it! There have been welcome changes in the direction of racial groups learning to work together, and towards according equal pay to equal work for women. But the growth in crime, vandalism, addiction, exploitation, suicide and the pain of family breakdown in Western societies illustrates that Utopia is stubbornly refusing to get any closer. Nor is there any evidence that new technology – warp drive, transporters or replicators – will end sin. As we have seen before, all experience shows that technology cuts both ways: from the simplest implement to the most up-to-date computer, we find the same technologies used as both cultural aids and as weapons.

As for encountering Vulcans, it is certain that meeting an

advanced alien race would bring significant cultural changes to human civilisation. But it is rather less likely they would help us abolish human wickedness. Anyway, even *Star Trek*'s future Utopian humans are no more Vulcan in outlook (with dispassionate logic) than today. *Star Trek* places great faith in the future. It is a wonderful fantasy, but it is not true to life. Most of the technological marvels dreamed up are far more likely than the possibility of people freely giving up rivalry.

Individualism

The second and third films, where Spock dies heroically saving the crew, and where the crew risk their lives to enable him to survive after all, feature humorous banter between Kirk and Spock. Spock argues that it is logical that the needs of the many outweigh the needs of the one (an individual should die to save others). Kirk argues that friendship means that for the needs of the one, the needs of the many should be set aside (the crew should risk dying to save their friend). In many ways, Kirk's view is the philosophy of *Star Trek*, where an extreme individualism is promoted in the context of friendship. Thomas Richards' insightful and provocative literary criticism of *Star Trek*, especially *TNG*, in his book, *Star Trek in Myth and Legend* (Orion, 1997), pursues this further than we can here. He points out how virtually every *TNG* character has bad relations with any family they have. For example:

▶ Riker's father.
▶ Data's brother.
▶ Deanna's mother.

Some have tragic relations:

- ▶ Worf's mate K'Ehleyr dies.
- ▶ Beverley Crusher raises Wesley after her husband dies.
- ▶ Geordi's estranged parents.
- ▶ Tasha Yar's upbringing among rape gangs.

And those who get romantically involved usually immediately see the one they love die:

- ▶ e.g. Riker, in *Silicon Avatar*.

Where family is presented more positively it turns out to be a fantasy:

- ▶ Picard's experience of the culture of the planet Kataan through seeing the life of Kamin and his doomed culture in *The Inner Light*; his experience of 'family' in the Nexus, in *Star Trek VII: Generations*.

When crew heroes are threatened, everything may be sacrificed to save them:

- ▶ In *Man of the People*, Picard is spared having to go through with it, but looks prepared to save Deanna Troi's life, even though the population of a planet will die if he does.

As the individual is so important, the integrity of the personality is frequently a theme. We have many splits, twins and take-overs:

▶ The good Kirk/bad Kirk of *The Enemy Within*.
▶ Kirk's personality abduction in *Turnabout Intruder*.
▶ William Riker/Thomas Riker.
▶ Data's malevolent twin Lore.
▶ The whole *Mirror, Mirror* universe with the bearded Spock in *TOS*, and Kira as the Intended in *DS9* stories.
▶ The more peaceable usurpation of Picard by Kamin in *The Inner Light*.

But in every case, the personality seems to recover fully by the end of the episode or story. The only exception is where Picard has become Locutus of Borg, and he needs a few days' rough and tumble rivalry with his brother in *Family*. Perhaps, Richards suggests, these frequent alien attacks on personal identity 'are often stand-ins for the dark forces of the mind'. He then goes on to discuss 'demonic possession' – a recurring theme in science fiction, which we'll turn to in our chapter on the struggle with evil.

There is a limit to *Star Trek*'s individualism: it resists personal spirituality. Though meditation exists in the *Star Trek* world (unlike any god or gods), it tends to be frowned upon. Vulcan meditations are possible, but Spock must forgo them to save Federation/Klingon peace; Worf may pursue Klingon spiritual exercises, but discovers fraud by Klingon priests (in *Kahless*), and so on. The more positive spin on Bajoran spiritual exercises in *DS9* and Tuvok's Vulcan meditations in *Voyager* show how things have changed since the early 1990s. But in *TNG* spiritual individualism is shunned. Instead, every story promotes social camaraderie among the crew. It's there throughout: the absolute freedom and rights of the individual *and* the values of social harmony.

What is our true humanity? *Star Trek*'s individualism emphasises the personal element that is part of our experience, and also the teamwork of friends and colleagues, but under-estimates the role of family in providing a context where, in better cases, people can experience love and affirmation, and be helped to grow towards maturity.

Our true humanity is shaped not only by our memories of the past and experience in the present but also by our hopes for the future. Earlier cultures did not look to the future in the expectation of change. This is actually a feature of the Jewish and Christian tradition, rooted in the Bible. Other civilisations tended to see history as going in cycles. But the Bible speaks of history moving in a forward direction. It speaks of God acting in history (as in freeing the Israelites from slavery in Egypt) and of history changing as a result. And it teaches hope for the future. A Messiah will come, the Old Testament proclaims. That the Messiah is Jesus is the key Christian claim: God has acted and changed all history – and he will act again, and then bring in the world where war, suffering and evil have truly ended. This hope of heaven rightly inspires *Star Trek*, but is beyond governments and technology.

What is our true humanity? Spock is not human – not fully, anyway. But his very difference, like that of *Star Trek*'s other near humans, highlights quintessential human experience: the tensions between reason and emotion; the problems of humour and tragedy; the need for solitude and friendships; the problems of identity and personality; and much else.

Life is rich and diverse. Indeed our cultural life is amazingly varied. *Star Trek* illustrates this diversity well, as does

Babylon 5, with its belief in the benefits of 'a diversity of voices'.[4] However, the celebration of such diversity is a Christian way of thinking, to glory in the richness of creation, including especially that of our humanity, and it reflects the Christian command to love our neighbour, even our enemy.

• 19 •
Transporter Malfunction

Imagine the scene: 'Transporter malfunction, Sir. We were transporting the Captain back to the ship, but we sort of lost his soul!' *Star Trek* is full of amazing problems for humanity caught up in far-flung space; problems caused by anomalies of physics interacting awkwardly with our fragile humanity. But is this also a problem for us? Could we lose our souls, literally?

What is humanity?

Lawrence Krauss gives us an entertaining trawl through many technological marvels in *The Physics of Star Trek*. He gives us the relative probabilities, or in some cases downright impossibilities, of the physics assumed here and there. Occasionally challenging for those unused to physics, it is nonetheless a great read. He raises this very question in the best context: 'What comprises a human being? Are we merely the sum of all our atoms? More precisely, if I were to recreate each atom in your body, in precisely the same chemical state of excitation as your atoms are in at this moment, would I produce a functionally identical person who has exactly all your memories, hopes, dreams, spirit?'[1]

That's the question: Are we complex mechanical objects that could ultimately be artificially manufactured, whether by the transporter or in other ways? Or is there something more to us, something intangible, some soul or spirit that is beyond being reproduced? Krauss again:

'There is every reason to expect that this would be the case, but it is worth noting that it flies in the face of a great deal of spiritual belief about this existence of a "soul" that is somehow distinct from one's body. What happens when you die, after all? Don't many religions hold that the "soul" can exist after death? What happens then to the soul during the transport process? In this sense then, the transporter would be a wonderful experience in spirituality. If a person were beamed aboard the *Enterprise* and remained intact and observably unchanged, it would provide dramatic evidence that a human being is no more than the sum of his or her parts, and the demonstration would directly confront a wealth of spiritual beliefs.'

Called 'teleporting' in *Blake's 7* and 'T-Mat' in *Doctor Who* (*The Seeds of Death*) this SF dream is unfortunately (or perhaps fortunately!) one of the least likely *Star Trek* technologies ever to happen, as Krauss makes clear. The physics either requires heating the bodies to 1,000 billion degrees – a bit too hot to be ten feet away from – or power for each teleportation equivalent to 10,000 times the entire energy output of the whole planet Earth today. This theological question won't be sorted out by technology anytime soon!

But there's another question. What does *Star Trek* actually assume is the answer to this puzzle about humanity – materialism (we're just matter and energy) or Platonism (beyond matter, there is the soul)? Most times its answer must be materialism. Those transporter accidents, and other technologically induced transferences, where Kirk or Riker duplicate, or where Kirk swaps bodies with the jealous Dr Janice

Lester in *Turnabout Intruder*, all assume that the personality is there in the buffers to be mixed up or copied. Then again, transporters are effective every time (almost!). EEGs already tell the difference between a living brain and a dead one, and the same difference would have to be in the transporter buffers, to avoid transporting live people but only beaming down corpses! So the teleport controls would have to register the differences between a living person and a corpse. This is represented by Krauss's comments about the 'chemical state of excitation'. The soul, the livingness of the person, would be that 'excitation' and would be beamed. Most *Star Trek* stories assume that the person gets beamed along with his or her body!

Having said that, some *Star Trek* stories tend to give the opposite, Platonic picture, that the soul is a detached part of the person, a non-material 'ghost'. *Emanations*, the *Voyager* story, goes down this road. When the Uhnori woman Ptera and Harry Kim change places, they interrupt a funeral with a supposed transfer to the after-life. Is the Uhnori 'after-life' just a morgue? Or is it real? Truly visiting the next life by dying totally and then coming back is beyond even *Star Trek* technology (though Harry has to die momentarily and be revived in a way consistent with current recovery techniques for cardiac arrest). But no one, apart from Jesus, has faced death deliberately, been well and truly dead, and come back days later to tell us! Janeway notes their 'neural energy in the ambient field'. Might that show something after death? She articulates what we are supposed to think. Although it can't be proved, maybe these people do move on to the next life – as energy, as souls, yet also as detectable entities. *Voyager*'s Chakotay, with his Native American religious traditions, ancestral spirits and the like, shows another move in the Platonic direction of body and separate soul.

But the strongest expression of this is the plot device right at the heart of the film *The Search for Spock*. Spock is dead but he projects his soul (his *katra* in the Vulcan) just before death into McCoy (by Vulcan mindmeld, of course); meanwhile his body is revived by the eventually doomed 'Genesis Project' planet. Pure hokum, of course, with suspension of belief dependent on Spock's supposed alien biology (and spirituality), and because of fandom's determination to see Spock in the remaining films. However, Spock also uses the transporter, so we can ask: Does Spock's *katra* get transported every time he uses the machine? Presumably. Spock does not die, or even change personality when he is transported. So his *katra* goes with him. Maybe, like the Uhnori's post-mortem 'neural energy', it would be detectable in the transporters after all. So the 'soul' would merely be a detectable part of the body!

This is no minor quibble. In one picture the body is material (including energy, chemical states of excitation, etc.) and at death these chemical and physical processes merely stop. The other view sees something extra, above and beyond physical processes, which departs the body at death. It is either above and beyond the body, in which case it can't be transported, or it is part of the body, in which case if it leaves the body it could be detected on a tricorder – or maybe even a humble EEG.

Perhaps the frequent *Trek* motif of highly evolved energy-type entities also shows this desire to see something soul-like in us as our evolutionary goal. But are we just transportable matter, or creatures with a spirit or soul that no transporter can touch? Is *Star Trek* running with a non-material soul that is above and beyond anything physical that can be transported? Transportation would suggest it isn't, while *The Search for Spock* and *Emanations* imply that it is, but in an odd way.

What if the two ideas are mixed together? Can Spock's *katra* register on the tricorder? *The Biology of Star Trek*[2] points to problems of transporter biofilters removing biologically helpful bacteria. What if Spock's *katra* was left in the buffers by accident, and only the 'rest' of him was beamed aboard? The implication of the film is that the boy Vulcan had no *katra*. He could not speak, but he was far from totally reactionless, let alone seemingly dead. Is the *katra*, the Vulcan soul, just the speech centre? In any case, how could your transporters lock on to a soul that was neither matter nor energy?

Belief in transporters versus belief in the soul

So if you believe in the possibility of transporters, do you have to reject the soul? Is this question a religious nightmare? Not for biblically based Christianity. Many religions view the spiritual dimension of humanity as a soul or spirit separate from the body, which detaches itself at death. Roman Catholics have usually followed a version of this pattern. However, it's more Greek than biblical Hebrew. This idea is undermined by what philosopher Gilbert Ryle termed the problem of the 'ghost in the machine'[3] (i.e. how can the 'ghost', the soul, operate the personality if it is not connected?).

Now a surprise for many is that Plato's idea of the soul as a separate entity to the body is not the Bible's picture. Old Testament words especially show a person as an integrated whole: 'body', 'soul', 'flesh' and 'spirit' refer to the whole person, but as seen in different aspects of our humanity. 'Flesh' refers to the whole person as a physical and mortal being. 'Soul' refers to the whole person as a living creature. 'Spirit' refers to the whole person as relating to God (or failing to), and so on. The picture of life with God in the afterlife is a picture of the whole person, transformed by the power of God so as to be capable of immortality, living with God, and indeed with other people, for ever.

Teleportation, if it ever became possible, would pile up new problems for belief in a non-material but detachable soul. But it would have no impact on biblical belief in the integrated human person, whose whole humanity is lived in the material world, but also lived before God, here and now, and ultimately also in eternity.

• 20 •
Vorlons Versus Vader

Resisting evil – SF style

The Bible has a lot to say about the different experiences and expressions of all that is wrong in the world.

▶ There is the discussion about suffering, particularly in several psalms and Job, but also at the start of Luke 13, and in the various accounts of the crucifixion of Jesus, and reflections on it.
▶ There is the challenge of the world – that context in which we live. An ambiguous context, where as we saw (in Chapter 17) Christian values and beliefs have to vie with others in the public forum.
▶ There is the challenge for believers to set their minds against sin, wickedness, evil, temptation and so on.
▶ There is the acknowledgement that spiritual evil, both in the demonic and in the personal form of the devil, is real and must be opposed.

Curiously enough, this theme of resisting the devil, and indeed the demonic, is one of the most widely presented themes in science fiction, and we will return to that in the next chapter. Here, however, we will look at *moral* evil rather than the spiritual and psychological evils involved in possession and mania. What is moral evil – the evil at work in temptation and causing so much suffering? Is it human personal evil? Set at the extremes of existence, and with alien exaggerations of human trends at every stop, SF has the option of exploring the struggle with moral evil in much sharper terms than more mundane drama can. This can lead to terrible simplifications in which the heroes have no flaws and the villains no redeeming features, no desires at all except as Douglas Adams put it 'to destroy the universe for no good reason'. But at its best, as in *Babylon 5*, SF can have both the alien, cosmic, larger than life expressions of light and darkness, and also the subtle struggle of people just like us with moral issues and problems.

Absolute evil and good?

SF occasionally has its figures that represent absolute, unmitigated good – like Superman – but more often it portrays absolute evil. The idea is imaginable enough: what if a computer with artificial intelligence, or a cybernetic organism, were developed which was so powerful that it could not be out-thought or destroyed, and if it were programmed to destroy all other life-forms? This could be by accident or design, but it would be the ultimate nightmare – the undefeatable foe that will destroy us all – though most SF falls short of such total pessimism.

Daleks are a clear example of this nightmare, particularly as reconceptualised in *Genesis of the Daleks*. Here, mad scientist Davros causes a genetic mutation to occur as a form of biological warfare: life-forms genetically programmed to destroy all creatures other than themselves, but otherwise exemplifying all the intellectual brilliance that Davros can foster in them, and encased in largely impregnable personal tank structures. The original Daleks were accidental mutations caused by nuclear warfare, but this story reinvents them as GM humanoids. It is this imaginable element that gives them a degree of credibility and makes them doubly fearsome.

But even Daleks can become good! In what many fans see as the best of the pre-Davros Dalek stories, *The Evil of the Daleks*, the Doctor manages to secure the reprogramming of most ordinary Daleks with the 'human factor', a moral centre, with appreciation of friendship, courage and other virtues. These are attacked by unchanged Daleks, pursuing their mission to destroy all divergent life, with the resulting battle that leaves their planet, Skaro, and most or all Daleks destroyed.

In the interests of dramatic tension, Daleks (and other monsters) need to present a credible threat of terrible evil and destruction, but they also need to present a degree of ambiguity and unpredictability. Earlier *Doctor Who* stories tried to solve that by putting them with misguided allies, like Mavic Chen; later ones had them fighting various renegade Dalek factions, with Davros the destabilising factor. Brian Hayles solved the similar problem with the Ice Warriors by surprising us in their third appearance far in the future as allies of humanity.

Darth Vader and the Evil Empire

Doctor Who rarely allows breadth, depth and ambiguity to its villains, though as we have seen Sharaz Jek in *The Caves of Androzani* is a strong exception. In the same story, Timmin is similarly complex. The character who overthrows the arch-villain (Morgus) and survives to lead the people is usually a clear hero in *Doctor Who*. But she simply proved a better

THE MEASURE OF A MAN

opportunist, and whether she would be just as bad as the tyrant she replaces or far better is left unclear.

We have also seen how *Babylon 5* pictures its heroes with ambiguity and personal struggles. It also shows its villains with redeeming features. Vendetta-minded G'Kar changes radically; Londo eventually accepts his responsibility both for causing a degree of genocide of the Narns and the eventual terrible damage to his own planet, accepting his tragic fate to save his people. Even Mr Bester, the chief Psi Cop, the creep everyone loves to hate, is shown his human side in *Ship of Tears*. This reminds us that even Adolf Hitler had his human side. He was fine if you were Eva Braun! Even the seemingly demonic Shadows argue their case that their grand scale evil is in the social Darwinist cause of promoting the survival and progress of the fittest.

Star Trek, of course, glories in this redeemability of its villains. Klingons may be the bad guys in one series only to emerge as allies and heroes in the following series. Ferengi are the next villains turning heroes in the third series. Later, the Maquis turn allies in *Voyager*, and even the hated Borg become allies – at least in the person of Seven of Nine. *Star Trek* has learned to develop more ambiguity in its villains, and even its heroes to a modest extent, in *DS9* and *Voyager*.

Perhaps *Star Wars* villain Darth Vader shows this redeemable element most famously. In the first two films he is pictured as the embodiment of evil, the personal face of the Evil Empire. He seems to be utterly lacking in compassion, without the faintest trace of humanity. The viewers can 'safely' see him as a worthy candidate of Orwellian 'two minutes' hate'.[1] But as later films reveal him as the father of heroes Luke Skywalker and Princess Leia, the stakes are raised. Both his humanity and his betrayal are uncovered. Ultimately he repents by taking action to save his son against Palpatine. He is redeemable. Meanwhile the prequel trilogy, showing Vader as a precocious but likeable boy in *The Phantom Menace* and no doubt exploring his seduction by the 'dark side of the Force' in the two forthcoming films, will heighten the ambiguity. We will see motives, where before in *Star Wars: A New Hope* we saw only evil, pure and simple.

This reminds us of an essential insight in the Christian faith. Our temptation is always to see 'the other guy' as the villain, and to justify our total anger. SF, particularly in its crasser manifestations, is commonly prone to this. But as it develops depth, it sees beyond the simple identification of 'our foes' with absolute evil. Perhaps this too, in some modest way, reflects a shift from the 1950s to 2000, from the simplicities of the cold war and McCarthyism towards a more pluralist global world, especially in relations between communist or former communist states and the West.

The Christian insight is well put by Paul:

'For our struggle is not against flesh and blood, but against the rulers, against the authorities, against the powers of this dark world and against the spiritual forces of evil in the heavenly realms.'

Ephesians 6:12

So our struggle with evil is not against people, but against the spiritual forces of evil.

Vorlon philosophy

The impression that *Babylon 5* might become a simple allegory of light versus darkness was clearly dispelled early in
Season 4, where in practice problems not only with Shadows
but also Vorlons rapidly emerge, and both are fascists. The
Shadows have a Hegelian model of 'evolution through conflict', a social Darwinism, promoting violence and war as a
means to progress.

But what about the Vorlons, those lofty and secretive
opponents of evil, who manifest themselves to humans and
other races alike as angelic? Shadow agent Morden calls them
'control freaks'. They are indeed law and order authoritarians
who must be obeyed, and they must destroy everything and
everyone who falls short of their standards (i.e. those tainted
by the Shadows). The Shadows fight for 'conflict' and the
Vorlons for 'order', but have forgotten why they are fighting.

Straczynski comments:

'Left unfettered, they would have destroyed
what they were setting out to save, in the same way that we
bombed villages in Vietnam to save them. You don't do it
that way. We had to be shocked out of Vietnam, and they
had to be shocked out of what they were doing.'[2]

So it is not a simple allegory of light versus darkness. It may
be that we identify more with one group than another, but
none of Straczynski's creations, human or alien, are simply
going to be the good guys. Instead, the Vorlons are more a
parable of Vietnam – what happens when the 'good guys'

allow the end to corrupt the means.

The philosophy of *Babylon 5* is sharp realism. It is filled with shades of grey. Yes, there can be heroes, but even the heroes will be flawed people. And in a way, that is very consistent with the general outlook of the Bible. For the Bible is very much an epic story, with lots of individual stories en route. And all its characters, including its heroes if we exempt Jesus, are clearly flawed. Moses murders someone and fails to cover it up, then tries to refuse his chance of greatness, before it is thrust on him. David commits adultery after he's made it as king, then arranges for the woman's husband to be killed in battle to cover it up. Paul is initially a religious bigot who hates Christians, contributing to a lynch-mob killing. Peter says he would die for Jesus, but that rash promise is challenged and he finds himself lying and denying his Lord to save his skin.

Again, it is an essential Christian insight, which Christians need to be reminded of as much as anyone, that just as much as we must resist seeing evil in 'the other guy', so we must resist locating goodness in ourselves. Jesus told a parable to highlight that in Luke 18. A Pharisee (representing the good believer) prays, but only parades his own supposed virtue before God. Meanwhile a traitor who collects taxes for the Roman occupation forces (representing the bad guy) prays, admitting his evil with acute conviction. It's the second one who gets straight with God. It's only when we admit our lives need to change that we can begin the right life.

Future moral maze: life begins at 40 weeks?

SF, then, shows up moral conflict, and at its best shows its complexity well. As we have seen, as in episodes like *Tuvix* in *Voyager*, it also has a brilliant context to raise present and future possible moral dilemmas. However, one moral problem is largely overlooked despite the fact SF is well placed to touch it if it dares: abortion. The big difficulty comes as we reflect on the idea of Mr Spock successfully mindmelding not just with an extraordinary but sentient alien like the Horta, but with Gracie, the non-sentient whale in *Star Trek IV: The Voyage Home*, where he discovers from her that she is pregnant. It is at least imaginable that if abortion were still an issue in the twenty-third century, pro-life groups would invite him to mindmeld with a foetus. If a whale could communicate her pregnancy, perhaps the foetus could communicate his or her desire to live. An episode with such a mindmeld could be hard-hitting. But so far this is one area into which SF has not boldly gone.

• 21 •
Doctor Who *and the Daemons*

Resisting the devil – SF style

One element of the call to resist evil is to resist the tempter, Satan. Biblical writers were clear about this: 'Resist the devil, and he will flee from you' (James 4:7) and, 'Your enemy the devil prowls around like a roaring lion looking for someone to devour. Resist him, standing firm in the faith . . .' (1 Peter 5:8–9). Surprisingly, this aspect is strongest in SF, but in a different way.

Quatermass and the Pit

Story outline

Quatermass and his colleagues Judd and Roney face increasingly paranormal phenomena, poltergeists and the like, on a tube station building site, where workers have found mysterious alien remains, amid a prehistoric spacecraft. These prove to be extinct Martians, insectile, horned aliens, seen as lying behind our image of the devil. Roney's equipment reveals ancestral human memories of their impact on early humans. Their prehistoric evils included a cull of all abnormal Martians. In the climax, tampering activates a giant 'devil-figure' who begins another cull of all abnormal Martians, so all humans will die. But Roney's heroic self-sacrifice saves humanity.

The BBC's various *Quatermass* stories were a landmark in TV SF, its eponymous scientist being the first TV hero to transfer into films. The third story, *Quatermass and the Pit* (1958–59), is usually seen as the best of the three. As often happens, the films were better resourced but inferior to the originals, which have all been destroyed, except for one episode. *Quatermass* proved the inspiration for various elements of *Doctor Who*: the scientist as misunderstood hero, the sinister problems, and the paranormal phenomena given an alien explanation. Amid the twin troubles of aliens and the paranormal, Bernard Quatermass cuts the exemplary figure of rigorous scientist who shows integrity and insight. The 'devil' is seen to be real, a Martian and the cause of paranormal phenomena. All images and memories of the devil are seen as rooted in this figure; so the final, total defeat of this ancient foe implies that the devil and all evil has now been destroyed for ever, by human courage and scientific determination.

Doctor Who: the Daemons and other psychic evils

In almost every *Doctor Who* story, the Doctor arrives, finds evil and defeats it, so it was only a matter of time before he was put up against the devil to defeat him too! *Star Trek* devils are only opportunistic con artists (e.g. Picard's problems with Ardra in *TNG: Devil's Due*). But in *Doctor Who*, like *Quatermass*, the 'devil' is both an alien and the real devil. This alien is the 'real' origin of all belief and experience of the demonic. The Doctor goes one better than Picard: he both outwits the alien, and in the process also defeats the 'real' devil!

Some occult features occurred in early *Doctor Who* stories: telepathy (*The Sensorites*); possession (*The Abominable Snowmen*); and mind control (*Spearhead from Space*). The first time the Doctor really encounters black magic is in the 1971 Pertwee story, *The Daemons* (its version of the *Quatermass* story). Differences are many but trivial. For example the aliens are 'Daemons from the planet Damos', as *Doctor Who* has enough Martians. A more amusing divergence is provided by the addition of the Doctor's nemesis, the Master, who poses as the new vicar with his new guise as the Revd Mr Magister!

But if the 'existentialist priest' is in league with the devil, the most extraordinary figure is Miss Olive Hawthorne, the village white witch, presented as the expert on how to oppose the occult! Miss Hawthorne, portrayed as the eccentric English village lady, is generally shown as being right, except when the Doctor corrects her. *K9 and Company* (1981) and *The Curse of Fenric* (1987) also follow similar themes. But *The Daemons* is the classic spin on all this.

A few surprises in *The Daemons*

1. The Doctor and the script support a 'white witch'

Miss Hawthorne says about herself, 'I have cast the runes; I have consulted the Talisman of Mercury; it is written in the stars. I tell you I'm a witch. White of course. And that is why you should listen to me, I know.' She also promotes the old fertility cult: 'We must do the fertility dance and celebrate.' Miss Hawthorne is shown as the only one in the whole village of Devil's End who understands the real problems, for the medical diagnosis proves to be faulty, but the witch's diagnosis is correct. The Doctor says to Miss Hawthorne, 'It's a great pity they didn't listen to you in the first place.' But what she calls 'magic' he insists is actually 'science'. She is also the only villager really able to resist the Master's hypnotism, brandishing her cross at him!

2. The Doctor uses magic

The Doctor points a trowel at the animated gargoyle, the mini-demon, and exclaims 'Klokleda partha mennin klatch!' This is explained later:

JO:	How did you do that?
THE DOCTOR:	Iron. It's an old magical defence.
(THE DOCTOR *holds up the trowel*.)	
JO:	But you don't believe in magic!
THE DOCTOR:	I don't. But he did . . . luckily!
JO:	And was that a spell you said?
THE DOCTOR:	No, it was the first line of an old Venusian lullaby . . .

Meanwhile all the paranormal phenomena are explained as really happening, but with an alien cause. The Master achieves telekinesis by somehow channelling the 'psycho-kinetic energy' caused by group strong emotions and group rituals. *The Daemons* is unusually full of technobabble (even $E = MC^2$) to imply that occult power, magic, can somehow be 'special science'. In many ways we're back to the idea of the Force, here the dark side, assumed to be possible within physics. But as we saw in Chapter 13, it's a mistake to confuse emotional and spiritual dynamics with physics.

3. The Master uses a satanic-type coven

The Master is in disguise as the Reverend Mr Magister. *Magister* is Latin for 'Master'. But Miss Hawthorne also states, 'Oh, I should have realised at once. Magister is the name given to the leader of a black magic coven.' And indeed, the Master has what is described as his 'coven', although this being a programme aimed at a family audience, the coven is adjusted from a strictly Satanist pattern. The Master declaims in mock ritual pose, 'As my will so mote it be,' and the coven responds, 'Nema' ('Amen' spelled backwards). He prepares to enact a real ritual sacrifice of a chicken, and when Jo interrupts it, he prefers to see her become a human sacrifice. Meanwhile he and his coven chant various sinister-sounding syllables. But the scriptwriters decided to fall short of open blasphemy.

Barry Letts: 'The spell the Master chants to raise the Daemon, Azal, is not something like the Lord's Prayer spoken backwards; it is in fact the nursery rhyme *Mary has a little lamb* spoken backwards . . . This isn't to say there was no research done for the story. I did read quite a few books about black magic to find out the sort of things Satanists did, but only so I could then invent my own rituals and my own words which would sound plausible without actually being the real thing.'[1]

The Master frequently uses hypnosis, here deceiving almost the whole village. But there's more:

▶ Mind-reading – he can reveal all the darkest innermost secrets of the villagers at will.

▶ Telekinesis of a poltergeist type (to scare the locals).

▶ Communicating telepathically with Bok, the animated gargoyle he commands (a mini-demon compared to Azal). It is of Bok, incidentally, that Brigadier Lethbridge-Stewart makes his most famous gung-ho order: 'Chap with wings there. Five rounds rapid!'

▶ Mind control and possession – the Master's hold over Tom Girton goes beyond simple hypnosis. The mind control enables him to fly a helicopter 'like an expert', or as the Doctor comments, 'Like a man *possessed*, you mean.'

 Possession in *Doctor Who*

The Abominable Snowmen

A cosmic entity, the 'Great Intelligence', possesses and keeps alive for 300 years Tibetan monk High Lama Padmasambhava.

The Masque of Mandragora

Hieronymous, leader of the pagan 'cult of Demnos', is also possessed to the point of total absorption by Mandragora Helix Energy.

Pyramids of Mars

Egyptologist Marcus Scarman is possessed to the point of totally losing humanity to the god/alien evil Sutekh (said to be Satan).

Kinda and *Snakedance*

An Eden-like world in which paradise, as in Genesis 1–3, is interrupted by a snake-like evil, the Mara, which possesses Tegan. Later it possesses her again.

---

4. The Daemon Azal – not your 'mythical devil', but real

One key factor in this story is the degree to which the devil himself is the evil seen and defeated. A 'BBC3' announcer, in setting the scene, makes it clear that what is encountered is the force behind witchcraft:

FERGUS: The witches of Devil's End – the famous curse – the notorious cavern underneath the church where the third Lord Aldbourne played at his eighteenth century parody of black magic . . . In this cavern pagan man performed his unspeakable rites; in this cavern the witches of the seventeenth century hid from the fires of Matthew Hopkins, witch-hunter extraordinary. . .

Like Quatermass, the Doctor presents his evidence that images of horned gods and demons and the devil are caused by ancient aliens that gave humanity a cultural kick start and a fear of horned demons: 'Daemons from the planet Damos . . . 60,000 light years away. . .'. Meanwhile when Jo asks if either the gargoyle, Bok, or Daemon Azal is the devil, the Doctor replies, 'No, not your mythical devil, Jo, no. Something far more real.'

So is the devil real? According to the Doctor, Azal is real, but the devil is 'mythical'. Such horned, fearful beings have been seen as 'Gods . . . or devils. But they are neither. They are, in fact, creatures from another world.' Azal is eventually defeated at the moment when he is about to kill the Doctor and hand over total power over humanity to the Master. Jo is desperate and jumps in the way, trying to sacrifice herself to save the Doctor. But the demonic alien explodes in on itself in confusion at this moral act. Commentators are not impressed at this resolution: 'This denouement is risible.'[2]

'It is arguably one of the story's few weak points that in the end he [Azal] is defeated relatively easily, simply self-destructing when faced with the apparent illogicality of Jo's willingness to sacrifice her own life to save the Doctor's. Clearly the writers were drawing a religious parallel here.'[3]

Stephen James Walker

Walker is right that from a dramatic angle *The Daemons* suffers the fate of many SF stories (though not the best), that having set up a number of taxing problems, the resolution is weaker than the development of the problem. Critics have also railed at the unsympathetic, patronising attitude the Doctor shows, and the 'pseudo-science'. However, if physicists can enjoy pointing out the most glaring of errors in their field, maybe it's fair game to point out the rather large holes in the assumptions made about spiritual evil.

The nitpicker's guide to the philosophy and theology of *The Daemons*

1. The Doctor destroys the real devil more than once. He doesn't merely scupper a pseudo-diabolical poseur, he actually destroys the one and only 'real' devil in *The Daemons*, but also destroys the one and only 'Satan' alias Sutekh in *The Pyramids of Mars*, defeats Omega (Satan in *Paradise Lost*), the Destroyer, Fenric, etc.

2. Such stories forget that if Satan the devil is real (a real alien), he is then really the inspiration of all evil. So if he is finally destroyed, mankind is now freed from all evil, and heaven has arrived on Earth. There is no more temptation; no more evil. The Doctor's task of saving the universe is complete! He can take his pension.

3. This script does not allow belief in the devil and the demonic, even as 'one possible interpretation'. No, conventional religious belief in the reality of the devil is misplaced faith in 'myths' people have made up. Instead, real, super-powerful and amoral aliens who look like the conventional devil inspired these folk memories. It's back to 'Was God an astronaut?', except that this time it's 'Was the devil an astronaut?' But if all evil is caused by aliens, what caused the aliens to be evil?

4. It's not just evil. Even odder, major cultural advances were 'caused' by these demonic aliens. This implies that throughout history humans could not progress but for alien-prompted memories. This robs humanity of any creativity, and leaves us with the assumption that now the alien inspiration is ended human progress will end.

5. The Master succeeds in hypnotising villagers and even bluff military types, but fails with the spiritually sensitive Miss Hawthorne.

6. The practising white witch brandishes a cross. While many treat the cross superstitiously, a practising fortune-teller who calls herself a white witch would be very unlikely to use this symbol, and use a pagan one instead. We will explore this oddity later in the chapter (see the comments on 'white magic').

7. Actually, this one is a gaffe by the commentators, not the

scriptwriters. *Doctor Who: The Discontinuity Guide* states: 'The last witchcraft statute in England was repealed in 1736, not as recently as Miss Hawthorne suggests.'[4] The commentators call this a 'goof' in the programme. However, the *Guide* itself has goofed. The 1736 act only replaced the death penalty for witchcraft with a year in prison. The virtual decriminalising of witchcraft was in the Fraudulent Mediums Act of 1951, just as Miss Hawthorne says. Indeed, the last time someone was convicted under the 1736 act occurred during the Second World War. By communicating with a dead sailor and passing on what the deceased had allegedly said, she was seen as in treasonable communication of state secrets, and was convicted and jailed.

In general, *Doctor Who* reveals its 1960s–80s mindset, where most religion, including occult religion, as we saw earlier, is presented as primitive and superstitious, and as evil when it engages in human sacrifice. The running implication throughout it is that it has no basis in reality, except as alien activity. It is certainly presented as having no spiritual reality. This means any threat posed is seen as nil. Of course if it were to return to our screens now, then like the *Auton* trilogy of 1998–99, with its tones of *The X-Files*, then different assumptions might prevail.

In effect, *Doctor Who* trivialises spiritual evil. In *The Smugglers*, the Doctor knows Tarot. In *Timelash*, Herbert (supposedly H. G. Wells) is shown as playing with the Ouija board, at which the Doctor turns up and takes him through space and time. This is laughable if you think Tarot or Ouija is just pretend, but dangerous once you have seen the long track record of such 'games' seriously afflicting people. Even the real Miss Hawthornes of this world warn against Ouija.

The other key oddity is in the methods that supposedly rout evil in *Doctor Who*.

How the Doctor defeats the devil

1. **Science**. Quatermass and the Doctor see applied scientific knowledge as the most effective weapon.
2. **Technology**. The Doctor's oscillator succeeds against the Daemons' powers. In *The Web of Fear*, he 'reverses the polarities' on the Great Intelligence (the entity that had possessed the High Lama). K9 fires to stop human sacrifice by witches in *K9 and Company*. The Destroyer is killed by silver bullets in *Battlefield*. Fenric is killed by toxins in *The Curse of Fenric*. The Doctor uses mirrors to banish the snake from the Garden of Eden-like planet Deva Loka, freeing Tegan from possession.
3. **Magic**. Though 'nonsense', sympathetic magic is used effectively with the Doctor's trowel and Miss Hawthorne's witchcraft.
4. **Sacrificial heroism**. Roney and Jo save the day: 'that a man lay down his (or her) life for his friend' destroys evil.
5. **Speaking in tongues**. Well, Venusian lullabies! There is a feeling that strange unknown words will be effective in combatting evil, just as strange words (backwards chants) effectively raise it.
6. **Faith in something**. Confidence, according to the seventh Doctor in *The Curse of Fenric*.
7. **Mystical defences**. A medium has brought an alien life-feeding force to Earth, and a practitioner in black arts has

activated it in *Image of the Fendahl*. The Doctor is able to capture the evil force using 'mystical defences', and destroys it by depositing it by a supernova! The Doctor can destroy the evil Mara with a ceremony in *Snakedance*.

8. **Combinations**. In *The Awakening*, the Malus has been using psychic projections to feed on villagers' fears. The Doctor defeats it by a combination of persuasion, generating an energy field and causing it to blow itself up. Trying to persuade victims to break free from alien mind control is a frequent strategy.

What is the reality of evil, and how is it really overcome?

Science and technology

These head the *Doctor Who* list. Indeed, together with general common sense, they play a role – though not in the gadget-driven way imagined in these stories. A scientific mind – a concern for truth and a rejection of superstition – plays a helpful part.

Using magic

Even if you don't believe in it, magic is not productive or helpful. In fact it can be counterproductive. Lies and deceits are corrosive. Using something you disbelieve varies from useless to dangerous. One episode from early Christian history (Acts 19:13–16) tells of non-Christian Jews who superstitiously copied Paul's words to free people from evil spirits. Although they didn't accept Jesus as Messiah, they would say, 'In the name of Jesus whom Paul preaches, I command you to come out.' Perhaps they made some headway with the easiest cases. But on one occasion 'the evil spirit answered them, "Jesus I know, and I know about Paul, but who are you?" Then the man who had the evil spirit jumped on them and overpowered them all. He gave them such a beating that they ran out of the house naked and bleeding' (Acts 19:15–16).

For this reason the memorable scene in the 1953 film of *The War of the Worlds*, where the Martians have invaded, so a priest goes out, cross in hand, trying to exorcise them, is theologically ridiculous! Priests and other Christians do not confront physical threats in this way. To do so would be using the cross as a superstitious thing. Where the cross, Bible, prayer, communion and so on come in is in facing *spiritual* evil, and even here they are only relevant as an expression of faith, not a substitute for it.

White magic

The script assumes that Miss Hawthorne, as a white witch, is the strongest opponent of black magic. Even more oddly it assumes that she is both a white witch and supportive of the church. She uses a cross and consults the priest ('at least he is a man of the cloth'), but prefers the real vicar. Is she supposed to be an active church member? Some people do attempt to mix Christianity and witchcraft, but it can't be done. Both black and white witchcraft are in conflict with the Spirit of Jesus Christ. Witches shun the cross, preferring pagan symbols. As occult power rests in the devil, whose ultimate defeat is through Christ's death on the cross, those immersed in witchcraft tend to be uneasy about or hostile towards the cross. It is a further gaffe to assume that as Miss Hawthorne is a *white* witch she must be opposed to black witches. The difference between white and black magic is their different aims behind their openness to spiritual occult power and knowledge. Black magic is used with malevolent intent – curses, voodoo dolls, deliberate blasphemy – while white magic uses the same power for purposes it sees as good, like telling fortunes, 'faith healing' and the like. In practice, this power can't be used without cost, without the user being affected.

So fighting one magic with another in real spiritual struggles means exposing your inner self to a force that is not the God and Father of the Lord Jesus Christ. So what is it? Certainly for Christians the issue is clear: spiritual life can only be from God, through faith in Jesus. The Bible has the strongest things to say about avoiding idolatry and witchcraft, including all contact with spirits, through mediums and wizards or without them. The only trustworthy spiritual power is God.

Sacrificial herosim

This is far more positive both as a personal act and, for Christians, central to faith, where Jesus, the Son of God, sacrifices his life for us, his friends. The cross, the shed blood of Jesus at Calvary, and Holy Communion are therefore powerful, prophetic symbols of this, and special to Christians. Not for nothing do Satanists centre their blasphemy on this in the black mass. In desperation they are trying to scorn God's decisive victory over the one they worship, Satan.

Speaking in tongues

In *Doctor Who* this consists of uttering any odd words, like Venusian. But the real thing for Christians is a spiritual *language*, even though its words make no intellectual sense to the speaker. It seems mysterious to those not used to it, but natural for those who are. People praying to free the demonised, in the name of Jesus, find it is helpful, if not essential. It can help those praying to get more in tune with God, and so become more effective in confronting the evil. It is a divinely guided prayer, which can prove effective in dislodging the evil. One emergency I was called into was a difficult situation of demonic affliction, which had developed into 'temporary possession'. Ordinary prayers and words were not making much impact. The entity spoke through the afflicted man, scorning everything I said as a 'waste of time'. But when I felt myself guided to pray out loud in tongues, and did so, the reaction was instant. The man outwardly screwed up into a foetal position, and the voice shouted, 'Stop those curses!' Words that praise Jesus, and God the Father, will no doubt be 'curses' to an evil spirit.

Faith

It should be obvious by now that it does matter what our faith is in. Evil will not retreat because we have a faith in Soviet communism, as the seventh Doctor suggests in *The Curse of Fenric*, as if faith were a kind of negative pheromone we exude that repels evil ('a belief a day keeps the devil away'). The vulnerability of the vicar in that same story, because his faith in God is only a kind of vague, polite faith in the reality of God and the need for goodness, is far more realistic. The 1940s vicar no doubt believes in God, but like many vicars and ordinary believers his confidence in the ability of God to help him when he is confronted by evil may be pathetically weak. In a real confrontation with real, spiritual evil, all dimensions of faith are relevant: faith as confidence; faith as true belief in the true God; and faith as relationship, as trust in the Lord as Saviour.

Mystical defences – or prayer

The Doctor's use of indiscriminate mystical defences has the same ambiguity as faith in 'anything'. Prayer to 'anything' is just as unhelpful. Faith in Jesus, and prayer in his name – that is, not just a set of words, but openness to him – is vital.

• 22 •
Resistance Is Futile

Telepathy in *Star Trek* and *Babylon 5*

Star Trek exchanges the Doctor's mission to defeat evil and save the universe, with its well-known call 'to explore strange new worlds, to seek out new life and new civilisations'. So aliens are regular, but pathological monsters are rare. But it is with the Borg that we hear the classic words of attack, 'Resistance is futile!', resonating through many a *Doctor Who* storyline. The Borg's chilling 'You will be assimilated' matches the Cybercontroller's words in *The Tomb of the Cybermen*, 'You will be like us!' It is the phrase of every evil dictatorship, ideology, seducer, and indeed the devil – 'Resistance is futile'; give in now! Though the battles of history are real, these evils *can* be resisted and eventually overcome. 'Resistance is futile' is a lie!

More generally, in *Star Trek*, psychic awareness is seen not as a threat but a gift, pursued in a benign way, from Mr Spock's mindmeld with the rocky Horta, to Deanna Troi's empathic counselling, used mostly to help her clients reach more harmonious personal fulfilment. In this context, Spock's forced mindmeld against Vulcan female Valeris in *Star Trek VI: The Undiscovered Country* is such an exception that some Trekkers have accused him of 'mental rape'.[1] But in *Babylon 5*, the Psi Corps is far more sinister. *B5* largely avoids the doubtful suggestion that telepathy is possible today. Instead, it pictures it genetically engineered into human and other races by the Vorlons, emerging among humans in the twenty-second century. Once the Vorlons' role changes from defenders to bullies, their manipulative danger is exposed. The Psi Corps, and even more the Psi Cops, are seen as a very sinister development on Earth. (Oddly, Centauri and Minbari telepaths aren't shown to be as sinister.) While regulation is introduced to prevent telepathic intrusion, this leaves their powers concentrated.

A tragedy of telepaths?

► Susan Ivanova's mother Sophie is a casualty of regulation. Taking powerful suppressants to avoid having to join the Corps, she ends up committing suicide. Susan is scarred and fearful of the Corps.

► Talia Winters, commercial telepath on B5, turns out to have been implanted with an alternative personality without knowing.

► As for Mr Bester, head of the Psi Cops, he is a smooth but nasty piece of work; though even he has his domestic side.

► Byron, the pacifist leader of a breakaway community of telepaths, dies as Bester's Psi Cops suppress his attempted settlement, fearing loss of hegemony.

► Lyta Alexander plays the most striking role. Originally a mid-grade commercial telepath like Talia, she breaks with Psi Corps, and gets taken under the Vorlons' wings, gaining unparalleled powers.

During the ascending struggle against the Shadows, it is discovered that telepathy disables them. One very evocative scene (so hard to project on television) has a group of telepaths all concentrating their mental energies against the powerful, evil and invisible Shadows – to great effect.

Although in the fullness of the 'story arc' of *B5* we see more than an allegory of the struggle between light and darkness, this element is centre stage over this period. To the Christian mind, this picture of people struggling in their thoughts against an invisible enemy of powerful evil is very evocative of the struggle involved in prayer, particularly in spiritual warfare.

The X-Files: the paranormal cover-up

The Andromeda Strain was a tense drama, not in the action sense but as a film gripping the mind with an unsettling idea: what if the sample returned by a deep space probe contained an unknown fatal virus that began to spread and seemed to be incurable? The alien invaders would be microscopic rather than monsters, and this made the film tense conceptually. Chris Carter, creator of *The X-Files*, said he wanted his show to work in a similar way: 'scary in the way that speculation pushes beyond scientific credibility to enter a realm of extreme possibility'.[2] And while most of his extreme possibilities centre on aliens and rumours of aliens, together with the all-pervasive atmosphere of government denial and cover-up, a fair number of paranormal stories crop up. As with *Doctor Who* we have possession, evil spirits jumping from one person to another, vampiric creatures, and telekinesis. In addition we have a wider range of unexplained phenomena such as spontaneous combustion and channelling spirits. Unlike *Doctor Who*, *The X-Files* avoids pseudo-scientific explanations. In *Doctor Who*, nothing really paranormal, nothing truly supernatural, occurs. But in *The X-Files*, these events are presented as 'extreme possibilities' – not really facts, because of confusion and obstruction of the truth. But a viewer watching these programmes will be left with the feeling that these paranormal events, together with alien abductions, clandestine government experiments and so on, are real.

To that extent, this programme presents an open face to the occult, as much for the viewer as for anyone in any particular story. And if occult spirituality is real and contains dangers for those open to it, then a programme like this can facilitate these dangers for the viewer. As for how the paranormal is fought, this is a show centring on FBI agents, so there are lots of scenes with guns at the ready and also a fair bit of shooting. In the scenes of alien abduction and strongly paranormal phenomena, these are shown to be just as ineffective as the Brigadier's 'five rounds rapid!'.

Resisting evil in reality: sin

Evil is real, and standing up to it is a real challenge. One aspect of evil is sin. The devil is traditionally seen as the tempter, an aspect curiously missing from most SF, though Ardra, Ventax II's pseudo-devil, tempts Picard sexually – and fails. The devil in the real experience of most people is the figure behind temptation. It is important to recognise that while the devil tries to seduce us into various forms of sin, we are free agents. Having said that, our experience of freedom varies enormously. A person interrogated by the KGB or the SS has the free will to stand up to the treatment, but many would find the odds against them too hard. Not everyone has the resolve of Sheridan. A person may, like Garibaldi, have a problem with drink, a problem that undercuts his performance, but his ability to withstand the temptation to drink to the point of incapacity will be rather weaker than the ability of others – even, paradoxically, Londo Mollari's. Resistance traditionally is against 'the world, the flesh and the devil'. The concept of sin includes succumbing to the world and the flesh – sins of money, sex and power, any of which can be used appropriately, or corrupted.

In science fiction, as in newspaper headlines, only mega-evil is seen as sin. The Yorkshire Ripper, Hitler, Davros, Bester, the Borg: they are sinful; they are evil. But me and my mate next door – well, we're no worse than anyone else, so we're not the problem! SF, particularly of the *Doctor Who* kind, is good at presenting the moral challenge to have courage. In *The Dalek Invasion of Earth*, Campbell asks if the Daleks 'dare to tamper with the forces of creation'. 'Yes, they dare!' the Doctor replies. 'And we must dare to stop them!' This part of the equation works well enough. We cannot be indifferent to evil or complacent about it. We cannot be equivocal, or the battle is lost. Evil must be fought. The problem is the other half of the equation. Our struggle with sin and evil rarely faces us with a megalomaniac trying to wipe us out, along with everything we have ever believed in. In the majority of people's experience, most suffering is caused by ordinary people. While our tendency is to see evil in simple newspaper headlines, we should try personalising it and asking who in our own experience has caused us more hurt than anyone else. In most cases, we will find it is not some evil monster, but an ordinary person. This is true in some 99 per cent of cases. And if you were to put everyone on the scale of evil to good from, say, Adolf Hitler to Mother Teresa, most people would say the person who hurt them most was actually someone in the crowded middle on this scale. So if sin and evil are really going to be resisted, we have to drop the unrealistic black and white picture that paints them as the isolated problem of maniacs. The problem with causing suffering to other people is found in each one of us. Sin is not usually mega-evil: it's in ordinary people like me.

This might seem a very pessimistic conclusion, but it's only the downside. There is another dimension. In the Bible, Satan is also called 'the accuser of the brethren'. In fact, 'satan' is a description, meaning 'accuser', rather than a name, and this points to his role in condemning us for the ways we fall to temptation to sin. This is why forgiveness is central to Christian faith; not just human forgiveness, but forgiveness by God, meaning freedom from the penalty of sin. This overrides Satan's accusation and condemnation. For Christians, every sin is committed against God, and he can therefore forgive.

The devil and demonic possession

The devil is real, and so is the problem of the demonic. Sci-fi stories regularly take the theme of possession. Is that real? Let's be a little more precise. In *Doctor Who*, we see different forms of possession:

▶ total possession;
▶ total possession giving unnatural powers;
▶ temporary possession.

Total possession to the point of the extinction of personality we see when Sutekh possesses Scarman, and where the Mandragora energy possesses Hieronymous. *Unnatural pow-*

ers for the possessed are seen in Padmasambhava living for 300 years, and Hieronoymus 'becoming' faceless energy, and being able to kill using energy bolts from his hand. And *temporary possession* happens, for example, where Sutekh controls the Doctor briefly. The best example of this is where, in a dream, Tegan is possessed by the Mara in *Kinda*, a story unusually full of religious allusions, both Buddhist (e.g. the wheel of life) and Christian (e.g. the snake in Eden).

Possession – past and present

Possession is certainly recorded in the accounts of various religions. Ancient historian Plutarch tells of a prophetess, a medium, whose attempt to contact the spirits during a consultation, a 'channelling', went wrong, and the medium got taken over for real. All ended in chaos and confusion, and she died.

In the traditions of Christian Europe, for a long time the terrible excesses of the witch-hunt period (*c*.1450–1650) led to an over-correction in rejecting all spirituality, all accounts of witchcraft, possession, spirits, ghosts, angels, and in the end God. What could be repeated in the labs at will was the only test of truth, so spiritual phenomena as non-physical and often non-repeatable were dismissed as medieval superstitions. In the following centuries, most people still believed in God, and steered clear of idolatry. But since the 1840s, the increasingly complacent assumption that the whole of spiritual reality was make-believe has led to a gradual rise in spiritism, with many assuming that seances, Ouija and Tarot couldn't affect anyone – they were just old superstitions and only a game. In recent years, naïve curiosity has led some people to dabble, in search of surprising thrills. As more dabble, problems of possession and exorcism have resurfaced, with many accounts of people being badly affected by these supposed 'games'.

In practice there is more overlap with the SF pictures of possession than might be expected, if we don't overdo the exactness of the parallels. Very rarely, there is total possession. This is where a person seems to have lost their personality permanently to evil. The most frequent suggestion made by those with the widest experience here is that Charles Manson, guilty of killing Sharon Tate and others, may be possessed in this total way.

Unnatural powers

While we rarely see unmitigated total possession, the use of unnatural powers by people during demonic fits is more common. In the worst case recorded in the New Testament, the man was regularly chained up by locals and his demons boasted they were a 'Legion' of evil spirits (officially 6,000). We are told that when he was taken over in a demonic fit, he had super-human powers to break any chains the fearful locals might put on him. This unfortunate man was at the extreme end of what is also, if fairly rarely, experienced today. However, he was freed by Jesus, and such people have also been freed today.

I am not aware of real possession resulting in the power to live for 300 years, nor of people acquiring the ability to kill with energy bolts! What's more, the afflicted person is not even in control of their surge of strength. It is a demonic fit, and the person is seemingly under control. But during such seizures, especially in more extreme situations, abnormal physical strength is sometimes displayed, as is speaking with an abnormal voice, and so on.

Temporary possession

One of the features of severe demonic attacks is that afterwards the person is often unaware of what happened during the attack. It's worth adding that various things can provoke such a demonic attack in a person, one of the more striking of which is the recognition by the evil spirit that it is up against the power that can expel it and free the person from it. So in the accounts of Jesus moving among people and meeting people afflicted by such evil, we find time and again that the evil presence manifests itself as Jesus turns up. The first occasion has a man in the synagogue of all places, where Jesus has spoken with authority, suddenly shrieking out, 'What do you want with us, Jesus of Nazareth? Have you come to destroy us? I know who you are – the Holy One of God!' (Mark 1:24). Jesus, more than any other, would simply by his holy presence provoke such evil unwillingly to display itself, but similar things can happen to Christians, as with Paul in Acts 16:16–19. This form of self-display, when the chaotic evil of an evil spirit shows itself, continues today, as Christians, particularly those with an experience of praying against such evil, and with a degree of personal holiness, also experience similar things.

I remember one such occasion when I was called in an emergency to help someone I know well, whose personality had been eclipsed in this way. To be frank, I was singularly unprepared for this late night call. My father had just died, and my youngest son had just had a heart operation, so I was rather distracted! This man was in a state of temporary possession, and knew nothing of what was happening at the time. The entity my colleague and I faced caused the man to behave chaotically and unresponsively – until we decided to say a simple prayer. I was barely a few seconds in, when the demonised man sprang up, fists flailing, and growling, 'What are you doing here, man of God? You don't know what you're up against!' I did not feel like a 'man of God' at the time! However, despite my feeling emotionally drained and spiritually very distracted, this thing reacted to prayer, and eventually the man was freed, the positive change being clear and permanent. The detail of this encounter is better left to another occasion, along with discussion of how people and God interact in such situations, but the striking thing was how, once we prayed for the man to be free, the evil manifested itself and made its last ditch take-over bid.

In practice, most people are not obviously or extremely affected by occult spirituality as in the situations we have mentioned. Usually a person is unaware and perhaps lightly affected. Generally, people are affected because they have deliberately opened themselves to the occult, but in some cases they are the victims of witchcraft (e.g. family members, those who have been formally cursed, etc.). Some are more spiritually sensitive and vulnerable.

There is another aspect of this theme of possession and affliction by evil in science fiction. SF explores situations of a possession-like nature. However, where it trivialises the occult, or glorifies it, it facilitates the very danger exposed in such stories. The danger of the occult is real.

A 1998 headline from my local newspaper (the *Leicester Mercury*) read: 'FAN OF X-FILES KILLED HIMSELF', pointing to obsession with the paranormal. First of all, there is a danger with such 'guilt by association' headlines. The headline 'Tory MP killed himself' might make a good headline, and make people rethink their politics, but that inference would hardly be 'logical', as Mr Spock might say. And the headline 'Headteacher killed himself' would certainly not justify the reaction, 'Oh, dodgy thing, teaching children. You never know where it might lead!' At best, in context, it might be fair to argue, 'Look how stressed teachers and heads are getting!'

Having got that proviso out of the way, let's state that there is a long track record of danger with Ouija, openness to Satanism and so on, and people who allow themselves to get heavily immersed in such occult things are not simply in psychological but also *spiritual* danger. And the effect of such danger can be demonic episodes like the ones mentioned earlier, which in extreme cases can lead to attempts at suicide and, very rarely, murder. With a programme that deliberately trades in the occult, as *The X-Files* sometimes does, there is some danger that viewers might soak up a degree of openness to the occult from the programmes. This can apply to other programmes that express openness to 'unclean spirits'. In practice, the extent to which someone might be badly affected depends on the degree of occultism in the programme. So an occult horror film like *The Exorcist* is likely to make a stronger damaging impact than the things we have discussed.

The way you are affected also depends on the extent to which you, as viewer, welcome the occult element, and also on your level of spiritual sensitivity at the time. During a time when I was praying with people in spiritually troubled circumstances on an almost daily basis, and felt called most times to fast and pray in preparation, I reasoned that as I'd already had to fast on Monday and Tuesday, surely God wouldn't want me to fast again for the difficult situation I was due to face that Wednesday evening! Unfortunately, however, if you tell God what you would like him to say, it can dull the hearing! So I began to eat, and decided to catch up on a videoed episode of *Voyager* (*Initiations*). Suddenly, as I was faced with Chakotay and his ancestral spirits, I began to feel spiritually and physically affected. This is rare for me, and such a theme would not normally affect me. *But on this occasion it did.* This was because my context required me to be spiritually focused without ambiguity. I knew I had to stop eating and viewing, and get praying. God *did* want me to fast and pray. Another time it would be OK to watch it, and indeed eat, but not that time.

The conclusion I draw from this is that some people will find that exposure to even the milder occult implications of the TV we have discussed in these two chapters could have an unhelpful effect. And others not normally affected might need to back off at times of spiritual sensitivity. If you find your relationship with God is being harmed by a TV programme, switch it off!

Censorship?

There will be those who are disturbed by that conclusion. Doesn't it reek of censorship? Censorship is very unpopular these days. However, a degree of self-censorship is necessary, and there is a case for censorship generally. The standard case against censorship argues that plays, films, TV shows and so on can't 'pervert' anyone. People should be allowed to watch whatever they want to. This case depends on the idea that such shows can't affect anyone, can't change the way they feel and act and are as people.

This bizarre argument fails because in practice the aim of all great art is to do precisely that: to affect people, to change them! To watch something and be moved, to be intellectually challenged, inspired and have your way of seeing things fundamentally deepened so that having seen it you will not be the same person again, is the aim, and the achievement of the greatest art. The downside is that violent, degrading and disturbing material *can* affect people harmfully.

Does it matter?

R. L. Dione told us that Jesus' exorcisms were an alien 'brain manipulating device'[3], and telepathy is electromagnetic power. But his 'flying saucer God' is more incredible than real SF. Jesus is at work today, as Christians experience answers to prayers. Dione's thesis depended on ignorance of Christian experience of prayer, where people are freed from evil.

But does it matter if people believe in alien visits and abductions? Alien abduction is a favourite theme of *The X-Files*. It's also a growing belief generally, which is why TV runs it. But there is an unhealthy overlap with the terrible suicide of the Heaven's Gate cult. They believed that Comet Hale-Bopp had come for them. Their astral deception turned science fantasy into ghastly tragedy. As Scully says, 'The truth is out there, but so are the lies.' It *does* matter if we mix them up.

So is the best response to stay cool and believe in nothing? Scully once said that she is 'afraid to believe' in paranormal things. This is after she has had overwhelming evidence of their reality. Many people behave in a similar way towards

God. A healthy dose of common sense is good, but recognition of the truth is a vital step towards faith. Our culture has a long tradition of doubt as the route to knowledge, but it's possible to doubt *everything*, philosophically – even existence. Doubt is ultimately arid; useless to help us through life. The proper response to the paranormal is neither doubt nor faith; it is to accept it can be real, but to keep a healthy distance from anything occult, and trust in God with openness to *him* to guide us.

'Resistance is futile' is the time-honoured mantra of mindless monsters; that humanity is irrelevant is their repeated boast. But the classic SF story also tells how, with considerable cost, they are resisted. Humanity is worth fighting for. 'Resistance is useless' is also the taunt of the evil against us. Just before the man I mentioned earlier was freed from evil, the spirit boasted, 'You don't know what you're up against!' and threatened, 'We will meet again!' But evil deceives. It does not have the final victory. Though the battle between God and evil is real, the days of the power of evil are numbered, and the victory has been secured, in the death and resurrection of Jesus.

Part Six:
It's Eternal Life, Jim!

 IN THIS SECTION

▶ **But not as we know it**

Is the meaning of life unknowable, absurd, like '42'? What about the struggle for purpose in so much SF?

▶ **At the end of the universe**

Millennium, Armageddon, the end of history – the language of SF is littered with religious pictures, especially the ultimate pictures. So are the Borg right to declare 'Death is irrelevant'?

▶ **Dimensions in time**

Prophecy was until recently widely dismissed as impossible. But *DS9*, *Babylon 5*, *The X-Files* and *Farscape* have shown a resurgence of interest. Time travel, the alienness of aliens, and other SF ideas have helped provide a context. What about the next century, or about humanity's ultimate future?

▶ **SF and Christian faith**

A checklist on how SF and Christian faith work together, or conflict.

• 23 •
The Undiscovered Country

The meaning of life: 42

Douglas Adams began the second set of six episodes of his classic radio series, *The Hitch-hiker's Guide to the Galaxy*, in typical pose:

 'There is a theory which states that if ever anyone discovers exactly what the universe is for and why it is here it will instantly disappear, and be replaced by something even more bizarrely inexplicable.

'There is another theory which states that this has already happened.

'There is yet a third theory which suggests that both of the first two theories were concocted by a wily editor of *The Hitch-hiker's Guide to the Galaxy* in order to increase the level of universal uncertainty and paranoia and so boost the sales of the guide. This last theory is of course the most convincing, because *The Hitch-hiker's Guide to the Galaxy* is the only book in the whole of the known universe to have the words 'DON'T PANIC!' inscribed in large, friendly letters on the cover.'

Douglas Adams was script editor for the seventeenth season of *Doctor Who* (which began the notable combination of Tom Baker as the Doctor and Lalla Ward as female Time Lord Romana), and he also wrote several of the stories. In *The Hitch-hiker's Guide* he presses his anarchic humour into SF spoof. Standard *Doctor Who* sees our hero saving the

Earth; Adams' series sees it demolished early in Episode 1. *Doctor Who* will see the Doctor solving the mysteries and complexities thrown up against him; but in *The Hitch-hiker's Guide* everything just gets 'even more bizarrely inexplicable'.

At the heart of the first series, the most phenomenal computer in galactic history (Deep Thought) has set itself the task of finding the answer to the meaning of life, the universe and everything, much to the consternation of the Union of Philosophers and Allied Trades. Seven million years later, it produces its answer: '. . . though I'm afraid you're not going to like it: 42.' In response to the howls of protest, it tells the crowd that to make proper sense they will need to have the right question. For this, what is needed, this electronic John the Baptist says, is 'the Computer that is to come after me, the one whose parameters I am not worthy to compute'! This turns out to be the Earth, manufactured on a 10-million-year programme to produce the right question, but destroyed by the Vogons to prevent the emergence of this result 'five minutes before the programme was complete'. The answer 42 is absurd. And the Earth as the means of finding the answer to 'life, the universe and everything' is deliberately ironic. We, who among all the species on Earth (in the real world!) see ourselves as uniquely searching for the meaning of life, are portrayed in that series as merely a complex organic computer for someone else to sort it all out – an exercise doomed to failure anyway!

Is the meaning of life absurd? Is it a hopeless exercise, the only fitting response being to treat it with irony? Must we see the universe as simply 'even more bizarrely inexplicable' and give up on it? Or is that 'to increase the level of universal uncertainty and paranoia'?

Fluid links

In this chapter, we will look *subjectively* at what the meaning of life is for our SF heroes on TV. What is it, first, for the Doctor?

1. For the first Doctor, who felt 'cast adrift in the fourth dimension', this seemed to be the joy of discovery, science, exploration, curiosity. Only later did he become galvanised by the moral challenge that confronted him in the cosmic evil of the Daleks.
2. The second Doctor pressed this moral crusade with anarchistic relish: 'Bad laws were meant to be broken.'
3. For the third Doctor, imprisoned on Earth, the wander-bug seems top priority; but he too is quickly drawn into an upright stance against evil.
4. The fourth takes this for granted, while laughing dismissively at those megalomaniacs he seems destined to thwart.
5. The fifth returns us to a straight moral character.
6. The sixth finds the meaning of life in himself! But even he is portrayed as a moral crusader in *The Trial of a Time Lord*: 'Daleks, Sontarans, Cybermen: they're still in the nursery compared to us. Ten million years of absolute power: that's what it takes to be *really* corrupt!'
7. The seventh, far more interventionist than the first, has a clownishness reminiscent of the second, but a manipulative determination to prevent the machinations of evil galactic powers, particularly those seeking to disrupt the flow of time. What is his motivation?

It is striking, reading the *New Adventures* novels that centre on the seventh Doctor and Ace, plus Bernice (Benny) later, how this Doctor's motivation and personal coherence come increasingly centre stage. These novels have far more opportunity to explore personality, relationships, motivations and the like. Ace and Benny find themselves ever more frustrated with the Doctor, who is secretive, plotting. What is his motivation? He saves planets and the universe, but can't save his friends, or at least the friends his companions get to know and like. Ace is so cut up she decides to leave him (only to return). Benny is just as angry: why can't they be let in on the secret? He can muck around chasing Exxilon ships, while the Aztecs are sacrificing 20,000 people in front of him, and only protests when the cosmic force he is up against (disguised as a local god) crops up.

Perhaps this is inescapable in such novels. Episode after episode had the Doctor amid great dangers saving this and that world. In the process good people got killed – even three companions. The requirements of the next story meant that no realistic time was spent grieving. The second Doctor's homely conversation with Victoria in *The Tomb of the Cybermen* (a whole two episodes after the death of her father at the end of *The Evil of the Daleks*) is very much the exception. But once the real feelings and motives of the characters are explored in any depth, the impossibility of saving the universe week by week begins to tell, the character looks increasingly incredible, and the other characters have to express that incredulity. It seems as if a similar problem with the humanity of a character saving the world week by week sent the writers of *Lois and Clark: The New Adventures of Superman* in the opposite direction. Saving the world from Lex Luther's villainy became less central, and the personal relationships of Mr and Mrs Superman became the focus.

In the original series of *Star Trek* the meaning of life, subjectively, is very much in the adventure of life, the expression of the rugged spirit (declaimed by Kirk in many end of episode speeches) with freedom and camaraderie. The technological Utopianism of the original series and Starfleet's Prime Directive are both firmed up and become unambiguously both the goal and the expression of the quest for the meaning of life in *TNG*. Forget the next life, heaven has arrived on Earth! Picard, who exemplifies this Starfleet outlook, is clearly motivated by the challenge to find new lifeforms, and, however unlikely, integrate them into civilised life. Only his terrible encounter with the Borg causes him to run counter to that.

In a way, *DS9* hits similar problems to *Doctor Who: New Adventures*, as the picture shifts from seeing a new planet every week. Losing the constant change of focus, to stay with the same space station and, more to the point, with the same alien race, the Bajorans, requires the same asking of questions as to what makes these people tick. As a result Utopia is called into question. Though the Prime Directive continues apace, the problems of reality start crowding back in. And the Utopian answer unravels. Quark deals in money – gold-pressed latinum, no less. He also deals in the holosuite. The assumption in *TNG* that the holodeck would be solely used for wholesome pastimes is naïve in view of the way Kirk and Riker are seen as womanisers. But this has given way to the more realistic assumption in *DS9* (if implied modestly to ensure this remains family viewing) that Quark's holosuite would be used for rather more obviously sinful intentions: the porn of the twenty-fourth century. Further, by Season 7 (1999), Utopia has been replaced by the bleak problems of all-out war (see *The Siege of AR-558*).

With the decline of Utopia comes a new journey of exploration by Sisko. *DS9* departs a bit from the pattern of its predecessors, where characters underwent amazing events only to appear unchanged next episode. In *Rapture*, the Season 5 episode with Sisko's amazing visions and fulfilled prophecies, Sisko endures life-threatening 'odd neural patterns', but after being 'doctored' by Bashir, he seems 'back to normal'. For the next few episodes he is. But Season 6 (*Far Beyond the Stars*) and Season 7 (*Shadows and Symbols* and *What You Leave Behind*) see these changes recur and deepen. Finally, *Voyager* combines the outlooks of both *TNG* and *DS9*, adding its own special setting of previously hostile crews working as one, whether Federation/Maquis, or later crew/Borg drone Seven of Nine. Their subjective 'meaning of life' and goals are twofold: the desire to get home, and fostering the sense of belonging together as a team.

Babylon 5 presents a different profile. There is a greater realism than saving the universe every week, or boldly promoting Utopia. As we saw earlier, individual characters struggle with the battle for meaning, sometimes finding it in a moment of destiny. However, the five-year series as a whole does imply answers to the question of the meaning and aim of life. It gradually builds up, and comes to a head during the 'Shadow War arc'. Despite all the ambiguities, those working for democracy, freedom, truth, decency and goodness find themselves facing an Armageddon-like battle against the forces of the superior Shadows, first with, but later also against, the arguably even more powerful Vorlons. All the while they have to take difficult decisions in relation to surrogate wars between the Centauri and the Narn, and against the Shadow-influenced EarthGov (the government of the Earth Alliance).

The implications in this epic are that the battle for democracy, freedom, decency, truth and goodness is rightly fought, and fairly won. Leaders Sheridan and Delenn, despite their limitations and mistakes, manage to do the right, even heroic, things. And everyone is the beneficiary. This was a strikingly positive message in the cynical 90s, and well worth articulating. In the 60s there were moral crusades: for the left, against apartheid; for the right, against communism. But by the early 90s they had succeeded, and with nothing particularly wrong for anyone to fight against (or so it seemed), the climate of relativism deepened.

In the city of Prague, Vaclav Havel (now President) and his friends took risks to fight for what they believed was right, setting up Charter 77 in the days of communist dictatorship. And they were right to fight for democracy, freedom, truth, decency and goodness; right to take that risk. What is the meaning of life, subjectively? For Havel, it was to end the nightmare of his people, which had been so graphically illustrated by the Soviet invasion that ended the 'Prague Spring' in 1968. And Sheridan and Delenn are about similar business in *Babylon 5*. The very fact of interstellar solidarity – the ability to transform relationships of war into partnership, as Minbari, human and Narn and ultimately even Centauri, together with the rag-bag of non-aligned worlds and races, become allies and colleagues – provides an allegory of how the various countries and races, major and minor powers can and should learn to form a patchwork of co-operation and partnership.

The X-Files delights in pivoting between its lead characters. Is the truth out there? Is the meaning of life ever going to be found? The programme deliberately projects both faith and scepticism in equal measure to convey an ironic feel for the 90s and beyond. But do Scully and Mulder have personal guiding beliefs as to the meaning of life for them? In practice their motivations vary. Mulder is the believer in aliens and cover-ups, Scully the sceptic about these. However, Mulder is pagan, post-Christian and postmodernist; Scully is the Catholic with a degree of renewed Christian faith. Again, Mulder is the passionate conviction agent, who risks so much to get through the lies and nail the truth; Scully lives for her science, but finds these convictions disturbed by her experiences, while her work, despite the chaotic circumstances, helps in this search for truth.

Subjectively, the heroes in science fiction have their goal, their feeling about the meaning of life for *them*. But not everyone is quite as motivated as such driven people. The stories also have their implied visions: saving the universe; promoting post-colonial paradise with the Prime Directive; struggling for democracy, freedom and inter-racial, international civilisation; and battling for truth even in a world that obscures it, criminally. At one point, Marvin the Paranoid Android tells his humanoid companions in the restaurant at the end of the universe that he can explain the answer to their search for the meaning of life (why 42 is supposedly the answer). He can see it in the human's brainwave patterns. But before he answers, the crew is distracted, and Marvin comments, 'I could tell you weren't really interested.'

What is the meaning of life, *objectively* – the real answer? Can we ever know? Do we *want* to know, or will we, like Marvin's listeners, ignore it? That is our next theme.

• 24 •
'On the Edge of Forever'

The end of history?

So what *is* the meaning of life? There is a long line of thinking to the effect that we will only really know at its end. G. W. F. Hegel, the early nineteenth-century philosopher, argued that history was a process; a continuing sequence of event, reaction and conclusion, which he famously termed a dialectic of thesis, antithesis and synthesis. Karl Marx then remodelled this as an economic conflict. Hegel himself suggested evocatively that we could only know the meaning of history at the end of history.

Martin Heidegger was a mid-twentieth-century existentialist. He argued that for an individual person death marks the boundaries of existence, and gives to life its urgency. He called life a 'being-toward-death'. To anticipate your own death is to give your life an authentic existence. Here, in an individual way, we would know meaning of life at the end – or indeed afterwards, when it seems too late. But significantly, he reminds us that we can begin to discover meaning now, by being honest about the overall, unfinished picture of life.

More sinisterly, in *Mein Kampf*, Adolf Hitler claimed to have grasped 'the meaning of history', which for him was a struggle between the races. At the height of the Second World War, two Nazi leaders commented to each other that history would either give them the highest honours or denigrate them utterly. We now know which!

Francis Fukuyama's controversial idea shortly after the collapse of Soviet communism, that the end of history had come, is another variation. He said that the last historic battle, between capitalism and communism, was clearly over – capitalism had won. From now on, there would be no more 'history', just minor variations of detail.

Logical positivism claimed that all questions of art, morality and religion were meaningless because they could never be proved, only believed. Life after death, and God, could never be proved. In response, John Hick pointed out that after the end of life, if we find ourselves alive and with God, that would be pretty decisive proof for the reality of both! Generally, humanism sees the meaning of life and history in humanity. Therefore it tries to deny the death of the human race. Gene Roddenberry's *Star Trek* has many ultra-advanced aliens who tell Kirk they were once humanoid, like us, but have evolved to become eternal spirit beings. And J. Michael Straczynski's *Babylon 5*, in the episode that tells of the ultimate future of mankind, *The Deconstruction of Falling Stars*, pictures mankind 'a million years' into the future evolving into Vorlon-like angelic creatures, able to survive the end of the Sun, and survive in space. But the truth is, the ultimate future of mankind, historically, must be death. In that context the meaning of life must be limited.

In contrast, the Christian claim is that the meaning of life is not based on future human progress towards perfection, but on God. Individuals, humanity, heaven and Earth – the whole of reality – will end. But God will create 'a new heaven and a new earth'. Eternal life begins now, and is not ended by death, and it is secure in God alone.

In different ways, each of these explanations for the meaning of life reminds us that if we could know the end of history we'd have a better idea of what it's all been about. But can we know the end of history?

The restaurant at the end of the universe

In typically absurd fashion, Episode 6 of *The Hitch-hiker's Guide to the Galaxy* sees the heroes apparently die, as a computer bank explodes. This scene follows their 'death'.

WAITER:	Good evening, gentlemen, madam. Have you a reservation?
FORD PREFECT:	Reservation?
WAITER:	Yes, sir.
FORD PREFECT:	You need a reservation for the after life?!
WAITER:	The after life, sir?
ARTHUR:	This is the after life?
FORD PREFECT:	Well I assume so – I mean, there's no way we could have survived that blast, is there?
ZAPHOD:	I certainly didn't survive. I was a total gonner . . . Wham! Bam! and that was it!
FORD PREFECT:	I mean, we didn't stand a chance. We must have been blown to bits! Arms, legs, everywhere.
WAITER:	Erm, erm. If you would care to order drinks, I'll show you . . .
ZAPHOD:	Here we are . . . lying dead . . .
TRILLIAN:	Standing!
ZAPHOD:	Standing dead in this er . . . restaurant!
FORD PREFECT:	Bit odd, isn't it?
ZAPHOD:	Er, yeah!
TRILLIAN:	Nice chandeliers, though.

ARTHUR:	It's not so much an afterlife, more a sort of *après vie*.
ZAPHOD:	Hey, hang about, I think we're missing something important here, something that somebody just said.
TRILLIAN:	About the chandeliers?
ZAPHOD:	No. Something *really* important. Hey, hey, hey, you!
WAITER:	Sir?
ZAPHOD:	Did you say something about drinks?
WAITER:	Certainly, sir. If the lady or the gentlemen would care to take drinks before dinner . . .
ZAPHOD:	Yeah, great!
WAITER:	Then the universe will explode later for your pleasure.

They turn out to be in a manufactured time bubble at Milliways which, we are told, is 'the restaurant at the end of the universe – one of the most extraordinary ventures in the entire history of catering'. This protected bubble rocks back and forth round the moment of the end of everything, and people commute by time travel to view it!

Second Coming

A cabaret atmosphere is pictured, and the MC asks, 'Do we have . . . lastly, a party of devout believers from the Church of the Second Coming of the Great Prophet Zarquon?' and adds to general laughter, 'Well he'd better start hurrying, because he's only got eight minutes left!' Later still, just seconds before the end, Zarquon suddenly appears to the Hallelujah Chorus. The MC continues, 'Oh? What? What's happening here? Who's this? I don't believe it! A big hand please for the Great Prophet Zarquon!' The prophet's words at his Second Coming? 'Er, hello, everybody. Sorry I'm a bit late. Had a terrible time, all sorts of things cropping up at the last moment. And how are we for time? . . . erm . . .' And the universe explodes into nothingness.

This is of course another of Adams' absurdities: the end of time as another meaningless party, and the Second Coming a photo-opportunity that makes no difference whether or not it happens.

But what is the Second Coming, really? The Second Coming of Jesus is not so much an event happening *in* history as an event happening *to* history. This does not mean it is a non-event, but it does make it hard to describe in straight prose – which is why so much of the language the Bible uses (Mark 13, and especially Revelation) is poetic, the colourful language of symbolic prophecy.

Millennium

In Christian history, those who have taken the words of the Bible seriously at this point, with its imagery of both Armageddon and Christ reigning a millennium (1,000 years), have reached different conclusions, because the symbolic pictures can be interpreted in several ways.

▶ *Post-millennialists* take the optimistic view: Christ's return follows his millennial reign, as the church expands his rule of love; eventually, after a short last-ditch revolt by evil, which is easily put down, heavenly paradise ensues.

▶ *Pre-millennialists* promote the pessimistic view: Christ's return and then millennial reign are future, only coming after the difficulties of church history, which would end with the most cataclysmic take-over bid by evil, the totalitarian dictatorship to outdo all, led by the devil himself.

▶ *A-millennialists* follow the neutral, more realistic view: history has its ups and downs, and Christ's reign of peace is no literal 1,000 years, but began at his resurrection, is revealed and actualised fully when he returns, and lasts for ever.

These different pictures come from trying to iron out poetry into prose – always a precarious exercise! However, the constant in all this is that the future is not faceless, uncertain or unknown, but is in the hands of Jesus. He is the Lord of the ultimate future. As such, we can be certain that the ultimate results of the future – the 'Day of Judgement' of life, the universe and everything! – will be according to his standards, as revealed in his life, death and resurrection. So they will be consistent with his 'way' of love and justice.

The Second Coming of Jesus is not some space-time event like Zarquon turning up a second before the 'Big Crunch', which is just another 'so what?' event. It is the end of the space-time continuum as we know it, and the introduction of a new form of reality (a new heaven and a new Earth). If Jesus ends history and transforms the whole of reality, then it is through him that the whole picture emerges, and through him that the full meaning of it all is disclosed.

'Death is irrelevant!'

What about the problem of death, where life and everything

ends for us as individuals? And what of the remarkable claim of the Borg? In the *TNG* story, *The Best of Both Worlds*, the Borg have captured Jean-Luc Picard. He defies them:

PICARD:	I will resist you with my last ounce of strength!
BORG:	Strength is irrelevant. Resistance is futile.

PICARD: Impossible. My culture is based on freedom and self-determination.

BORG: Freedom is irrelevant. Self-determination is irrelevant.

PICARD: We would rather die!

BORG: Death is irrelevant!

To the human mind, this response is truly shocking. How can you fight an enemy for whom death is irrelevant? They stand against everything humanity believes in. No doubt the writers meant the machine-like element, the 'cybernetic' part of the 'cybernetic organism', here: machines can't feel, and can't be bothered by emotions like the threat of death. A similar mechanical relentlessness is portrayed with the Cybermen in *Doctor Who*, for example in the story *The Five Doctors*. Death doesn't matter to machines; so how can you fight a killing machine?

In practice, this has been exaggerated in the interests of a scary story. Death does matter, even to the Borg and the Cybermen! They are portrayed as sentient realities for whom there is a difference between existence and non-existence. Indeed, most Cybermen stories are based on the very need for survival. In *The Tenth Planet*, Mondas is dying, and the

Cybermen with it, so they plan to kidnap Earth. In *The Tomb of the Cybermen*, the Cybercontroller defiantly protests, 'We will survive!' In fact, the whole reason for the complex trap they spring to ensnare logically adroit humans is to kidnap their bodies and cybernetically alter them to ensure their race does not die.

Similarly, in *TNG* and *Voyager* the Borg seek new worlds to assimilate. Given the choice of survival or the complete elimination of all Borg, they don't consider it a matter of indifference. In practice, in all stories, notably in the film *First Contact*, they work very hard to stay alive. The only way in which the defiant boast 'Death is irrelevant!' is true is that death is irrelevant for any particular *individual* so long as the hive as a whole thrives. This is certainly realistic. Many life-forms would take that attitude. Our highly individualistic culture recoils at the loss of personality, where the hive is all, the individual nothing. But even here we consider it heroic when a person risks death, and dies for another. In family life we see it at its strongest, where parents act recklessly to save their children.

But in the full-blooded sense implied, death is far from irrelevant to the Borg. And it is not irrelevant to us. It is worth recalling, however, that there is both this individual element and the collective. It *does* matter to us whether others live or die. (Just imagine eternity on your own, stuck on the Moon, if you doubt that!) The meaning of the universe is not simply a selfish concern for personal survival! And as the Bible says in 1 Corinthians 15:26, death is the 'last enemy', the last evil to be overcome. But that is also part of the ultimate victory of Jesus at the heart of the Bible's message.

Regeneration, reincarnation, resurrection

What comes after the end? The end is personal death, and is far from irrelevant! But in SF, as it becomes fantasy, death has a habit of not being the end. Leonard Nimoy commented once in *Star Trek Memories* that this being science fiction, Spock's death in *Star Trek II: The Wrath of Khan* may not turn out to be the end after all! Sure enough, the next film resurrected him. As we have seen, Spock's soul (*katra*) separated from the body and, together with the Genesis planet, brought Spock back from the grave. Not to be outdone, William Shatner has not been satisfied to see Kirk dead, and in his *Star Trek* novels has had him somehow resurrected.

Doctor Who has famously turned this into a saving feature of its story. The Doctor is held to be an alien, from Gallifrey, whose race has a facility at the point of 'death' to rejuvenate or regenerate. Is the resulting 'new' Doctor basically the same as his predecessors, with a few minor superficial changes, or a radically different person, with a personality vastly at odds with his previous selves? That's one of the debating points among *Doctor Who* writers.

Terrance Dicks is a prolific writer of *Doctor Who* scripts and novels, including *The Eight Doctors*, which takes place immediately after the 1996 film, in which the latest Doctor is seen as chaotically drawn by time travelling politics into meeting each of his previous 'selves'. Dicks is of the school that emphasises continuity between the Doctors. By contrast, the story *The Trial of a Time Lord* has a kind of materially realised amalgam of the twelfth and thirteenth versions of the Doctor supposedly expressing the darker side of the Doctor, a Machiavellian personality no better than the Master. So this can clearly be argued both ways by Whovians!

Life after death – the real thing – is one of the big questions. In a way, this picture of regeneration has some similarities to reincarnation, which is one of the major answers to the question of what happens after death. Reincarnation is an increasingly fashionable belief in Western societies. As it has its roots in Eastern religion, it is worth noting that what it means to Westerners is almost exactly the opposite of what it means to Hindus and Buddhists. These religions talk of the cycle of return – the idea that in life we are trapped, and will not achieve the salvation of immersion into the Ocean of Being or Nirvana if we fail to achieve enlightenment. In the case of failure, we are obliged to return to life all over again. Reincarnation in the Eastern tradition represents failure to achieve the true goal of the after-life. It is the failure to find salvation. Among those Westerners taking it up, it has an altogether different resonance. The Western tradition of beliefs about life after death has been dominated by the doubts philosophers have raised concerning the Christian picture of personal salvation into community with God and all the redeemed in heaven. The atheistic tradition has gathered pace and helped bring about an increased sense of disengagement from God, and so from the sense of life with him after death.

However, most people don't want to think that after they die, that's it. So the idea of reincarnation comes in as a replacement. They like to think that just as the Doctor (Sylvester McCoy) dies having been shot and then regenerates into the new Doctor (Paul McGann), so when they die they'll have another attempt at life.

That is an odd view because it doesn't even have the virtue

of the Eastern picture that if we finally get to sort out the meaning of life, achieving enlightenment, we will escape this otherwise endless pattern, and reach a real goal beyond life as we know it. In this Western reincarnation picture, the aim is to keep on repeating life as we know it, without achieving anything. What's more, there are serious philosophical problems about the continuity of the personality, the identity of the self, in reincarnation: who *am* I, if I could previously have been both Francis of Assisi and Adolf Hitler? Evidence for reincarnation is popularly held to come with memories of previous lives, and previous-life therapy is in vogue in some circles. The first famous case of this in the West, a lady with the assumed name of Miss Hélène Smith, began revealing memories of previous lives, like Marie Antoinette, but also included memories of a previous life on Mars. She spoke 'Martian' and described the Martian landscape. Unfortunately for devotees, her descriptions are nothing like what we now know Mars is like, and her Martian was suspiciously close to French.

This occult knowledge is pseudo-knowledge. The main characteristic in such situations, even those with a genuinely supernatural element, is that what is revealed is what the listeners want to hear. Michael White recalls a similar personal story in *The Science of the X-Files*.[1] He tells of really getting interested in Ouija experiments when his group of 15-year-old boys made contact with 'Alan Kalak 7' who allegedly came from Saturn. White comments that this was not the real Saturn, but one 'in a parallel universe, in which the planet was inhabitable'. Double-think, of course, but what such boys wanted to be told.

One vital thing to spot about reincarnation, both versions

of it, is that it is very different from the picture of the Jewish, Christian and for that matter Muslim picture of the after-life. This comes at its sharpest in the Christian faith of the New Testament, as pictures of life after death in the Old Testament are rare, and come more by implication than statement. Jews by the time of Jesus were famously divided on the issue, with Sadducees heading up the traditionalist view that since heaven is not mentioned in the earliest books of the Bible, it's a new-fangled idea that a true believer ought to reject. Pharisees were strongly committed the other way, accepting among other things the reality of resurrection from the dead.

The central Christian claim is that Jesus of Nazareth, after his crucifixion in front of religious and political leaders, rose from death. And he didn't simply achieve resuscitation, re-emergence after death for an extra few weeks or years, but resurrection, the proper conquest of death, which precipitates resurrection for all; the way to eternity with God for all.

Resurrection is different from reincarnation. It says that the person who died is the same one who rises again in the next life. There is a degree of discontinuity: the previous body was mortal, and subject to the ravages of time, it was only a 'living body'; the resurrection body will be immortal, free from such deterioration. It will be a 'spiritual body'. And to be a spiritual body means to be in unbroken harmony with God and all others.

• 25 •
Tears of the Prophets

In the hands of the prophets

One clear sign of change in SF during the 1990s was the place of prophecy. *Star Trek* itself is of course a kind of predictive prophecy of the future. For Roddenberry, the fantasy element helped to develop the drama, but the whole point was to imagine what he expected the future to become. However, when we look in the original series, we are hard pressed to find prophecies of the future unless they are placed in the past. Perhaps the strongest example is the speech Roddenberry has Harlan Ellison's Sister Edith Keeler give. Ellison's character is from the 1930s and a mixture of suffragette, Pentecostal preacher and Salvation Army worker. Kirk and Spock enter a time-travel porthole into that era. Roddenberry has her make a rather unlikely speech to the unemployed, where she speaks of a future of interstellar space travel.

But prophetic predictions and other marks of prophecy lie at the heart of *DS9*. The almost godlike powerful aliens that live in and sustain the stable wormhole near *DS9* are held to be 'the Prophets' for the highly religious but also ancient and advanced Bajoran people. They have given various 'orbs of prophecy' which have been treasured by the Bajorans, and which foster religious experience. These include deep personal insight into oneself, visions of the future, and prophetic insight ('words of wisdom and knowledge') into the present and best future for others.

Babylon 5 also holds a variety of prophecies at the heart of its story, with its 900-year-old prophecies central to Minbari culture, and Centauri prophecies of personal fate.

Dimensions in time and eternity

What is the rationale of prophecy in SF? Is it religious, occult, alien, scientific or some mixture? In *DS9*, the fact that the wormhole aliens are non-temporal, i.e. timeless, is significant. If non-temporal aliens were possible, they could see events in time together, including what for us is the future. If we could somehow communicate with them, we might be able to hear the future. In this way what is basically a religious idea – faith for the future, because the prophets have foretold the way ahead for us – is given a science fiction context.

One of the contexts for prophecy in *B5* is time travel. Although time travel is not routine, as in *Doctor Who*, or regular, as in *Star Trek*, its one instance is central to the overarching story of *B5*. *Babylon 4* disappeared mysteriously just after becoming operational. Then, in a Season 1 story, it reappeared just as suddenly four years later, only to disappear again. A couple of years later this is explained as instabilities in the fabric of time promoted by the 'great machine of Epsilon 3'. The upshot of all this is that original *B5* captain, Jeffrey Sinclair, knows he has to go back in time on a one-way journey taking *Babylon 4* with him, to enable the historic defeat of the destructive Shadows 1,000 years earlier (*c.* AD 1260). Because he knows the future, his prophecies, which are treasured in Minbari society, all prove true. Similarly, the instability in time allows Delenn to glimpse a moment a few weeks hence, and Sheridan to pre-live a dangerous time 17 years ahead of time. So the first *B5* answer is through time travel.

The second is left far more open. Various societies are portrayed as having telepaths – a facility apparently instigated in each case by the Vorlons. Also several races, particularly the Centauri, are shown as having prophets, seers. Whether this is an aspect of telepathy or separate from it is not spelled out. But these prophecies follow the religious pattern, and turn out to be valid.

In the *B5* story, *Point of No Return* (3:9), the prophetess Lady Morella (strikingly played by Majel Barrett, the widow of *Star Trek*'s Gene Roddenberry) appears on the station at the request of Centauri Ambassador Londo Mollari, who wants her, as a seer, to 'see' for him: 'I believe . . . I am meant for something greater,' he says. 'A greater darkness or a greater good I can no longer say.' She tells him that fire lies ahead, but he has three opportunities to avoid it: 'You must save the eye that does not see. You must not kill the one who is already dead. And at the last, you must surrender yourself to your greatest fear, knowing that it will destroy you.' She then adds the killer punchline that both Londo and Vir will become Centauri Emperor – the one after the other has died.

In the fullness of time the prophecy becomes clear. 'The eye that does not see' refers to G'Kar, who loses his eye to Centauri mad emperor Cartagia. (Later Dr Franklin gives him an artificial working eye, after the Narns are freed in Season 4.) Shadow agent Morden is revealed as 'the one who is already dead'. That Londo should surrender himself could mean:

▶ his readiness to die to avoid Vorlon destruction of his world;

▶ to be controlled by a Drakh keeper, to save his world;

▶ his acceptance of death at G'Kar's hands to enable Sheridan and Delenn to escape Centauri Prime, and so, perhaps, begin to instigate the freeing of that world from Drakh control.

Vir becomes emperor after Londo's death. Also, Londo's prophetic dreams come true, like his 'seeing' of the Shadows above Centauri Prime.

Doctor Who played prophecies purely as a feature of knowledge gained through time travel. In this way, Vicki can play prophetess in *The Myth Makers*. No mystery here. By contrast, *The X-Files* plays up the mystery. The sense that there are mysteries beyond science, or at least beyond current science, is dominant. But the angle tends to be uncanny insight into present feelings and past experiences of others rather than predictive prophecy. In *Beyond the Sea*, the criminal character Boggs 'channels' a variety of people with uncanny results. In *Miracle Man*, healer Samuel tells Mulder the truth about his feelings for his missing sister, with what Christian charismatics might call a 'word of knowledge'.

What is prophecy?

Babylon 5 and *DS9* develop something nearer real prophecy. Londo Mollari experiences what was dreamed and prophesied. What's more, this true element is not made dependent on fatalism either: the future remains open. Captain Sisko is obliged to be the Emissary, bringing religious and cultural renewal to Bajor, and in his visions and prophecies fulfilled in *Rapture* and later stories.

In *DS9*, room for uncertainty is left, and this provides the opportunity for a naturalistic 'scientific' explanation to squeeze through, both through the deliberate cracks in the stories ('odd neural patterns', 'odd synaptic potential') and the powers of timeless aliens. But the implication of the story is that prophecy happens and is sometimes amazingly true, even though we don't know why. This is far from the old approach, which always gave a clear implication that a 'prophecy' would only come true because the speaker had used a naturalistic (but hidden) means of securing the knowledge it paraded as 'prophecy'.

Biblical prophecy always has two main dimensions: foretelling and forth-telling, and they are connected. Forth-telling concerns the words spoken as God's message to the people now. It might be a word of comfort (e.g. Isaiah 40:1ff.), a call to repentance (Isaiah 1:1–17), or a bit of both (Hosea 11). But it also implies action for the future, which is where the foretelling comes in. Foretelling in the Bible is not straight prediction, because that implies a fatalistic world in which, whatever we do now, the future is irredeemably fixed. The whole point of the famous story of Jonah is that it isn't.

The point of prophecy is to change attitudes and behaviour, not to show fate at work. Jonah is told to give the hated Ninevites a prophetic message: 'Forty more days and Nineveh will be destroyed.' A bit of a bleak sermon! Jonah wants to avoid doing this – hence his famous escapade with the big fish. This is not because he is against declaring the destruction of his enemy, but because he fears that they might actually hear and repent, and then God would not destroy them. He is right: 'When God saw what they did and how they turned from their evil ways, he had compassion and did not bring upon them the destruction he had threatened' (Jonah 3:10). Prophecy leads to changed behaviour, so the doom prophesied never happens.

Biblical prophecy is not fate. It declares God's will – and that turns on human response. Jonah is famously huffy because the Ninevites repent: 'I knew that you are a gracious and compassionate God, slow to anger and abounding in love' (Jonah 4:2). Jonah wants them destroyed, not forgiven. God then gives him an object lesson in care. He shows that Jonah is concerned for a mere plant, and then says: 'Nineveh has more than a hundred and twenty thousand people . . . Should I not be concerned about that great city?' (verse 11). The prophecy of doom is lifted because they repent. Indeed, the prophecy of destruction is given in order to provide them with the opportunity to repent and make the prophecy false!

That doesn't mean prophecy is subjective – that just what a person *feels* is right – and the stories we have looked at show this well enough. Londo is troubled by the vision he is given of being killed. He doesn't see it as only feelings. But the futures expressed in Centauri prophecies have that provisional aspect: it depends on what you do about it. To use a philosophical word, it is 'contingent' rather than fixed, and to that extent is similar to prophecy in the Bible.

So prophecy can be true, within its context, with the proviso that responses to it can affect it. But in the Bible true prophecy can and should be distinguished from false prophecy. Deuteronomy 13 and 18 give the two main litmus paper tests in the Bible:

▶ Deuteronomy 18:21 gives the obvious test: predictive prophecies that don't happen are false. That is the test of factual truth.

▶ The other test is of spiritual truth. Deuteronomy 13:1–4 says that a prophet may predict something that actually happens, but if he or she urges people to follow and worship other gods, then that is also false prophecy. False prophecy can come true! But it is a false prophecy because it calls people to worship a false god.

The false gods of that time bound the people up in a nature/fertility religion, which included cultic prostitution and infant sacrifice. In our time, prophecies are a growth industry, including in esoteric and dangerous cults. When comet Hale-Bopp shone brightly in 1997, the Heaven's Gate sect followed the prophecy that it was a visitor from the heavens to take them off into heavenly realms. All they had to do was commit suicide! For people who say that all beliefs are of equal value and truth, it is vital to emphasise that wrong beliefs and wrong choices can be catastrophic.

However, *true* prophecy also happens today. There's the forth-telling element, in preaching and prophetic social comment. And there's also the foretelling element. Both can overlap. Christians commonly experience a number of things we might call prophetic:

▶ The sense of being guided to do something or to say something in prayer; something that proves to be right and helpful to someone, and is shown to be just what they needed.

▶ Words of strikingly relevant encouragement.

▶ Surprising practical wisdom to help solve a problem.
▶ Special knowledge or insight to help a person.

The last three are often called 'words of encouragement', 'words of wisdom' and 'words of knowledge', on the basis of Paul's words in 1 Corinthians 12:8; 14:3, 6, 26. They are rather like Sisko's words in *Rapture* to Bajorans keen to receive prophetically inspired guidance. The difference is that the Christian claim is not just about mental powers facilitated by alien powers, Vorlons or non-linear aliens, 'prophets' of the wormhole, or even by spirits or natural human psychic abilities.

The claim is that the God who made every wormhole and every species, no matter how advanced or different, and who made every human and every spirit, is the one at work in Jesus and in the Holy Spirit. God himself guides and inspires, in prophecy as elsewhere. True prophecy comes only from God. All other prophecy, supernatural knowledge or power from a source other than God is therefore openness to the reality that is opposed to God, i.e. the demonic.

Life and faith at the end of the twenty-first century

Trying to anticipate the future is far from easy! What if H. G. Wells had built a real time machine in 1895, not just a story, and had been able to take Queen Victoria forward 100 years? What would she have made of the changes in this century? Maybe SF's predictions are among the easiest. To have predicted air flight or even space travel is one thing. I suspect she would not have guessed at the political changes, still less the social ones. The last century has been described as the sexual century, and I guess the changes here would have staggered the Queen.

In practice it's easier to predict things that are a continuation of the present than it is to foresee radical changes. Few people expected apartheid to end so relatively peacefully. Just a few did forecast the collapse of communism, like Andrei Amalrik, who was sent to a labour camp in 1970 for writing *Will the Soviet Union Survive Until 1984?* He was only seven years out! When I heard a Czech dissident in the 1970s say of Prague Spring leader Alexander Dubček: 'And then an extraordinary thing happened, a one in a hundred chance: a genuinely good man became the leader of the Communist Party!' I thought, 'Yes, but it's not enough to happen in Czechoslovakia. The way communism will end throughout eastern Europe is when a genuinely good man becomes leader of the Soviet Union.' It was just a private thought. Effectively, with Mikhail Gorbachev, that's what happened. Again in the 1970s a friend of mine openly predicted the Shah would fall five years before it happened.

But can we predict not five but 100 years on? We assume all the changes taking place today will simply be extrapolated indefinitely into the future. But will they? Predictions of this kind in 1900 would have been wildly out, with assumptions of ever-increasing European empires, and sexual restraint, and only predictions of air and space travel, the SF predictions, proving true! Will democracy thrive as most assume, or collapse under the increasing weight of voter selfishness, media manipulation or forces completely unpredictable? Will the family continue to collapse, and be replaced by people leading increasingly isolated lives, as we see now, or will it reach a point where this collapse sets new social processes, forcing either new collective groups or a resurgence of supportive and committed families? Will religion and the institutional forms of church continue their twentieth-century decline in the West, or have the changes leading to new vibrant forms of Christian faith and life only just begun? Perhaps a new form of religion will dominate, as Islam came to dominate North Africa and Turkey in the seventh and fifteenth centuries. Will advanced aliens (if they exist), Vulcan or otherwise, decide that now is the time to make first contact? How that would change us is hard to predict! Or will Jesus return, ending history before 2100?

The destiny of humanity

What is the destiny of humanity? What is our future? Can it be prophesied – or even guessed at? We could ask this in a cultural way. Is our destiny to make our way among the stars? Could it be in discovering alien races of comparable or even greater sophistication than ourselves, or in discovering thousands of planets, and finding that none of them has any signs of life? Or could it be to destroy ourselves by abusing weapons of mass destruction, ecological disasters, or even some of the more exotic disasters SF has conceived, allowing some form of machine to corrupt, enslave or destroy us? Could it be in experiments with institutions aiming towards world government, where we find newer and better ways of helping all our peoples to work together, embracing the whole world with a democracy through which everyone votes, and no one is left in poverty and famine? Or could it be in forms of world government coupled with new technologies that permit the development of a totalitarian nightmare unparalleled in history? Or will the current split between the rich world and the poor world deepen? These and many other issues are the proper stuff of science fiction. It is well placed to hold these dreams and nightmares before us, to challenge us and remind us of where we are (or could be) headed.

In this book we have seen that the question of life elsewhere in the universe has largely shifted from the solar system to the planets just being discovered outside it. Maybe within 20 years it will be possible to determine whether any terrestrial-type planets with oxygen atmospheres (M-class in *Star Trek* jargon) exist on nearby stars. Alien sightings and abductions say more about the spiritual vacuum in our culture than new scientific discoveries. We are only beginning to acknowledge our ability to destroy ourselves by long-term climate change, or worse by Chernobyl-type disasters, with nuclear waste problems rumbling in our oceans and under our soil for millennia. The more exotic nightmares dreamed up purely to alarm and entertain probably won't happen. But the more prosaic ones probably will.

We could treat this in a more philosophical way: What is our true destiny as a species? Above and beyond the actual ups and downs of history, what is the final truth about us as a species? Who are we, and where should we be heading in order to fulfil our destiny? The Doctor is not human. In *The Ark in Space*, he soliloquises:

'Homo sapiens. What an inventive, invincible species. It's only a few million years since they crawled up out of the mud and learned to walk. Puny, defenceless bipeds. They've survived flood, famine and plague. They've survived cosmic wars and holocausts. And now, here they are, out among the stars, waiting to begin a new life. Ready to out-sit eternity. They're indomitable.'

Who are we? What is our role? What is our destiny? Those evocative words at the start of the Bible spell it out: 'God created man in his own image, in the image of God he created him; male and female he created them. God blessed them and said to them, "Be fruitful and increase in number; fill the earth and subdue it. Rule over the fish of the sea and the birds of the air and over ever living creature that moves on the ground."'

We have a destiny that in this life includes an earthward and a heavenward – a physical and a spiritual – dimension. We are to rule as God does, by looking after this planet, and perhaps others. We are to be ecological stewards – those who rule with knowledge. We must develop our science, not just in the sense of acquisition of straight facts, but also the development of wisdom. We are set as physical creatures to relate to one another in expression of that highest quality in God that is to be reflected in his image in us: love for one another. This is where the physical and spiritual intersect, because as spiritual beings we are called to this love that is God. We are called to love God, and to be changed for ever by that love, learning to love all others – a task to take us through life and beyond.

We could also take this spiritually. What is our destiny before the court of eternity? I have argued that God is no alien, but real. So what is our future before him, both individually and as a community? The heart of Christian faith is that Jesus, the Son of God, became a human being. His mission is for our salvation. And that means bringing humanity into the very presence of the Godhead. Our destiny, achieved in principle by Jesus, is to be a redeemed people, with God and in God, totally taken up in the reality and enormity of his love for ever. It is a personal destiny, and it is a community destiny.

Resurrection pictures each individual transformed for eternity. Heaven pictures us together for eternity.[1] The truth is out there. It really is. Not just a fact or two, however extraordinary, but a truth to change each one of us for ever.

• 26•
The Voyage Home

Science fiction and faith

So how do SF and faith match up? Are they hopeless enemies of each other, each aiming to occupy the same ground?

I hope by now it has become clear that the relation has more positive potential than that. Science fiction raises questions. Its roots are firmly in humanism, both that of the Renaissance (the human hope) and that of the Enlightenment (the future of science). But there are other aspects to all this. Christians need to hear some of the questions that the best SF provokes. In turn, SF raises questions for which Christians have some very interesting answers. Many of the themes we've looked at have, I trust, shown something of this potential. What's more, as we have seen repeatedly, *DS9* and *B5* in particular have shown a less rigorously negative humanistic and atheistic outlook.

Either way, the questions remain open.

I. How Christianity scores in SF

There remains the continuing fascination within much SF with the 'What if?' questions and in particular, 'What if aliens have already visited this planet and surreptitiously interfered with our (religious) history?' *Stargate SG-1* is just as full of this one as *Doctor Who*. Even *Babylon 5* assumes this, though with characteristic subtlety. (The Vorlons have been to many worlds posing as angels, and took Jack the Ripper, along with others, for their purposes.) The path from this 'What if?' to assuming that the old gods were aliens is rapidly travelled. And the implication that you can assume all modern gods are also alien con tricks is not far behind. But you hit trouble when, as with the aforementioned *Xena* programme, you turn implication into explicit statement that a godlike Krishna, worshipped by today's Hindus, is part of your fiction. And Gene Roddenberry was very keen to rubbish the biblical God this way. Table 1 shows how earlier episodes treated Christian interests. But more recent programmes at least often recognise that religious belief is real and important to believers. They also assume that such belief will continue into the interstellar age. And with a programme as well thought out as *Babylon 5*, the ways that such beliefs will work out, and how believers and others interact, are well portrayed.

Table 1: How religion scored in SF 1960–90				
Programme	*Star Trek: TOS* and *TNG*	*Doctor Who* and *Blake's 7*	*Hitch-hiker's Guide*	*Star Wars*
Old gods as aliens	✓	✓	✗	✗
Today's gods as aliens	✓	✗	✗	✗
Angels as aliens	✗	✗	✗	✗
Religion as primitive	✓	✓	?	—
Aliens have visited Earth	✓	✓	✓	—

Future Earth religions	X	X	✓	—
Some heroes are Christian	X	X	X	—

Table 2: How religion scores in SF 1990–2000

Programme	Star Trek: DS9 and VOY	Doctor Who (books)	B5	Stargate SG-1	X-Files	Far-scape
Old gods as aliens	X	✓	X	✓	X	X
Today's gods as aliens	X	X	X	✓	X	X
Angels as aliens	X	?	✓	?	X	X
Religion as primitive	X	?	X	✓?	X	X
Aliens have visited Earth	✓	✓	✓	✓	✓	✓
Future Earth religions	✓	✓	✓	—	—	✓
Some heroes are Christian	X	✓	✓	X?	✓	X

2. How SF scores with Christianity

Even more significant is the way in which issues important to Christians are played out. It is worth recognising that for some Christians, SF would be seen as a no-go area, not because they happen not to be interested in it, but because they see it as likely to be spiritually misleading.

In some ways, this can be a bit like the attitude that rejects rock music. It is sound to recognise that some rock music, like some SF, can be rooted in heavily occult ideas and can be spiritually unhelpful. But that is just as true of some classical music and some examples of other forms of fiction. So the attempt to advise Christians to avoid all SF is only consistent with avoiding all culture – a ghetto attitude that is arguable (as we saw in Chapter 17) but unhelpful. Instead we should promote Christian engagement with SF, rock music and other forms of culture, modern and classical. Our view is that Christian faith and life is true to itself not when it hides in the ghetto, but when it claims the market-place in free, open discussion with the cultures of the world. 'Be as shrewd as snakes and as innocent as doves' (Matthew 10:16). Meanwhile, a comparison of shows from the secularising 1960s (see Table 3) with those of today's spiritually more ambiguous climate (see Table 4) shows far less change. Instead the contrast is between *Star Trek*'s continuing optimistic humanism, and the more realistic or even pessimistic picture elsewhere.

Table 3: Issues for Christians in SF 1960–90

Programme	Star Trek: TOS and TNG	Doctor Who	Blake's 7	Hitch-hiker's Guide	Star Wars
What it believes in	Science; human goodness	Doing good	Fighting tyranny	Humour	The Force
Evolutionary humanism?	✓	✗	✗	✗	✗
Occult elements?	✗	✓	✗	✓	✓

Table 4: Issues for Christians in SF 1990–2000						
Programme	*Star Trek: DS9* and *VOY*	*Doctor Who* (books)	*B5*	*Stargate SG-1*	*X-Files*	*Far-scape*
What it believes in	Science; human goodness	Fighting monsters	Working together	Adven-ture	Duplicity	Getting through
Evolutionary humanism?	✓	✗	✗	✗	✗	✗
Occult elements?	✓	✓	✗	✓	✓	✓

What's more, SF themes can usefully and naturally raise issues important to Christians. Some programmes will be more appropriate than others. *Star Trek*, because it is the most well known, is probably the easiest to adopt, but as allegory or to raise issues. The same is possible with *Star Wars* and *Doctor Who*. But for me, the best of the lot is *Babylon 5* (and its successor, *Babylon: Crusade*), a truly extra-ordinary programme for its depth, richness and subtlety. Unusually, it is one where a second or even third viewing can be more enriching than the first, because of the number of subtle features you only really see the second or third time. This takes it beyond the level of SF soap and into SF epic status. So it will be fitting to close with something from that series.

Conclusion: a sermon according to *Babylon 5*

I gave extracts of this book to a conference of Baptist theologians in ministry in August 1999, at which one participant, the then Baptist President Michael Bochenski, suggested that some of the themes from SF on TV are today's sermons. One example that has provoked a sermon thought for me comes from the Season 1 episode *Signs and Portents*. This is the first appearance of the Shadow agent, Morden. He appears with his deceptively simple question, 'What do you want?' The other crucial question is, 'Who are you?' Earlier, G'Kar highlighted this by commenting, 'Everyone here is not what they seem.' Straczynski explains the force of this and the other repeated question:

 'The show is built around two fundamental questions for the first couple or three years, the first being "Who are you?", the second being "What do you want?" – on the theory that the answers to those questions can either make you or they can destroy you depending on the order in which they are asked or answered. If you know who you are before someone asks you what you want, the answer will probably be fairly constructive. If you had not gone through that process of self-examination and somebody asks you "What do you want?", that answer might lead you into a more destructive path. So those questions are pivotal.'[1]

So pivotal that those who have seen the successor series *Babylon: Crusade* will know they come explicitly in the title sequence. 'Who are you? What do you want?' These questions can be asked of the key characters.

Who are you?

▶ Delenn: victim instigating the Earth/Minbari war, becoming the agent of reconciliation.

▶ Sheridan: scourge of Minbar, becoming the reconciler, President of the Alliance, on Minbar.

▶ Sinclair: uncertain and driven, until he discovers his calling to be Valen.

▶ Franklin: runs away from the question into work, until literal workaholism overtakes. Only then does he face the question directly.

▶ G'Kar: begins as victim seeking revenge, later is ready to be the vicarious sacrifice, his Narns dying that others might live.

▶ Londo: answers 'What do you want?' with Centauri glory, at the expense of a holocaust, only later beginning to hear 'Who are you?' to be the agent of a greater good or a greater evil.

▶ Vir: unwitting helpless assistant, later risking being a force for good.

We could press this further with Marcus, Garibaldi, Bester and so many others. But this question can also be asked of the leading characters of the Bible.

▶ Abraham: uncertain prince then man of faith.

▶ Moses: fugitive then Israel's liberator.

▶ Elijah: loner then leader.

▶ Peter: reactive, volatile loudmouth then reliable, inspirational leader.

▶ Paul: religious bigot then apostle of love.

Above all, Jesus faces the questions 'Who are you?' and 'What do you want?' directly and in the right way when tempted in the desert as recorded in Matthew 4. The devil twists the 'Who are you?' question ('If you are the Son of God . . .') into a 'What do you want?' question: Do you want things for yourself such as fame and power? Jesus turns it back into a 'Who are you?' question, answering in effect: Since I am the Son of God, I will hear God, obey him, worship him.

What do you want? (for self)	**Who are you?** (Son of God)
Self-seeker? (bread)	Seeker after God's word
Publicity-seeker? (jump off temple)	Seeker after God's will
Power-seeker? (world empire)	Seeker after God, to worship him

But this question is profoundly important for Christians too. We need to recognise that the question 'Who are you?' comes first. And the answer is that we are made in the image of God; we are children of God, for whom Christ died in love; we are a new creation in Christ. If we recognised this before we pressed the question 'What do you want?' more often, we would be truer to our Christian faith. We need to hear this question in general, but also in detail. Sinclair has a specific calling, and so does G'Kar. But they are different. We need to ask the question not only in general, but personally. Who are you? Who are you, as an individual before God? Are you called? Have you a sense of mission? Are you running away from yourself, like Franklin? Hiding behind a sense of martyrdom, like Marcus? 'Who are you?' And then, having understood that, we ask, 'What do you want?'

This insight from Straczynski, particularly in its Christian application, certainly is a rich sermon. The same is true of the extended questions in the opening sequence to *Babylon:*

Crusade, with the questions 'Where are you going?' and 'Who do you serve and who do you trust?' Used selectively, with integrity, wisdom and discernment, there are many such insights we could apply.

Appendix One:
Six Christian Youth Talks

1. All Alone in the Night? (Are we alone?)
2. Is the Truth Really Out There? (Truth claims such as Jesus saying he is the truth.)
3. Man and Superman. (Why supermen save us.)
4. The Search for Spock. (Spock and the question of our humanity.)
5. Resistance Is Futile. (The struggle with evil.)
6. The Voyage Home. (The ultimate, final questions: meaning, the end, heaven, etc.)

I followed these main themes for a series of talks to our church's Boys' Brigade: a group of lads aged 10 to 15. Not all are fans of *Star Trek*, but by including *Star Wars, Doctor Who* and *Babylon 5*, the interest of the boys was maintained with good, engaging interaction. This gives one example of how SF questions might be worked through in a Christian context. So here is a brief summary of these talks.

1. All Alone in the Night?

Do aliens exist? Share a discussion and help them to express their viewpoints.

If aliens do exist what do we think they are like? Again, obtain viewpoints.

Who made God? It's a classic question. Some people say that God was an alien in disguise, but if so, who made him? And if a superior alien made him, who made that superior being? And so on. What's at the end of the line? Are we alone in the universe? The discovery of aliens will not meet the human need for company any more than Columbus's discovery of alien humans did. God alone meets that ultimate need.

2. Is the Truth Really Out There?

What do people believe in? Present various models of aliens including Ferengi, Klingons, Daleks, Darth Vader, etc., and ask about what they believe in. Obtain obvious answers: Ferengi believe in the Rules of Acquisition (commercial greed); Klingons believe in glory, courage, and above all honour; Daleks believe in exterminating everyone, so they alone rule the universe, etc. Then encourage them to join you on a flight of fancy. What if we were actually to meet such aliens, and as a result one of these creatures decided to become a Christian? What difference would it make? What about a Ferengi no longer believing in Rules of Acquisition, but in Jesus and his two great commandments of love? A Klingon no longer thinking honour and death in battle the most important thing, but loving your neighbour? A Dalek no longer exterminating, but being compassionate? What difference does it make for us?

3. Man and Superman

What saves people? Is it technology? Or an alien (like Superman)? Salvation is about the ultimate future, but also about the change that happens in our lives. What if we've got our lives in a real mess? Who or what can save us? Develop and comment briefly on the *B5* answer outlined in Chapter 15: people face problems and gain help, e.g. from friends, leaders and ministers. Christian experience is that God helps us in real ways. He gives us insight and inspiration through his Spirit.

4. The Search for Spock

Show pictures of Spock, the eighth Doctor Who, Delenn and Q. Who is the odd one out? (Q – the others are half-human; Q isn't.) Then Davros, Darth Vader, Borg and Data. Who is the odd one out? (Data – the rest are part living/part machine; he is all machine trying to be human.) Lead towards discussion of Spock. Is he human? Is he like anyone you know? Who does he spar with? (Bones.) What's he like? How human is Data? Or Odo? The Emergency Medical Hologram? These nearly human characters show us in a different way what *we* are as humans. Ask what the differences are between such characters and humans. Daleks and Cybermen (and Borg) show us we can lose our humanity. Our humanity is in our relationships. God has made us that way because that's the way *he* is. He is the God of love.

5. Resistance Is Futile

Show picture of Darth Maul. Who's that? What's he look like? (Satan!) What is Satan/the devil? Discuss evil, and their images of it. Is Darth Vader ever good? (Yes, at the end of *Return of the Jedi*.) Are the Daleks ever good? (You'd have thought not, but the exception is *The Evil of the Daleks* where many are transformed by the Doctor, giving them the 'human factor'. What is that? Friendships, forgiveness, courage, compassion.) Who is worse, Darth Vader or Palpatine? (Palpatine. Darth Vader repents at the end.) How do people get to be so evil? (Discuss Anakin to Vader; motives for evil – power, anger, lust, etc.)

How can evil be defeated? A quick technical fix? Not really. With Luke Skywalker, it's by being ready to die. By war? Historically, after the First World War nations tried to make Germany pay for their evil. The Second World War resulted 21 years later, and far more countries were invaded. For Christians, evil is ultimately overcome by Jesus. In the desert he faced temptation and successfully resisted it. Throughout his life he showed obedience to his Father. Ultimately he faced evil down, on the cross. That is a victory of love.

6. The Voyage Home

What is the meaning of life? Part of it is the meaning we feel it has, and part is the real meaning. Let's take the question about what we feel is important first. What do we think is the most important thing in life? (Show relevant poster pictures for the following.) What's the most important thing for Palpatine? (Absolute power.) Or the Daleks? (To destroy all competition, all alien life.) What's most important for Data? (To be and become as human as possible.) For Spock? (To be logical.) For Bones? (To express human emotion.) What's most important for Janeway? (Getting home, making her team work.) For Kirk? (To boldly go – exploring, controlling and womanising.) For Doctor Who? (To save the universe from monsters, to explore and understand, to share the universe with his companions.) Now what about us? What's most important for us? Try to encourage them to answer.

Can we answer the bigger question? What really *is* the meaning of life? What should we be making the point of life? At the end of life, whether your life or the life of the whole universe, if somehow you could look at it all, would it be just a string of meaningless events, or would you know the answer? (Listen and respond to any comments.) If when it's all over we still don't get the point we never will! That's the time by which any meaning must have become clear! The Christian picture is that Jesus will end time as we know it, and that at the end we will see him and be with him for ever.

Notes

Introduction

1. Verity Lambert, 'Woman's realm', *Doctor Who Magazine* (no. 235, 14 February 1996), p. 38.

Chapter 2

1. A selection from Marc Okrand, *The Klingon Dictionary* (Pocket Books, 1992), pp. 1, 149, 170–2.

Chapter 3

1. Edward Gross and Mark A. Altman, *Great Birds of the Galaxy* (Boxtree, 1994), p. 109.
2. Mira Furlan, in 'Mira Furlan Minbari Moments'. An interview by Joe Nazzaro in *Starburst* magazine (Issue 210, February 1996), p. 27.

Chapter 4

1. See Tim Shawcross, *The Roswell File* (Bloomsbury, 1997).
2. Frank Lovece, *The X-Files Declassified* (Hodder & Stoughton, 1996), p. 4.
3. David Pringle (ed.), *The Ultimate Encyclopedia of Science Fiction* (Carlton, 1996), p. 168.
4. Lovece, *op. cit.*, p. 5.
5. *Ibid.*, p. 23.

Chapter 5

1. Helmut Thielicke, *The Ethics of Sex* (James Clarke, 1964), pp. 178ff.

Chapter 6

1. Joel Engel, *Gene Roddenberry: The Myth and the Man Behind Star Trek* (Virgin, 1994). Unless otherwise stated, this book is the source for quotations in this chapter from Gene Roddenberry.
2. Ed Gross, 'Star Trek The Lost Voyages', *SFX* (Issue 39, June 1998), p. 89.
3. Gross and Altman, *op. cit.,* p. 109.

Chapter 7

1. Erich von Däniken, *Chariots of the Gods: Was God an Astronaut?* (Souvenir Press, 1969).
2. R. L. Dione, *God Drives a Flying Saucer* (Corgi, 1973), p. 36.
3. *Ibid.*, p. 37.
4. Francis MacNutt, *Deliverance from Evil Spirits* (Hodder & Stoughton, 1996), p. 174.
5. R. L. Dione, *op. cit.*, p. 39.
6. *Ibid.*, p. 45.
7. Michael White, *The Science of The X-Files* (Random House, 1996), p. 193.
8. Martin Heidegger, quoted in John Macquarrie, *Martin Heidegger* (Lutterworth, 1968), p. 44.

Chapter 8

1. Immanuel Kant, *Critique of Pure Reason,* Second German edition (Riga, 1787), pp. 611–70.
2. Augustine of Hippo, *The Confessions* (published 400), Book 1/1.

Chapter 9

1. Engel, *op. cit.*, p. 46.
2. Ira Steven Behr, quoted in 'Faith in the 24th Century', *Star Trek Monthly* (Issue 41, July 1998), p. 31.
3. *Ibid.*, p. 34.
4. *Ibid.*
5. Michael Piller, quoted in Edward Gross and Mark A. Altman, *Captains' Logs Supplemental* (Little, Brown and Company, 1996), p. 56.
6. Daniel Leonard Bernardi, *Star Trek and History Race-ing Toward a White Future* (Rutgers University Press, 1998), p. 79.
7. *Ibid.*, p. 62.

Chapter 10

1. J. Michael Straczynski, quoted in Jane Killick, *Babylon 5 Season by Season 3* (Boxtree, 1998), p. 59.
2. *Ibid.*, p. 152.
3. J. Michael Straczynski, quoted in Jane Killick, *Babylon 5 Season by Season 1* (Boxtree, 1997), pp. 69–70.
4. Thomas Helwys, *A Short Declaration of the Mystery of Iniquity* (London, 1612).

5. Karl Barth, *Protestant Theology in the Nineteenth Century* (SCM, 1972), p. 50.

6. J. Michael Straczynski, quoted in Jane Killick, *Babylon 5 Season by Season 3* (Boxtree, 1998), pp. 47f.

Chapter 12

1. William Hartnell, quoted in Peter Haining, *Doctor Who: A Celebration. Two Decades Through Space and Time* (Virgin, 1983 and 1995), p. 39. See also David J. Howe, Mark Stammers and Stephen James Walker, *Doctor Who – The Sixties*: 'Hartnell always saw *Doctor Who* as a children's programme.' Hartnell is quoted as saying, 'The programme is a success because we keep it as a children's programme.'

2. Verity Lambert, quoted in Peter Haining, *Doctor Who: A Celebration* (Virgin, 1983 and 1995), p. 22. See also *Doctor Who Magazine* (no. 234, 17 January 1996), p. 6, where she says, 'Firstly, this was a children's show, aimed at eight- to fourteen-year-olds.'

Chapter 13

1. B. Moyers and G. Lucas, 'Of myth and men', *Time*, 26 April 1999.

2. C. S. Lewis, *Voyage to Venus* (Pan, 1960), p. 83.

3. Lawrence M. Krauss, *Beyond Star Trek* (Boxtree, 1997), p. 111.

4. Kimberly Cornish, *The Jew of Linz: Wittgenstein and Hitler and Their Secret Battle for the Mind* (Century, 1998), p. 153.

Chapter 14

1. Pauline Webb, *Salvation Today* (SCM, 1974), p. x.

Chapter 15

1. J. Michael Straczynski, quoted on the front cover of each *Space Patrol* video (1998). In the video *Space Patrol Volume 3*, Straczynski is interviewed, explaining how he still sees the programme (called *Planet Patrol* in the US) as genuine science fiction that happens to use puppets.
2. Roberta Leigh, quoted by John Ainsworth, 'Star Beat', *Dreamwatch* (no. 47, June 1998), p. 68.
3. Walter Koenig, quoted in Jane Killick, *Babylon 5 Season by Season 3* (Boxtree, 1998), p. 127.
4. J. Michael Straczynski, quoted in Jane Killick, *Babylon 5 Season by Season 4* (Boxtree, 1998), p. 159.

Chapter 16

1. Gene Roddenberry, cited in Joel Engel, *op. cit.*, p. 212, from an interview with Jesco von Puttkamer.

Chapter 17

1. H. Richard Niebuhr, *Christ and Culture* (Harper Torchbooks, 1956).
2. Stephen May, *Stardust and Ashes. Science Fiction in Christian Perspective* (SPCK, 1998). May's book concentrates far more on literary SF. Those looking for a theologically and philosophically reflective review of the

whole range of SF, especially literary SF, are well advised to explore May's book.

3. C. S. Lewis, *The Discarded Image: An Introduction to Medieval and Renaissance Literature* (Cambridge University Press, 1964), pp. 18f.

4. For the whole of this section, see J. R. R. Tolkien, *Tree and Leaf* (Unwin, 1964).

5. J. R. R. Tolkien, letter to Fr Robert Murray, 2 December 1953, in Humphrey Carpenter (ed.) with the assistance of Christopher Tolkien, *The Letters of J. R. R. Tolkien* (HarperCollins, 1995), p. 172. This letter is cited by Patrick Curry in *Defending Middle Earth. Tolkien: Myth & Modernity* (HarperCollins, 1998), p. 172.

6. Thomas Richards, *Star Trek in Myth and Legend* (Orion, 1997), pp. 174, 177, 178.

Chapter 18

1. Isaac Asimov, 'The Bicentennial Man' reprinted in *The Complete Stories Vol. 2* (HarperCollins, 1994), pp. 492–523. Asimov's comment that it was his favourite story is reported on the fly-leaf of that book.

2. Revd Robert Evans, in an interview with Jim Barclay, *Astronomy Now* (September 1988), especially p. 15.

3. H. Richard Niebuhr, *The Kingdom of God in America* (Harper 1937; as Harper Torchbook, 1959), p. 193.

4. J. Michael Straczynski, quoted in Jane Killick, *Babylon 5 Season by Season 1* (Boxtree, 1997), p. 69.

Chapter 19

1. Lawrence Krauss, *The Physics of Star Trek* (HarperCollins, 1995; Flamingo, 1997), p. 69. For more on this theme, concentrating more on issues of human identity and continuity during transportation, see also Richard Hanley, *Is Data Human? The Metaphysics of Star Trek* (Boxtree, 1998), especially chapter 4.
2. Robert and Susan Jenkins, *The Biology of Star Trek* (Boxtree, 1998), pp. 62f.
3. Gilbert Ryle, *The Concept of Mind* (Hutchinson, 1949 and Peregrine, 1963), pp. 17–20, 61–80.

Chapter 20

1. George Orwell, *Nineteen Eighty-Four* (Clarendon Press, 1984), pp. 165f. Orwell pictures a nightmare world where totalitarians have taken over, and telescreens show the opposition figure everyone is supposed to fear. They are to vent all their hatred onto this figure as the supposed embodiment of evil.
2. J. Michael Straczynski, quoted in Jane Killick, *Babylon 5 Season by Season 4* (Boxtree, 1998), p. 74.

Chapter 21

1. Barry Letts, quoted in Stephen James Walker, 'Background', *Doctor Who The Scripts: The Daemons* (Titan Books, 1992), pp. 11f.
2. Cornell, Day and Topping (eds), *Doctor Who: The Discontinuity Guide* (Virgin, 1995), p. 129.

3. Stephen James Walker, *op. cit.*, p. 13.
4. Cornell, Day and Topping, *op. cit.*, p. 127.

Chapter 22

1. See, for example, John S. Hall, 'Mental rape in Star Trek VI', *Dream Watch Bulletin* (a.k.a. *dwb*) (115, July 1993), p. 20.
2. Chris Carter, quoted in Lovece, *op. cit.*, p. 1.
3. Dione, *op. cit.*

Chapter 24

1. Michael White, *op. cit.*, p. ix.

Chapter 25

1. Theologian Wolfhart Pannenberg points out how, unlike secular versions such as Marxism, the traditional Christian future hope combines the individual and social hope in the 'idea of a resurrection of the dead, and that of the future kingdom of God'. See 'Can Christianity do without an eschatology?' in *S.P.C.K. Theological Collections 13: The Christian Hope* (SPCK, 1970), pp. 29, 32; see also his *The Apostles' Creed* (SCM, 1972), pp. 175–8.

Chapter 26

1. J. Michael Straczynski, quoted in Jane Killick, *Babylon 5 Season by Season 1* (Boxtree, 1997), p. 121.

For Further Reading

In addition to the literature outlined in the Notes, the main sources of my research (apart from the actual episodes on TV, film, video and audio, and as scripts and novelisations) are listed below.

The following magazines are normally available from larger newsagents and some bookstores, as well as specialist SF and fantasy shops:

▶ *Doctor Who Magazine* – originally a weekly magazine, but now monthly, published by Marvel Comics.

▶ *Doctor Who Classic Comics* (now discontinued), also from Marvel Comics, which along with *Doctor Who Magazine* published many of the recovered telesnaps of missing stories of *Doctor Who*.

▶ *Star Trek* – a monthly magazine published by Titan Magazines.

▶ *Star Trek Fact Files* (Paramount) – a regular series of supplements which go towards a whole set of files on a wide range of background features of the world of *Star Trek*.

▶ *Babylon 5* and *Crusade* monthly – formerly *Babylon 5* (Titan Magazines).

▶ *Star Wars* – every two months (Titan Magazines).

There is also a magazine for X-Philes. However, I have not yet seen magazines solely for the newer shows, so for information on series like *Red Dwarf, Earth: Final Conflict, Farscape, Stargate SG-1*, not to mention occasional features on short-term series like *Invasion Earth*, and on video releases of older material, for example *Space Patrol*, as well as regular articles on the main SF shows (often with material on other fantasy series, like *Buffy* and *Xena*, and sometimes on literature as well) see the following:

▶ *DreamWatch* – formerly *DreamWatch Bulletin* (a.k.a. *dwb*), this is a monthly magazine that has evolved over the years from a fanzine (fan-generated magazine) concerned principally with *Doctor Who*, to a wide-ranging magazine centred on SF, plus fantasy. Apart from *Doctor Who* only magazines, it gives the widest range of material the *Doctor Who* fan will want.

▶ *SFX* – a more recent monthly magazine with a fairly similar range of subjects to *DreamWatch* but with perhaps a slightly more laddish feel to it. However, its greater length provides a wide and effective set of book reviews.

▶ *Starburst* is another long-standing monthly magazine with a similar range, from Visual Imagination Ltd. Both in the UK and the USA.

▶ *Cult Times* reviews similar material, but as its title implies, with a considerably wider range, plus a month's TV listing. From Visual Imagination Ltd.

▶ *TV Zone* is also billed as a cult magazine, from Visual Imagination Ltd.

This is far from exhausting the range of magazines! Apart from some overlapping regular magazines, there is a wide range of fanzines which are harder to obtain (either found in more specialist SF shops or direct). Many of these are short-lived, but some have lasted as long as the high street magazines. Some of the *Doctor Who* based ones include:

▶ *Celestial Toyroom* – a long-lived fanzine from the Doctor Who Appreciation Society (DWAS).
▶ *Skaro* – a more recent fanzine, from Bath.

Other *Doctor Who* material covers various episode guides including: David J. Howe and Stephen James Walker, *Doctor Who: The Television Companion*, and Jean-Marc Lofficier's *The Programme Guide* and *The Terrestrial Index* (both Target, 1989 and 1991, respectively). There are many other books on monsters, artwork, eras (like the *Seventies* and *Eighties* sequels to Howe, Stammers and Walker's, *Doctor Who – The Sixties*), stories, and the annuals.

Insights into the world of *Star Trek: TOS* (and the films) can be gained from the many autobiographies, including William Shatner's *Star Trek Memories* and *Star Trek Movie Memories*, and Leonard Nimoy's *I Am Not Spock* and his (later!) *I Am Spock*. There are many books outlining the episodes of the various *Trek* series. As well as those mentioned in the Notes, these include:

▶ Allan Asherman, *The Star Trek Compendium* (Titan Books, 1987, 1989 and 1993).
▶ Larry Nemecek, *The Star Trek: The Next Generation Companion* (Pocket Books, Simon & Schuster, 1992 and revised in 1995).
▶ Judith and Garfield Reeves-Stevens, *Star Trek Phase II: The Lost Series* (Pocket Books, Simon & Schuster, 1997).
▶ Lou Anders, *The Making of Star Trek: First Contact* (Titan Books, 1996).
▶ A fascinating if typically expletive-ridden account of the original award-winning script for the much changed for

TV episode is provided in Harlan Ellison's *The City on the Edge of Forever: The Original Teleplay That Became the Classic Star Trek Episode* (Borealis Legends, White Wolf Publishing, 1996).

In addition see:

▶ James Van Hise, *The Unauthorized History of Trek* (HarperCollins, 1997).
▶ James Van Hise, *The Unauthorized Trekkers' Guide to The Next Generation and Deep Space Nine*.

Further *Babylon 5* material includes:

▶ David Bassom, *Creating Babylon 5* (Boxtree, 1996).
▶ Andy Lane, *The Babylon File* two volumes (Virgin, 1999).
▶ Edward James and Farah Mendelsohn (eds), *The Parliament of Dreams: Conferring on Babylon 5* (The Science Fiction Foundation: Reading University Press, 1998).

Christian writers, apart from Stephen May, include David Wilkinson with two books: *Alone in the Universe? The X Files, Aliens and God* (Monarch, 1997) and *The Power of the Force: The Spirituality of Star Wars* (Lion, 2000). Larry Kreitzer, New Testament Lecturer at Regent's Park College, Oxford, has also written lectures and other material on *Star Trek* especially, and I am particularly grateful to him for some of his material and insights, especially concerning the *Star Trek: TOS* story *Bread and Circuses*.

Shortcuts

This index shows the more substantial discussions of the various TV, radio and film series, authors and subjects.

A Closer Look at Harry Potter

by John Houghton

J K Rowling's *Harry Potter* series is uncontested as the greatest children's book phenomenon of all time.

Yet, while the world applauds, Christians are divided, and many are calling for the books to be banned from state schools and public libraries.

John Houghton himself is a writer of fantasy for children. In this book he offers an alternative to the secular wisdom on the conflict between good and evil. His considered critique offers timely and valuable insight for parents, teachers and all those involved in children's ministry.

This book is a must for all those who want to encourage a culturally literate, wise and godly generation who know how to have fun without regrets.

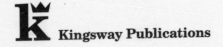 Kingsway Publications